Empire in the Age of Globalisation

Critical Introductions to World Politics

Series Editors:
Alejandro Colás (Birkbeck College, University of London)
Richard Saull (University of Leicester)

Empire in the Age of Globalisation

US Hegemony and Neoliberal Disorder

Ray Kiely

Pluto Press

LONDON • ANN ARBOR, MI

First published 2005 by Pluto Press
345 Archway Road, London N6 5AA
and 839 Greene Street, Ann Arbor, MI 48106

www.plutobooks.com

British Library Cataloguing in Publication Data
A catalogue record for this book is available from the British Library

ISBN   0 7453 2449 5 hardback
ISBN   0 7453 2448 7 paperback

Library of Congress Cataloging in Publication Data applied for

10   9   8   7   6   5   4   3   2   1

Designed and produced for Pluto Press by
Chase Publishing Services Ltd, Fortescue, Sidmouth, EX10 9QG, England
Typeset from disk by Stanford DTP Services, Northampton, England
Printed and bound in the European Union by
Antony Rowe Ltd, Chippenham and Eastbourne, England

Contents

Series Introduction

Critical Introductions to World Politics
Series Editors:
Alejandro Colás (Birkbeck College, University of London)
Richard Saull (University of Leicester)

World politics in all its socio-economic, cultural, institutional and military dimensions affects the lives of billions across the globe. Yet international relations is still an area of study associated with the 'high politics' of statecraft, strategy and diplomacy, or with distant and seemingly uncontrollable global flows of money, people and commodities. Critical Introductions to World Politics aims to reverse this prevailing elitism by illuminating and explaining the causes and consequences of these diverse aspects of international relations in an accessible way, thereby highlighting the impact of international processes and developments on the lives of ordinary people. The series will bring together a range of theoretical and empirical studies into the workings of world politics, while also identifying areas for political intervention by those seeking not just to interpret the world, but also to participate in political struggles to change it.

The series engages with key areas, providing succinct, informative and accessible overviews to central debates in global affairs. It draws mainly, although not exclusively, on Marxist approaches to international relations concerned with the analysis of, among other issues, transnational class formation, the role of international organisations in sustaining global capitalist hegemony, the sources of violent conflict and war, and the nature and evolution of state sovereignty. Empirically, it focuses on such issues as the origins of the modern international system, the Cold War and the consequences of its end, globalisation, and the character of American global power.

Critical Introductions to World Politics builds on a new, distinctly historical materialist approach to global affairs, serving as a key reference point and resource for those studying and teaching international relations from a critical perspective, as well as those involved in the various movements for a more just, equal and sustainable world.

Acknowledgements

Thanks to David Castle, Roger van Zwanenberg, Robert Webb and Melanie Patrick at Pluto, for seeing this book through to completion, and Alex Colás and Rick Saull, the series editors of Criticial Introductions to World Politics. Thanks also to Denis Cattell, Robin Cohen, Paul Kennedy, Jens Lerche, Subir Sinha and Damian White, for constructive criticism, debate and support. Most thanks go once again to Emma and Will.

1
Introduction

The purpose of this book is to examine the relationship between US hegemony, contemporary imperialism and globalisation. Specifically, it examines the claims that the more belligerent foreign policy of the US state since the terrorist attacks in September 2001 constitutes a significant departure from 'globalisation'. In order to address this question, we need to examine what is (was?) meant by globalisation; consider the practices of the Bush administration, and relate these to claims made concerning the nature of globalisation; and deliberate on the extent to which these constitute a break from globalisation.

In order, in turn, to address these questions we need to consider in detail the claims made about globalisation, and a critique of some of these claims is central to the book's overall argument. Specifically, the book challenges the claims made by a body of thought that can be called globalisation theory, focusing on the flawed methodology of this theory and its problematic interpretation of the decade of globalisation in the 1990s. This critique is then used to challenge the argument that post-'September 11' US foreign policy represents an unambiguous and regressive retreat from the potential of globalisation. While there are crucial differences between the 1990s and post-2001, there are also considerable continuities. Crucial to these continuities is the neoliberal character of contemporary globalisation. In making these arguments, the relationship between the US state and imperialism will also be addressed.

Globalisation was undoubtedly central to political debate in the 1990s. This was true in the academic social sciences, but equally in mainstream (and alternative) political discourse. But the precise definition of globalisation was less than clear. Briefly, globalisation refers to a set of processes that have increased interconnectedness across the globe, and where, crucially, these connections in many respects transcend the narrow boundaries of the nation-state. Central to this argument is the idea of a widening of 'spatiality' through the severing of the intrinsic connection between territoriality and polity. These contentions have enormous political implications: globalisation is said to have given rise to such far-reaching changes that the 'international' – or relations between nation-states – may be a thing of the past. Certainly, no globalisation theorist actually argues this point, and most qualify statements such as Giddens' (1999: 18) contention that 'following the dissolution of the Cold War, most nations no longer have enemies', or indeed Scholte's (2000: 61) claim that '(w)e no longer inhabit a territorialist world'. Nevertheless, some globalisation theorists[1] have drawn particular, optimistic conclusions from the deepening and stretching of social relations that was said to characterise globalisation. In particular, the argument was made that the stretching of social relations across national borders provided the basis for a new cosmopolitanism, in which a genuinely global, universal interest could result (Held and McGrew 2002). This was linked not only to the end of the Cold War, but also to the idea that there are genuinely global problems that require cooperation between states, which saw the rise of various institutions of multilateral global governance, and the emergence of a transnational civil society, in which global, non-state actors could put pressure on nation-states and international institutions in order to facilitate 'global justice'. This relatively optimistic perspective usually separated such issues from the dominance of neo-liberal economic policies (Held et al. 1999), although in some cases the claim was made that the 1990s represented a shift towards a post-neo-liberal world (Giddens 2000). This was usually associated with the 'third way' of the Clinton and Blair governments in particular, but also with many governments in the South that supported market expansion alongside appropriate institutional changes that could facilitate such expansion. Much was also made of the new post-Cold War extension of the principles of 'liberal internationalism' through expansion of the European Union (EU), the creation of the World Trade Organisation (WTO), and of new regional agreements such as the North American Free Trade Agreement (NAFTA). While these were considered to be far from perfect vehicles of global democratisation, they were also said to have some potential, in that they were at least preferable to an international order composed of self-interested nation-states.

For globalisation theory, the terrorist attacks of September 11, 2001 undermined this potentially better future. The attacks themselves were of course atrocities, carried out by reactionary political forces that would have little sympathy with the liberal cosmopolitanism advocated by globalisation theorists. But equally, the response of the Bush administration to these attacks laid the basis for what some globalisation theorists have called a 'regressive globalism' associated with the Bush II Doctrine. Globalisation theorists generally reject the Bush II Doctrine on the grounds that it breaks with the expansion of multilateral governance, using the United Nations (UN) as a simple tool of US state interests. In the case of Iraq, globalisation theorists generally reject the contempt that the Bush II administration (among others) showed for the UN and regard the war as an affront to the principles of international law and multilateral cooperation. Not all globalisation theorists agree – Anthony Giddens, for one, has supported the actions of British Prime Minister Tony Blair in supporting the war in Iraq. But most globalisation theorists regard world events since 2001 with dismay, arguing that limited but real advances in 'global governance' have been reversed by the actions of the Bush administration. Indeed, this applies not only to the question of military action, but also to issues such as non-cooperation on arms limitation, the international criminal court, environmental regulation, and protection of US industries from foreign competition. The potential for progressive globalisation has thus given way to the self-interested, unilateralist foreign policy of the Bush II government.

There is plenty of evidence to support the idea of a radical break in US foreign policy from 2001 onwards. The Bush II administration has undoubtedly been more unilateralist than its predecessor. Moreover, the neoconservative defeat of the Democrats did represent an important shift away from Clintonite policies. This was rooted not only in the more overt unilateralism of Bush II, but was also the product of an 'America first' strategy that combined the idea of promoting forward thinking Americanisation abroad, while simultaneously restoring the values of a mythical America at home (Lieven 2004). These ideas are far from novel in US political culture, but they were central to the Bush II administration's critique of Clinton, who was accused of not pursuing primacy with enough vigour abroad (see Chapter 4), and who was regarded as a decadent liberal at home.

But this book suggests that the extent of the break may not be as great as is often suggested, and that indeed there are areas of substantial continuity and convergence between Democrats and Republicans. In particular, I will suggest that Clinton was not as multilateral, and that, equally, Bush II is not as 'anti-globalist', as is sometimes suggested. I will then move on to suggest that these observations have implications for understanding the reality of globalisation, under *both Clinton and Bush II* (and their predecessors dating back to Reagan), and that the central continuity is based on an intrinsic link between US hegemony and the *neoliberal* nature of contemporary global capitalism.

This argument has implications for understanding *both* the 'globalisation' of the 1990s *and* US unilateralism since 2001. This book argues that globalisation theory does not represent a convincing account *either* of the post-2001 period, *or* of the globalisation period of the 1990s. Indeed, Chapter 2 argues that globalisation theory all too easily accepts the political parameters established by the victory of neoliberalism in the 1980s, which argued for the primacy of market forces, free trade, liberalised finance and open competition. This neoliberal globalisation is neither inevitable nor desirable. At best, globalisation theory underestimates the neoliberal nature of the international order, and at worst it apologises for it. Moreover, even in its more critical variants, this theory does not provide a convincing account of the nature of the contemporary international – or indeed global – order. A critique of this view is undertaken through a consideration of international politics, economics and culture in Chapters 3, 4, 5 and 6.

Chapter 3 examines the debates in the discipline of international relations, and relates these to the issue of multilateral global governance. The main focus of this chapter is an assessment of the development of state sovereignty, the international institutions of multilateral global governance, and how these operate within a hierarchical nation-state system under US hegemony. The main argument made is that institutions of global governance have not transcended the deeply unequal international system of nation-states, and that the world can still *in some respects* be regarded as imperialist. These debates are further illustrated in Chapter 4, through a detailed discussion of international relations after 2001, and especially of the war in Iraq in 2003. Together, Chapters 3 and 4 also reconsider the relevance or otherwise of classical Marxist theories of imperialism and newer theories of transnational capitalism. The broad argument made is that contemporary globalisation has undermined much of the relevance of classical Marxist theories, with the partial exception of Kautsky, and that the current international order is best characterised as an ultra-imperialist world led by the US state, actively supported by other states and capitals. In the neoliberal era, this hegemony has changed its form, with a passage from Reaganite neoconservatism, through the Clintonite Third Way and back to Bush II's neoconservatism; but the underlying neoliberal content is similar.

These arguments are further considered in Chapter 5, through an examination of the global economy from Bretton Woods to the present. The chapter thus mainly focuses on the development of 'free markets' since 1945. In examining and challenging the claims that neoliberal global market expansion unproblematically promotes economic growth and poverty reduction, the contradictions and tensions of the global economic order – and the role of the US in that order – are highlighted. The chapter particularly highlights the unequal competition associated with the global 'free market', and the ways in which the promotion of 'free trade' undermines sustained capitalist development in the periphery. This is intensified by the dominance of financial capital, which further diverts funds from productive investment and increases economic instability in emerging markets, but which is also central to the continued hegemony of the US state. Once again, these arguments are illustrated through an examination of the policy process from the 1980s to the present, with particular reference to their relationship to the US state and international financial institutions. The dysfunctionality of these processes is illustrated through a consideration of global poverty and inequality, and of the concentration of capital in some areas and consequent marginalisation of other locations, which free trade intensifies.

Chapter 6 then reviews debates over the globalisation of culture, examining questions related to consumer culture, liberal rights, universalism and cultural standardisation. The argument is made that while the cultural imperialism thesis is deeply flawed, increased cultural flows are far from equal; and, more importantly, the expansion of the commodity is deeply implicated in specific power relations that do not transcend territorial place. Theories of global consumer culture too easily take 'the market' as a given, abstracting it from the social relations and territorial places that have the most power to direct processes of globalisation. This critique has implications related not only to the narrow concerns of specific cultural goods, but to wider issues related to questions of human rights and freedoms, of what constitutes 'progress' and the 'good life', and indeed who or what agency promotes the universal good. These debates are in turn related to US-led liberal internationalism (including neoconservatism), associated with this perceived universal good, and again the argument is made that while the form of US state power may have changed, there has been substantial continuity in terms of content.

These critical accounts are made not only as a contribution to the globalisation debate, and as a critique of mainstream globalisation theory, but also as the basis for providing a clearer understanding of the realities of the contemporary world order. In so doing, I attempt to provide an understanding of the contemporary nature of US hegemony, imperialism and globalisation. In conclusion, Chapter 7 revisits the debates set out and discussed in Chapters 2 to 6, and summarises the nature of contemporary imperialism and 'actually existing globalisation', and then moves on to discuss the question of alternatives to it. These alternatives are addressed, with specific reference to the questions of politics, economics and culture examined in the previous chapters. These issues are then finally related to the issue of *progressive*, as opposed to *reactionary*, alternatives to the current international capitalist order. As will become clear, this final question is not unrelated to the main focus of the book, which is how we theorise the relationship between US hegemony and neoliberal, capitalist globalisation.

2
Globalisation Theory or Capitalist Globalisation?

This chapter provides a broad overview of the globalisation debate, with particular emphasis placed on sociology and globalisation theory. It starts by examining definitions of globalisation, and some of the problems with these definitions. The focus in this opening section is on global interconnectedness, an increase in the intensity of this interconnectedness, and the intensification of what can be described as a global consciousness. In the second section of the chapter, I move on to an examination of the globalisation debate, focusing on the distinction (Held et al. 1999) between hyper-globalisers, sceptics and transformationalists. The debate here rests on the division between the hyper-globalisers and the sceptics over the degree of globalisation, which is measured in terms of such factors as capital flows, state autonomy and the fate of national culture. Transformationalists, on the other hand, focus less on quantitative measures (although these are regarded as important) and more on qualitative change, such as the intensity of flows and the prominence of international institutions. In this section I argue that there is much to be learnt from this debate, but in some respects it confuses a number of important issues, which essentially relate to the politics of globalisation. This issue is taken up in the third section, which does not completely reject the distinctions within the globalisation debate, but argues that an alternative approach may be more useful. This alternative attempts to place agency, power and politics (in the widest sense of the term) at the centre of the globalisation debate, and to define globalisation as not only a set of processes but also a *political project*. The main features of this project are briefly outlined, and related to the current neoliberal era of global capitalism. This discussion then sets the scene for later chapters, where there is a more detailed analysis of specific debates related to globalisation, and of how these relate to US hegemony and neoliberal capitalism.

DEFINING GLOBALISATION

Anthony Giddens' *The Consequences of Modernity* (1990) is one of the most important sociological works that attempts to construct a theory of globalisation. In this work, Giddens (1990: 64) defines globalisation as 'the intensification of worldwide social relations which link distant localities in such a way that local happenings are shaped by events occurring many miles away and vice versa'. In what is probably the most comprehensive examination of globalisation to date, David Held and his co-authors similarly define it as 'the widening, deepening and speeding up of worldwide interconnectedness in all aspects of contemporary social life, from the cultural to the criminal, the financial to the spiritual' (Held et al. 1999: 2). They then develop a more rigorous definition, arguing that globalisation is '[a] process (or set of processes) which embodies a transformation in the spatial organization of social relations and transactions – assessed in terms of their extensity, velocity and impact – generating transcontinental or interregional flows and networks of activity, interaction, and the exercise of power' (Held et al. 1999: 16). In these definitions, globalisation refers to increased interconnectedness across and beyond national borders, and an increase in the speed and intensity of these connections. These in turn have promoted an increase in global awareness – what Giddens calls reflexivity – which undermines localised social relations and consciousness.

Interconnectedness means that events in one part of the world will impact on different localities in other parts of the world. There are plenty of examples that support this idea: the impact of financial flows in one region on other regions, such as in 1997–98, when the financial crisis in East Asia had spill-over effects in Russia, Latin America, and ultimately the United States, when a serious global financial crisis was only averted by the actions of the US government and the International Monetary Fund (IMF); the destruction of rainforests in much of the world, but particularly Latin America, which has exacerbated the environmental problem of global warming; and 'local' wars, which, when they involve the actions of superpowers, can have all kinds of unanticipated consequences. The context for the atrocities committed on September 11, 2001, for instance, can be traced back to superpower intervention in Afghanistan, the US-led attack against Saddam Hussein's forces in Kuwait in 1990–91, and the subsequent decision to increase US troop numbers in Saudi Arabia.

Clearly then, the world is interconnected. But a note of caution is also necessary, for how novel is this interconnectedness? Events in one locality have always impacted on events in other places. One thinks here of old empires, the slave trade, and wars between competing powers. For those countries that were established in the move to independence after the Second World War, the idea that events in one part of the world impact on their own territories is hardly new, for they had experienced years of colonialism. But, for many writers and commentators, globalisation is supposed to be something that is a relatively recent phenomenon. Clearly it is not, and it may be that the notion of novelty is a peculiarly western one, for in the eighteenth and nineteenth centuries it was western countries that clearly directed the process of colonisation, whereas globalisation today may be a less clearly directed process (though this is a contentious point, as I show below). Seen in this light, those who claim that globalisation is novel may be betraying a western bias in their thinking, as it is only in recent years that the former colonial world has more directly impacted on the west – through, for example, post-war migration.

These points are not made to deny the reality of contemporary globalisation. As will become clear, I think the concept of globalisation does 'capture' some important changes in the world over the last 30 years or so. But we also need to remember that globalisation is in many respects much older, and so we need to be sensitive to what precisely is new in the current era of globalisation. Writers like Giddens (1990), Tomlinson (2000) and Urry (2002) have all argued that a novel feature of contemporary globalisation is that the direction and origins of global flows are difficult to pin down or locate, in contrast to earlier periods of globalisation, which were really about 'westernisation'. But I will argue that the contemporary period of globalisation is one characterised by the dominance of neoliberal capitalism, and that in some respects globalisation can be regarded as a project designed to expand this domination, in part through the actions of the US state. This dominance may be contested, above all by the rise of East Asia; but as we will see, this challenge can hardly be explained by globalisation theory.

Another way in which some writers have attempted to specify what is novel in the current period of globalisation is to emphasise the increase in the speed and intensity of global flows. Interconnectedness is not new, but what is novel is the amount, extent and rapidity of these flows, and the extent to which we experience them. Following Marx's prophetic analysis in the mid nineteenth century (see below), David Harvey (1989) calls this process 'time–space compression'. Put differently, we live in a shrinking world. Thus, air travel is faster, cheaper and more available (for some) today than in the past. The development of information and communications technologies (ICTs) means that we – or some of us – can communicate instantaneously with people across the globe through email and the World Wide Web, or immediately experience a far-off event through satellite television.

Manuel Castells (1996) argues that the development of this shrinking world has led to new social divisions, chiefly between those at the cutting edge of the new ICTs and those that are marginalised from them. The marginalised are still largely confined to their particular, localised places, and experience life mainly in what he calls the 'space of places': they are marginalised because they are insufficiently globalised. On the other hand, members of the global elite experience much of their life – both in work and leisure – in the 'space of flows', in which they link up with other, distant places, in order to make money and take expensive holidays. They still live in particular localities, but are abstractly – and literally – fenced off from those confined only to the space of places. For Castells, because power is increasingly globalised, it is increasingly difficult to find political opposition that can challenge these unequal and unjust power relations. What was often considered to be the main vehicle of opposition in the era of 'national capitalism' from the 1940s to the 1970s – the organised labour movement – is said to be too confined to the space of places in the era of globalisation, and so has been seriously undermined. In this globalised world of intensified information flows, there needs to be a radical reconceptualisation of our ways of thinking about this world, including a greater sensitivity to the fluidity of social structures, and a recognition that some of these have been seriously weakened. Thus, Castells argues that the old manufacturing working class of industrial capitalism is not as significant as it once was. At times – though he often qualifies this argument – he also argues that the nation-state, perhaps the key reference point for classical sociology, is also changing rapidly, and may even be in decline.

The French cultural theorist Jean Baudrillard takes these arguments even further, suggesting that attempts to understand 'the social' are doomed to failure, even perhaps that there is no longer anything that can be called 'the social'. Rather than focusing on power relations, as in sociological analysis (including Castells), he argues that the world is full of global flows, and that these are moving with such speed and intensity that it is impossible to find any deeper meaning or truth beyond them. Instead, the world of global commodities lacks any depth or meaning, and is simply one of surface appearances. We may experience distant local events on our television screens, but it is this very immediacy that leads to a lack of meaning or depth. These events are simply one more meaningless occurrence in an increasingly shallow world. Hyper-mobility means a placeless world, and therefore a meaningless world. Thus, to return to the definitions of globalisation above, the 'stretching' of social relations is so great that they have effectively snapped. There is no 'real' or 'social' anymore, just a proliferation of images and signs that represent or refer to nothing but other signs and images. Crucially, Baudrillard argues that we are not manipulated by some other power – be it the state, dominant classes including owners of media companies, or even advertising agencies. Instead, we are fully aware of the shallowness of global flows, but we do not care about their lack of meaning or correspondence to a supposed reality. For Baudrillard (1993: 17), 'we manufacture a profusion of meanings in which there is nothing to see'. Baudrillard's infamous and much misunderstood claim that the Gulf War of 1991 'did not take place' should be seen in this light. He was not literally claiming that the events that made up the Gulf War of 1991 did not occur, merely that this could not be described either as a war or a particularly meaningful event. It was less a real war than a spectacle.

There is obviously some truth in the notion of time–space compression. However, there is a danger of exaggerating the degree and significance of this phenomenon. Baudrillard is right to focus on the spectacular in the reporting of the 1991 Gulf War, which was a highly mediated event (as was, in a different way, the 2003 war). But to claim that because it was so mediated it was *simply* a spectacle, or that it was without *any* meaning, is too one-sided, and betrays a tendency in Baudrillard to over-generalise from his own cynicism. The deaths, political protests and conflicts that arose out of the 1991 war made it a far from meaningless event. More generally, the claim that global flows have intensified so much that we have witnessed the death of the social, and indeed the 'end of reality', is based on contradictory logic. As Strinati (1992: 78) notes,

if the 'real' has 'imploded', as Baudrillard argues, then what 'real' evidence can we refer to in order to show that it has done so? If we could find this evidence then the point would be disproved, but if we couldn't then we wouldn't know if it had or hadn't.

Clearly, then, Baudrillard's views are questionable, and even he seems to be developing a more nuanced (though still unconvincing) account in relation to the events after September 11, 2001 (Baudrillard 2002). But even the more carefully considered views of Castells need to be treated with some caution. Castells (1993: 20) has argued that 'the enhancement of telecommunications has created the material infrastructure for the formation of a global economy, in a movement similar to that which lay behind the construction of the railways and the formation of national markets during the nineteenth century'. But this view can be questioned. Certainly, information and communications technologies are important, but they may not be as important as Castells suggests. Commercial and financial transactions make up a tiny proportion of total world gross domestic product, with estimates ranging from a high of 1.25 per cent to a low of 0.3 per cent. In other words, 'old economy' activity constitutes around 98.75 to 99.7 per cent of world GDP (Thompson 2003: 194–5). Moreover, most internet traffic is focused on fairly mundane and/or leisure activity. Even the supposed indirect benefits of new technologies for the rest of the economy is hard to identify – there were certainly no unprecedented increases in productivity in the so-called new economy of the 1990s, and this in fact turned out to be a largely old-fashioned speculative boom (Henwood 2003; and see Chapter 4).

This is not to deny that new technologies have facilitated some changes, such as providing increased information in the provision of supplies and stocks to manufacturers and retailers, but their overall significance has been exaggerated. Golding (2000) usefully distinguishes between two different effects of new technologies. The first allows existing social processes and interaction to occur more quickly, while the second allows for completely new forms of activity. New information and communications technologies fit more closely into the former than the latter category. Indeed, the current vogue for describing a shrinking world is actually far from new, and was also seen in the nineteenth century, in the context of the disembedding effects of railways and the telegraph (Thrift 1996). It could even be argued that the telegraph – which 'shrank' communication times with distant locations from weeks to minutes and seconds – was more revolutionary than the web, which shrinks communications from seconds to fractions of seconds. Moreover, it could be claimed that this debate focuses too narrowly on one issue, and that the impact of technology on society is exaggerated in these accounts. Frankel (2000: 6–7) points out that

> there is a tendency to see globalization as irreversible. But the political forces that fragmented the world for 30 years (1914–44) were evidently far more powerful than the accretion of technological progress in transport that went on during that period. The lesson is that there is nothing inevitable about the process of globalization.

This can be illustrated by taking the example of financial capital, which in many respects conforms most closely to the idea that capital has now transcended the limits of place (O'Brien 1992). Implicit in this argument is the assumption that new developments in communications technologies have determined this process, as these allow people to switch money to new locations literally 'at the flick of a switch'. But this is too simplistic. It is more accurate to say that the new technologies have facilitated this process, but that its ultimate cause lies in decisions by states to liberalise financial regulation, and therefore end border restrictions on the movement of money – a point I will return to in the next chapter (see also Helleiner 1994). Time–space compression may therefore be facilitated by technological developments, but there are also underlying political causes.

Moreover, there are also limits to the degree to which time–space compression exists. The world has certainly 'shrunk', but it does not necessarily follow that the world is therefore made up of hyper-mobile global flows in which particular, local places become irrelevant. Mittelman (1997: 229) acknowledges the reality of increasing capital mobility, changing forms of state regulation, and wider patterns of globalisation, but, crucially, he also argues that 'the compression of time and space is limited because flows of capital and technology must eventually touch down in distinct places'. In other words, there are enormous costs to capital – particularly productive capital – in simply relocating from one place to another, and leaving behind plant, machinery, labour, suppliers and markets. It is certainly easier in some sectors than others, and mobility is greater in labour-intensive sectors, but this does not apply to most sectors.

The importance of place can also be understood by looking at the question of access. There is a great wealth of evidence that shows the reality of unequal access to cutting-edge 'global' technologies (as well as basics like food). For instance, there are more telephone lines in Manhattan than there are in the whole of sub-Saharan Africa. In the mid 1990s, the United States had 35 computers per 100 people, South Korea 9, and Ghana 0.11. Internet use remains heavily concentrated in Western Europe and the United States, and to some extent parts of East Asia (Kiely 1998a: 5). Some may claim that this information gap can be closed through the diffusion of technology to the developing world, presumably through a trickle-down process. But the question of *how* this will occur is not simply one of technological diffusion. The significance of social and political relations also demands some attention. Important questions have to be asked, such as how 'catch-up' can occur – either through incorporation into the world economy through a process of market-friendly policies, or through selective protection, whereby technology is borrowed from abroad and gradually unpacked and developed in new ways. To ask such a question leads us back to debates about the role of markets and states in the process of development, something that pre-dates the literature on globalisation, and which returns us to the question of agency. Neither should we lose sight of the fact that power relations can exist *within* the social relations that embody the new technologies. For example, the last few years have seen a sustained attempt by private companies to assert ownership of 'intellectual property rights' (see Chapter 5).

These points reflect a basic tension in Castells' work. On the one hand, he tends to suggest that power relations exist on the basis of people operating in the space of flows, rather than the space of places. The latter are therefore marginalised in relation to the former. But on the other hand, because the space of flows transcends the space of places, in principle the network society could operate anywhere. Indeed, for this reason Giddens effectively co-opts Castells' work for the global third way project, as he argues that every 'place' can effectively compete, provided the correct (neoliberal) policies of trade and investment openness are adopted. The problem here is that the very fact of marginalisation implies the continued importance of the space of places, as capital concentrates in some areas and marginalises others. In other words, to use the language employed by Castells, some places continue to matter more than others. The basis for this concentration coexisting with relative marginalisation is the competitive advantage that some locations enjoy over others, based on a clustering of socio-economic activity. Crucial here is the development of technological capacity, which does not involve simply the importing of machinery or information technology, but also the development of technological knowledge, so that the technology can be used efficiently and competitively. This involves the development of a state 'interventionism' that takes us far beyond the 'market-friendly' interventionist policies advocated under neoliberalism. This also suggests that the dominance of neoliberalism undermines the 'development' prospects for the developing world (Kiely 1998b: Ch. 9). I shall return to these issues in Chapter 5.

Taken together, the arguments so far suggest that globalisation is associated with a reconfiguration of particular economic, political and cultural conditions, but that it has not destroyed the importance of particular places (Dicken et al. 1997). Much of the debate on globalisation tends to assume that there is a 'global level' operating independently of particular places, and impacting on them in uniform ways. Even when lip-service is paid to the importance of the 'local' or 'particular' (as by Giddens), globalisation still tends to be seen as a free floating, agentless, and therefore placeless phenomenon. This culminates in the extreme arguments of Baudrillard, which most writers quite correctly reject. But this tendency is present in the work of Giddens (and to some extent Castells), and it has serious implications for an understanding of the politics of globalisation – a point taken up in the following parts of this chapter, and in later chapters.

Before moving on, however, we need to look at the third defining feature of globalisation. This is the notion that there has developed a global consciousness, so that we are more consciously aware of the notion of 'one world', first in terms of a common global fate, and second (and relatedly) in terms of the fate of 'distant others', and their awareness of us (Robertson 1992). This has implications for our understanding of the global, but also for how we perceive the local spaces in which we live. In terms of the former, a common global fate can perhaps be seen most clearly in terms of the environment, and specifically in relation to fears of global warming. In terms of the latter, the impact of global flows means that no 'local' society or culture can exist in a self-contained way, which in turn means that it cannot any longer justify its existence through appeals to 'local tradition'. This is what Giddens means when he refers to a process of disembedding, and he sees this as a progressive development. In some respects I share this view, but once again I think there is a need for caution. I argue this point in more detail in Chapter 6. For now, I would simply say that it is one thing to argue that this is a progressive development, but quite another to argue that it is a directionless or placeless one. For many of the processes of disembedding are products of free-market, consumer capitalism. This system is certainly not placeless, but is located most powerfully in the United States and a few other 'advanced' capitalist countries. To point this out is not necessarily to reject the products in question, nor to champion a crude anti-Americanism; but it is to suggest that, once again, globalisation is a process that lacks neither place nor power.

These issues are also reflected in debates over the question of human rights. The 1948 United Nations Declaration of Human Rights championed the principle of universal rights, though there existed a tension between the sovereignty of nation-states and the rights of individuals (see Chapters 3 and 4). There are also important debates over the question of which rights are important. Western governments have tended to see individual rights such as freedom of speech, freedom of movement (for some) and the right to own property, as most important. Some developing-country governments have tended to argue that collective rights, such as freedom from poverty and the right to development, are more important. Both sides in this debate have at times been hypocritical, sometimes being more concerned to justify their own existence than to extend any rights at all, individual or collective. In other words, important debates about global justice have all too easily become caught up in the messy reality of power politics. For example, Robert Mugabe's 'concern' for the landless in Zimbabwe now appears to be motivated less by an older commitment to social justice, and more by a desperate (and probably doomed) attempt at self-preservation.

But on the other hand, even leaving aside colonial history, western governments are far from benign. Concern for human rights is undoubtedly justified, but there is then a question of who polices human rights violations. A global concern for the rights of distant others presumably means protection for those others from serious human rights abuses, such as genocide. But this begs the question of how this protection is to be implemented and who defines the violations in the first place. Thus, in 2003, the initial justification for the war in Iraq was the existence of weapons of mass destruction, but when it appeared that these may not have existed in any immediately usable form, some apologists for war made the post-hoc justification that the war was necessary to oust the serious human rights abuser, Saddam Hussein. This begs a number of questions examined in more detail in Chapters 3 and 4, which include: Who has the power to decide that war is justifiable and necessary? What of those killed in the war? And what about the US-and British-led occupations after the war? More generally, there is also the question of human rights abuse: Why in 2003 was Saddam Hussein considered to be such a violator, when his worst atrocities were committed in 1988 (when he was an ally of western governments) and in 1991 (when retreating US forces effectively turned a blind eye to massacre)? Similarly, why were atrocities committed in the former Yugoslavia (eventually) deemed to be worthy of military intervention, while genocide in Rwanda in 1994 was not? Indeed, the US and British governments, among others, deliberately played down the atrocities in Rwanda in order to discourage intervention. The 2003 war was launched against Saddam Hussein's regime at a time when more pressing human rights abuses were being committed in the Democratic Republic of Congo. To note these examples is not to downplay the atrocities that were committed, nor to deny the murderous nature of regimes like those of Slobodan Milošević and Saddam Hussein. Still less is it an argument for ignoring these human rights abuses (though whether war is the best way to deal with them is another issue). It is, however, to suggest that the selective nature of interventions – which by definition means that some abuses are ignored – cannot be divorced from the question of power, including the continued power of nation-states. Moreover, what is to be made of action designed to promote other, more collective rights (such as development), which relate to issues of debt relief, increased aid and trade justice, but where it may be harder to pinpoint individual villains accurately, and which may actually cost more lives? At best, there has been limited progress on these issues; and at worst, western action has been negligent. These issues are taken up further in Chapters 3, 4 and 6.

This section started with three quite simple definitions of globalisation, and extracted three main characteristics: interconnectedness through flows that go beyond national borders; an increase in the intensity and speed of these flows; and an increase in global consciousness. We have also found, however, that these definitions and characteristics are very contentious. In my discussion we will continually return to the questions of agency, politics and power. This implies, at the very least, the need for a more in-depth consideration of theories of globalisation.

THEORIES OF GLOBALISATION/GLOBALISATION THEORY

This section examines a text that tries to provide a more theoretically rigorous account of the nature of globalisation. David Held et al.'s

Global Transformations (1999) is perhaps the most comprehensive account of the phenomenon to date, so it is worthy of some further consideration. The main purpose of the book is to look at contemporary manifestations of processes of globalisation, including the state and global governance, trade and production, the environment and culture. But also of interest is how the writers attempt to define the theoretical debate on globalisation, and it is this account that I will examine in this section. Held et al. identify three theoretical positions in relation to globalisation: those of the hyper-globalisers, the sceptics, and the transformationalists. Here I will examine in detail these three positions; But I will also provide a critical account of this way of dividing the globalisation debate, and thus return to the questions discussed in the first section, particularly those relating to Giddens's definition of globalisation.

The hyper-globalisation thesis

The hyper-globalisation thesis argues that globalisation represents an unprecedented change in recent years, so that global flows have undermined the existence of the nation-state. According to Kenichi Ohmae (1995: 5), 'traditional nation-states have become unnatural, even impossible business units in a global economy'. In other words, capital flows have eroded the capacity of the nation-state to regulate the market. Instead, we have a borderless world, in which capital effortlessly moves from one part of the globe to another. There is, however, considerable disagreement over the political implications of the development of hyper-mobile capital. On one side are the neoliberals, including Ohmae, who welcome this development; on the other are various radicals who see it as regrettable. To confuse matters further, there are also some radicals who welcome the development of hyper-mobile capital.

Neoliberals welcome it because they regard free markets as being more efficient than states. All individuals and countries, they contend, can develop through the exercise of comparative advantage – in other words, countries should specialise in producing those goods that they can produce most efficiently (that is, cheaply). The question of what to specialise in can be discovered through operating according to the principles of free and open competition. Thus, if country A can produce cars cheaply and country B computers, they should specialise in each and then exchange their surpluses with each other, which will mean more cars and computers in both countries. States should not intervene to protect economic sectors from foreign competition, which means that they should adopt low tariffs and eliminate other controls on their trade and investment policies (for a critique of this view, see Chapter 5). Quantitative increases in global capital flows, measured by such phenomena as increased foreign investment and trade/GDP ratios, are therefore welcomed, because they undermine the capacity of nation-states to regulate – and therefore distort – the global economy. In the long run, neoliberal hyper-globalisers maintain, a world economy determined by market forces will operate to everyone's benefit.

Radicals, on the other hand, draw very different implications. They argue that the undermining of the nation-state gives capital a free hand to promote a race to the bottom, based on undermining wages and social and environmental conditions, through a move from high-wage, heavily regulated areas to areas of low wages and worse social conditions. In an early formulation of this argument (Frobel et al. 1980), it was argued that the selective industrialisation of the former Third World had given rise to a new international division of labour. The newly industrialising countries of the former Third World had developed through the attraction of cheap labour, so that transnational companies relocated from expensive First World to cheaper Third World locations. This amounted to super-exploitation of cheap, Third World labour – a practice that states were powerless to stop. If states tried to regulate capital and improve social conditions, then capital would simply relocate to areas where wages and conditions were worse, and costs to capital correspondingly low. Insofar as states retain power, it is only to accept the new competitive conditions imposed by transnational capital. Hyper-globalisation is thus said to represent the triumph of exploitative capital, manifested most visibly in the resurgence of sweat-shop labour – a particular *bête-noire* of the anti-globalisation movement (see Chapter 7).

A small minority of radicals actually *welcome* globalisation, as it is said to increase the development performance of the former Third World. States, according to this view, entrench the power of already powerful countries; so the loosening of the ties of capital to particular nation-states means that the developing world is likely to benefit from an increasing share of world investment and trade. Of course this investment may be exploitative, but all countries that develop have to go through stages of particularly acute exploitation before economic growth secures social advances. Moreover, it is better to be exploited through capital investment than it is to be marginalised through lack of capital investment. The globalisation of 'cosmopolitan capital'

(N. Harris 2003), freed from ties to particular nation-states, therefore prepares the way for the ending of uneven development, and of the domination of weaker states by more powerful ones. Globalisation thus allows capital to fulfil its historic mission of promoting the development of the former Third World (Kitching 2001; Desai 2002). To borrow the words of Marx (at his worst), the rapid development of East Asia 'shows to the less developed world, the image of its own future' (Marx 1976: 91).

As should by now be clear, the hyper-globalisation thesis – in its neoliberal and radical (and dissenting radical) versions – tends to focus very much on political economy. But it is clearly possible to see that there is something like a cultural equivalent, which would not be so far removed from the strong notion of time–space compression discussed above. Although political economists would certainly reject Baudrillard's notion of the death of the social, where there is some common ground is in the idea of hyper-mobility. In the case of Baudrillard, this is so great that it undermines meaning; in the case of the views discussed in this section, mobility is seen as so great that it undermines the nation-state (Kiely 1999). This similarity gives us some clue as to the problems with this perspective. Leaving aside disagreement over the political implications of the 'death' of the nation-state, hyper-globalisers believe that capital can simply move from one location to another without cost. But the evidence does not bear this out – Chapter 5 demonstrates that there are significant costs associated with relocation (particularly for productive capital), and strong reasons for capital (including financial capital) to continue to concentrate in specific locations. Indeed, while the absolute amounts of capital investment going to the developing world have increased, the relative shares of global investment and trade have in many cases fallen, thus undermining any simplistic thesis based on capital effortlessly moving to lowest-cost areas. If capital is not as mobile as this approach implies, then clearly the state still has some economic role to play – even if this may have changed since, say, the 1950s and 1960s. Indeed, much is made of East Asia in the hyper-globalisation approach; or at least the rise of East Asia before the financial crisis of 1997–98. Neoliberals argue that the region developed because states played a limited role in these economies, and because their intervention was only market-friendly (World Bank 1993); or rather, this was the argument made until financial collapse led to a renewal of the claim that there was *too much* government intervention in the economy. Theories of the new international division of labour argued that the region developed as capital relocated in order to take advantage of cheap labour. And the theory of cosmopolitan capital argued that the rise of East Asia could be explained by the diffusion of the capitalist mode of production from the 'advanced' capitalist countries of the west. But each of these theories discounts the role that the nation-state played in the industrialisation processes in South Korea and Taiwan, where states targeted credit, protected particular industries from foreign competition, restricted foreign investment (relocation by transnationals was strictly limited in these countries), and limited the export of capital (Kiely 1998b: Chs. 7 and 8). Indeed, the gradual lifting of this regulatory framework in South Korea was one reason for its financial crisis, in striking contrast with the more heavily regulated Taiwanese economy. Moreover, the cheap labour argument is also problematic, because workers in both South Korea and Taiwan won large increases (from admittedly low starting points) without facing wholesale relocation of capital investment to lower-cost sites.

These comments hint at the basic problem with the hyper-globalisation thesis, which is that globalisation is held to have impacts on particular places in a one-sided way. Globalisation is active, while local and national places – including nation-states – are passive. Although in this case some agency is at least specified (transnational capital) – unlike in some of the approaches to globalisation discussed so far – it still does not stand up to critical scrutiny, as South Korea and Taiwan 'took off' with limited foreign capital investment; and more generally, capital flows show a strong tendency to concentrate in particular regions, rather than disperse across the globe.

The sceptical thesis

Sceptics are particularly concerned to challenge the notion of the death, or even serious weakening, of the nation-state. Once again, this account does not belong to any one political tendency, and can be associated with political realists, who see international politics as conflict between states (and differ among themselves on political implications); social democrats, who place continued faith in the hope that the state can continue to regulate capital; and some Marxists, who believe that the current internationalisation of capital is an expression of inter-imperialist rivalries.

Some of these debates are addressed in detail in Chapter 3. Here I want to outline broadly the reasons why the state is still seen as powerful in terms of its relationship to 'global markets', and then problematise some of their associated contentions. One major measure of the extent of globalisation is the degree of trade openness of countries, as measured by the ratio of trade to GDP. Hirst and Thompson (1999) argue that, compared to the year 1913, there is actually little change in the openness of many economies. Thus, measured at current prices, the 1913 trade/GDP ratios were 35.4 per cent for France, 35.1 per cent for Germany, 31.4 per cent for Japan, 103.6 per cent for the Netherlands, 44.7 per cent for the United Kingdom, and 11.2 per cent for the US. In 1995, the figures were 36.6 per cent for France, 38.7 per cent for Germany, 14.1 per cent for Japan, 83.4 per cent for the Netherlands, 42.6 per cent for the UK (for 1994), and 19 per cent for the US (Thompson 2000: 97). The US alone, therefore, has seen a sharp increase, while Japan has seen a sharp decline. The overall trend is one of little change, hardly amounting to a picture of unprecedented change to a wholly new era of globalisation. One common objection to this argument is that figures are measured in constant prices, and are therefore unadjusted for inflation. Once the measure is switched to constant figures (adjusted for inflation), then there is an unambiguous increase in trade/GDP ratios, such as an increase in export/GDP ratios from 11.2 per cent for all developed countries in 1913 to 23.1 per cent in 1985 (Held et al. 1999: 169). However, adjusting for inflation can be problematic, since it is in the traded goods sector that prices generally rise more slowly than the economy as a whole, because this sector tends to be the most efficient and to have the fastest rates of productivity growth. Adjusting for inflation for the economy as a whole cannot distinguish between sectors in the required way, and so the growth of trade relative to GDP may exaggerate the growth of trade relative to total output. It is also sometimes argued that, with the movement towards a service economy – at least in the 'advanced' capitalist countries – there is less likely to be international trade in this sector, and so comparing 1913 (when economies produced or traded more manufactured goods, and traded more primary goods) with the 1990s is not sensible. But this argument is unconvincing, because the fact that some countries have shifted to services, which are less likely to be traded across borders, highlights the fact that employment prospects in such sectors are not only subject to the pressures of international competition. The clear implication of this argument is that nation-states continue to have an important role in economic policy-making, and are not powerless in the face of transnational capital.

Moreover, it is not only in the economic sphere that nation-states continue to be relevant. The creation and maintenance of international institutions is ultimately sanctioned by nation-states, and they ultimately stand or fall on the basis of agreement between (at least) some states. As we will see in Chapter 3, this has given rise to an important debate over the nature of 'global governance', and whether international institutions can move beyond the interests of particular nation-states (realism), or whether states and other institutions simply reflect powerful capitalist interests (Marxism). A similar point can be made in terms of the fate of national cultures, which are not simply being swept away by a global culture, but are in some respects strengthening as part of the processes of resistance to perceived cultural homogenisation (often regarded as 'Americanisation'). This issue is taken up further in Chapter 6.

The sceptical account is useful. Above all, it reminds us of the continued centrality of the nation-state. Indeed, in one respect the world has changed enormously since the late nineteenth century, as the end of empires has seen the emergence and universalisation of the nation-state. Thus, one manifestation of globalisation is not the decline of the nation-state, but rather its universalisation (see Chapter 3). In terms of economics, states retain considerable leverage over taxation and expenditure decisions, the setting of interest rates, continued protectionist policies, research and development, education, and so on. More widely, two points can be made. First, states do not become irrelevant in the context of enmeshment in the institutions of 'global governance'; and second, national cultures retain considerable vitality even when faced with enhanced cultural diversity.

But in other respects the sceptical position is problematic. In particular there is a tendency to argue that nothing of great significance has changed in recent years. Indeed, the argument is sometimes made that globalisation should be seen simply as an ideology, a way of justifying unpalatable policies such as redundancies as necessary in the face of 'global competition'. I will argue later that much of the rhetoric on globalisation is ideological in precisely this way. But on the other hand, globalisation is not *just* ideology, and there have been some important changes in the last 30 years.

National cultures still exist, and these have always been in some sense open to flows from 'other' cultures. However, the intensity and immediacy of global flows in recent years does mean an increase in the likelihood and amount of cultural 'mixing and matching'

– what is sometimes called cultural hybridity. Similarly, the number of international institutions, and the recognition of the reality of the need for global solutions, no matter how contested, does mean that globalisation is not simply an extension of nation-state interests. In terms of political economy, there have also been important changes. Rather than being mainly a producer of primary products, the developing world has become increasingly involved in manufacturing. On the other hand, trading and production of these goods remains highly stratified, and developing world exports to the developed world are quite low (see Chapter 5). Production has in some respects been globalised, as unfinished parts of manufactured goods may be produced in a variety of countries. There has been an increase in global competition between companies and nation-states, but there has been no level playing field, and no unambiguous race to the bottom. Financial flows have been increasingly deregulated, so that many states now allow the more-or-less free movement of money across national borders. These flows can undermine state-directed policies, especially those that aim to boost economic growth through expansionary – and inflationary – policies, as these can undermine the confidence of financial investors and lead to a flight of capital. This may not be a new phenomenon, but it certainly represents a reversal of dominant policies from the late 1940s to the 1970s. The liberalisation of trade, production and finance of the last 25 years, associated with neoliberalism, does represent very real changes, even if they are not completely novel. Sceptics rightly point to an earlier period of 'globalisation', from the late nineteenth century to 1914, but do not sufficiently emphasise that this earlier period was not one that experienced *neoliberal* globalisation. Indeed, while there were significant rates of growth in world trade in this period, they were no higher than in the 1950–73 period, when, compared to contemporary globalisation, 'national capitalisms' were relatively closed (Baker et al. 1997: 6). Moreover, in the earlier period, from 1875 to 1913, average tariff rates among the more developed capitalist economies (except Britain) were higher than in the current era of globalisation – and, indeed, higher than they had been in the period from 1820 to 1875, which is not generally regarded as an era of globalisation (Chang 2002: 17). Sceptics tend to make these valid points in order to illustrate their argument that neoliberal accounts of nineteenth-century globalisation – and neoliberal arguments that the current era of supposedly unprecedented global interdependence forces neoliberal policies on all states – are equally invalid.[1] The question of agency in promoting these policies does of course need to be addressed, but a sceptical analysis that either denies real changes or suggests that states can simply reverse these policies is not particularly useful. Certainly, states can change policies, but then we need to address the question of why so many states, and above all the US state, adopted neoliberal polices in the first place. The sceptics are therefore correct to question the globalist assumption that an era of unproblematic state-centrism has given way to an equally unproblematic era of globalisation; but, on the other hand, they are wrong to deny that the neo-Keynesian era has given way to a new era based on the dominance of neoliberalism. These issues are addressed in detail in later chapters. For the moment, we need to return to the third and final theoretical perspective.

The transformationalist thesis

The transformationalist thesis argues that the debate between the hyper-globalisers and the sceptics focuses too narrowly on quantitative measurement of the extent of globalisation, when instead we should see globalisation in terms of qualitative change. This approach, pursued by Held and his collaborators, argues that 'at the dawn of a new millennium, globalization is a central driving force behind the rapid social, political and economic changes that are reshaping modern societies and world order'. They go on to suggest that 'contemporary processes of globalization are historically unprecedented such that governments and societies across the globe are having to adjust to a world in which there is no longer a clear distinction between international and domestic, external and internal affairs' (Held et al. 1999: 7). The direction of these processes of globalisation is uncertain and contradictory. Certainly the world is increasingly globalised, but this has not led to anything like global convergence. Instead, it has seen new sources of power and inequality, and the relative marginalisation of some parts of the world – some becoming more firmly entrenched in the circuits of global power, while others are simply left out. However, no single state has absolute power, since the nature of (unequal) interdependence compels all states to adapt to a globalising world.

There is undoubtedly something useful in the transformationalist account, particularly its tendency to define globalisation in terms of a set of processes rather than as an end-state (which is implicit in the debate between hyper-globalisation and scepticism). The direction of globalisation is in many respects uncertain and contingent, and it is true that globalisation is a process in which no single agent has overall control. However, much the same point could be made about capitalism – Marx's theory of alienation was based on the fact that neither workers nor capitalists were in control, even if capitalists had far more power in this anarchic system than workers. This is an important point, because the argument made by transformationalists that power is fluid (Held and McGrew 2002: 6–7), and that no one is in absolute control, is correct; but again, we have to question the view that this is entirely novel. Similarly, the transformationalists' attempt to transcend the debate between the other two positions is unconvincing. The claim that the transformationalist view based on qualitative change moves us beyond the focus on quantitative change begs the question, because a marked qualitative change presupposes quantitative change that is so great as to have produced it.[2] But I think the main problem with this account is more fundamental. The quotation above refers to globalisation as a 'central driving force' behind rapid changes in the world order. But is globalisation a driving force *at all*? Is it not, rather, simply a concept that attempts to capture some important changes in the contemporary world, without saying how they have come about? In other words, is globalisation a concept concerned only with a series of broadly related *outcomes* or *processes*, but which actually has little to say about the *agencies that lead these outcomes and processes*?

The force of this critique can be seen by returning to a consideration of Giddens' definition of globalisation. For Giddens (1999), globalisation is a revolutionary development, in which formerly locally embedded social relations break free from spatial and temporal boundaries, and abstractions such as science, markets and human rights come to replace local, traditional norms. Disembeddedness means that people no longer have their lives set out in advance, but are instead constantly faced with choices about how to live. The establishment of identity therefore becomes a life project of reflexive subjects. These processes reach a climax with globalisation, as nation-states lose control in the face of global communications, capital flows, shared aspirations, and so on (Giddens 1990: 76–8). Globalisation therefore becomes an established fact; in Giddens' words, it has 'come from nowhere to be almost everywhere', and is 'simply what we are' (Giddens 1999: 1; 1997).

Giddens' approach to globalisation therefore clearly establishes the argument that there is no alternative to globalisation.[3] In this approach the concept of globalisation is used to explain widespread social change. But at the same time, globalisation also refers to a set of processes. It is therefore not altogether clear what globalisation actually is in Giddens' account. Is it (i) a new theory used to explain important social changes; or (ii) a concept used to understand and clarify a number of important social changes? (Rosenberg 2000) This is not a semantic point. If globalisation is a theory used to explain the world, then it must explain the mechanisms that account for the change from pre-globalisation to globalisation proper. However, if it is a concept used to aid understanding of a concrete set of processes, then we need to look for other factors that might determine processes of globalisation. In other words, is globalisation determining (the first definition) or determined (the second definition)? Again, this may seem like the worst sort of academic pedantry, but in fact the distinction has enormous implications. For if globalisation determines, then there is no alternative to it; but if it is determined by other factors, then clearly globalisation is a contested process, to which there are clearly alternatives. Giddens' response may well be that there are alternatives, but that these are available within the context of globalisation – or else they betray a fundamentalism that seeks to restore 'local embeddedness'. He may well be right about this, although it does not really capture the complexity of global–local relations, or the contexts in which (very different) 'fundamentalisms' arise. But there is a more important argument to be made, which is that if alternatives take place within globalisation, then it is surely more important to talk about the nature of those alternatives then it is to assert the significance of globalisation. For example, some people support the free movement of money across borders, while others do not, arguing the case for capital controls by nation-states. Interestingly, Third Way British Prime Minister Tony Blair is in the first camp, while Third Way intellectual guru Anthony Giddens is in the second. The implications of this difference are enormous, as the free flow of money is central to neoliberal domination, while controls on the movement of financial capital constitute a major challenge to it. But such is the over-generalised discourse of globalisation – and of the Third Way – that such differences can easily be reconciled.

Ultimately, this reconciliation can occur because Giddens' definition of globalisation attempts to tell us a great deal about the contemporary world, but in fact tells us very little. In one sense it tries to do too much, arguing that almost all change in the world is a product of globalisation. But in another sense it tells us little, because it is theorised at such a high level of abstraction and generalisation. This problem pervades the work of another leading globalisation theorist, Jan Aart Scholte. Scholte goes to great lengths to distinguish globalisation from internationalisation, liberalisation, universalisation, and westernisation/modernisation. In contrast to these older, clearly defined concepts, globalisation is defined as deterritorialisation, which is said to refer to 'a far reaching change in the nature of social space' (Scholte 2000: 46). Whereas previous eras had seen a compression of time and space, which reduced the impact of location, globalisation is a 'supra-territorial' process, in which the only limit is planetary or global. In this definition, Scholte links the significance of globalisation to information and communications technologies, which have literally taken us (to cite Castells) beyond the space of places into the space of flows. This leaves Scholte open to the charge of technological determinism, whereby the focus is placed on the new technologies themselves rather than on the uses made of them by human beings in the process of carrying out social activities in particular places. Moreover, if the focus is only on new technologies, then one has a very restricted definition of globalisation, which begs the question of the significance of the so-called global transformation. Indeed, Scholte himself qualifies the significance of the transformation when he argues that globalisation has 'shown few signs of bringing an end to the predominance of capitalism in production, bureaucratisation in governance, communitarianism in community and rationalism in knowledge' (Scholte 2000: 5). As Rosenberg has pointed out, this leaves Scholte facing a catch-22 situation, in which he either defines globalisation so narrowly that its significance is limited, or relaxes his definition, but at the cost of re-introducing those definitions – internationalisation, liberalisation, universalisation, westernisation – previously discarded (Rosenberg 2000: 18–26). Scholte opts for the latter, and in doing so discusses various global phenomena – including trade unions, nuclear weapons, international institutions, and so on. At times the qualifications are so great as to render his theoretical analysis redundant – for instance, he argues that globalisation and territoriality are not diametrically opposed, and that, before contemporary ICTs there were earlier moments of globalisation (Scholte 2000: 8, 60). This latter argument is also made by Held et al. (1999: 415), which begs the question of the timing of the global transformation that they otherwise endorse. What is clear is that Scholte's (and for that matter Held et al.'s) empirical discussion, much of which is of great value, has re-entered the discussion only at the cost of dispensing with his theoretical approach. Indeed, substantive discussion is only possible because it breaks from the circular reasoning and spatial fetishism of globalisation theory.

The latter problem is also prevalent within the political analysis of globalisation theory. Much emphasis is placed on the changed context in which nation-states now operate, or the development of a global civil society beyond the narrow confines of national politics (Kaldor et al. 2003). The former is often linked to the question of US hegemony (Chace 1992), and the main argument made is that military might is no longer the main source of power in the post-Cold War, interdependent world order. The only effective means of exercising leadership (as opposed to hegemony) is to develop a truly liberal vision of collective defence, international cooperation, multilateral diplomacy (Nye 1990). This argument is sometimes explicitly linked to debates around 'liberal internationalism', and the argument is often made that globalisation provides an enabling context for such internationalism at last to be properly exercised. We will consider these arguments in detail in later chapters, but two critical points need to be made here. First, they ignore the capitalist and neoliberal nature of globalisation and liberal internationalism, and thereby also ignore the reality of uneven development and the limitations of multilateral institutionalism in this context. Second, they also closely parallel the logic of neoliberalism in its treatment of globalisation. Just as neoliberals talk of 'market imperfections' as being caused by 'external' interventions, so globalists implicitly point to 'global imperfections' caused by the same interventions. The implicit assumption is the market or the global could be effective in the absence of such interventions. The most serious intervention is the action of states that do not play by the rules of the game. But, given the uneven development of global capitalism and the intensified inequality associated with neoliberalism, such interventions are bound to occur (see Chapter 5). In other words, the 'imperfections' of globalisation (or of the market) are not external to it, but are an intrinsic part of the way it operates. Moreover, markets do not exist in isolation from states, since states play an important role not only in protecting, but even in *creating* markets. This point can be related to post-war US hegemony, since globalists argue that in the post-Cold War era the US state can play a new role in the international order. But this argument ignores the fact that the US was concerned not only with the containment of communism, but equally with liberal, capitalist expansion, which has intensified since the end of the Cold War. Indeed, this point was explicitly stated in one of the main National Security Memoranda of the post-war period, NSC-68 (see Robinson 1996: 15). The important point here is not whether or not liberal capitalist expansion is a 'good' or 'bad' thing,[4] but that this old question cannot be evaded by ideas like cosmopolitanism and global civil society; indeed, its proponents cannot avoid making implicit assumptions about a liberal capitalist order, and about the role of the US in promoting such an order.

Similarly, the assumption of an intrinsically progressive global civil society collapses a potentially useful analytical concept into an automatically desirable normative principle. Moreover, globalisation tends to be theorised as a linear process that outgrows the nation-state, and so politics is measured solely by the extent to which movements and ideas react to globalisation. Like the globalist position on US hegemony, this argument downplays the agencies involved in the processes of globalisation, and in seeing globalisation as largely progressive, ignores its predominantly neoliberal character. Moreover, as we shall see, neoliberal globalisation is a process that has been promoted in part by nation-states. Theorists of global civil society express regret that, since September 11, 2001, there has been a movement back towards 'nation-state thinking', particularly under George Bush (Kaldor et al. 2003: 7). The problem with this argument is that it exaggerates the 'non-nation-state thinking' before Bush, and sets up a false dichotomy of global good and national bad. It is not spaces in themselves, be they national, local or global, that are intrinsically progressive or reactionary, but the social relations and politics within and between such spaces[5] (Kiely 2004).

So, returning to the two definitions of globalisation outlined above, it is clear that globalisation is not a 'big theory' that can explain current events in the world. Rather, it is a concept that can be used to clarify a set of processes taking place in the world order. Globalisation thus refers to certain *outcomes*, themselves determined by other factors. This implies that processes of globalisation are the product of particular social and political agents, and that there are conflicts among these agents. This in turn implies that these processes of globalisation are intimately connected to relationships of power and domination. This section has therefore argued for a view of globalisation that refers to a set of concrete processes, promoted and resisted by different agents. I am therefore arguing against globalisation theory, but in favour of a theory of globalisation that explains certain outcomes and processes through a proper examination of social and political agencies. The final section in this chapter draws out the implications of the discussion so far, and argues for a thorough repoliticisation of the globalisation debate.

REPOLITICISING GLOBALISATION

My argument so far is that there are serious problems with globalisation theory. Globalisation is a useful concept, as it does capture the reality of certain globalising processes in the contemporary world. Indeed, transformationalists do a useful job in outlining what some of these are, even as sceptics draw our attention to their limitations. The following chapters will provide some illustration of this point by, for example, showing that capital does not disperse equally throughout the globe, and that institutions of global governance exist alongside the nation-state. But in later chapters these issues will be addressed in a different way from the threefold divide outlined above. Instead, they will be addressed in terms of agency, power and politics, bringing us back to questions of capitalism, neoliberalism and state power. I start by making a few brief comments about political confusion in the globalisation debate. I then move on to suggest that this confusion can lead to a conflation of two things – the 'reality' of globalisation on the one hand, and globalisation as a political project on the other – which again returns us to the question of agency. I will then conclude by making some suggestions concerning the relationship between capitalism and globalisation.

The globalisation debate has often conflated two issues: the extent to which globalisation is a reality, and the extent to which it is desirable. As we saw above, it is perfectly possible to accept the hyper-globalisation argument and to see its conclusions as good or bad; similarly, some sceptics will support continued US state power, while others will oppose it. But the confusion is most obvious in the transformationalist account, which accepts globalisation as a reality, and then insists that politics must take place within its framework. But the question that then needs to be asked is: What should we take for granted, or accept as given, when talking about globalisation? Do we simply accept its capitalist nature? More narrowly, do we accept the rise of neoliberalism, both empirically and morally, and the end of neo-Keynesianism?[6]

A few examples illustrate the point. British Prime Minister Tony Blair constantly asserts that global competitive pressures mean that we have to respond by increasing this flexibility of our labour market.

In Blair's tautologous thinking, this is a necessity because there is no alternative: it is a constraint on the state. On the other hand, together with former Home Secretary David Blunkett, he has also argued that the state must tighten its policies on entry for asylum seekers. In other words, the state can be pro-active in this case, and is not a prisoner of forces beyond its control – namely, wars and human rights abuses in other countries. Where then does this leave globalisation rhetoric? In the first case, globalisation is 'merely the way we are', but it clearly is not in the second. Discourses of globalisation all too easily conflate inevitability and desirability, reality and ideology, established fact and political project. Globalisation becomes so all-pervasive that there is little that we can do to change it, and we must work within clearly established political parameters. But crucially, these parameters are largely set by the victory of neoliberalism in the 1980s, which argued for the primacy of market forces, free trade, liberalised finance and open competition. Insofar as there is a theory of power in this approach, it is located in the discourse of globalisation, which is said to set the boundaries for debates about the limitations of politics. Power – in the sense of social and political actors promoting certain globalising tendencies – tends to disappear from view. Of course, the discourse of globalisation is important, but this is precisely because it is used by these same dominant social and political forces to justify the notion that 'there is no alternative'. In this way, contingency is redefined as necessity (Watson and Hay 2003). At the same time, there have been some concessions about the problems of the rampant neoliberalism of the 1980s, with a renewed focus on poverty reduction and institutional development at the World Bank, for instance; but these concessions remain firmly within a neoliberal framework (see Chapter 5). Similarly, there is also massive state intervention – both by nation-states (especially the US Treasury) and international institutions (especially the IMF) – but this is designed above all to protect investors when markets (especially financial markets) threaten economies with widespread collapse. State (national and international) regulation is largely market-expanding rather than market-restricting. Similarly, neoconservatism breaks with some core themes of the Third Way, such as (selective) commitment to multilateralism. But this break in terms of means hides substantial continuity over the ends of globalisation. In particular, I will argue that we can identify three broad projects that relate to the current period of contemporary, neoliberal globalisation. The first is associated with the move towards neoliberalism in the 1980s, the second with the consolidation of neoliberalism through the Third Way in the 1990s, and the third with the neoconservative moment in the US under Bush II.

But in order to understand the neoliberal nature of globalisation, we first have to understand its *capitalist* nature. This point is crucial if we are to grasp the fact that globalisation is not simply an established fact, but instead represents processes that are inseparable from relationships of domination, and are therefore contested. This argument can be illustrated by starting with a famous quotation from as long ago as 1848:

> The bourgeoisie cannot exist without constantly revolutionising the instruments of production, and thereby the relations of production, and with them the whole relations of society ... Constant revolutionising of production, uninterrupted disturbance of all social conditions, everlasting uncertainty and agitation distinguish the bourgeois epoch from all earlier ones. All fixed, fast frozen relations, with their train of ancient and venerable prejudices and opinions, are swept away, all new formed ones become antiquated before they can ossify. All that is solid melts into air, all that is holy is profaned, and man is at last compelled to face with sober senses his real conditions of life and his relations with his kind. (Marx and Engels 1977: 36–7)

This quotation from the *Manifesto of the Communist Party* captures something of the globalising processes that lie at the heart of the contemporary globalisation debate. There is discussion of the notion that the world is increasingly interconnected, that the intensity and velocity of these interconnections is increasing, and that distinct localities are thus increasingly 'disembedded'. There is also some notion (and too much optimism) that a genuine global consciousness is developing as a result. But what is also apparent from the first sentence is some notion of agency, related to the notion of competition between capitals. Marx and Engels (1977: 37–8) go on:

> The need of a constantly expanding market for its products chases the bourgeoisie over the whole surface of the globe. It must nestle everywhere, settle everywhere, establish connexions everywhere ... The bourgeoisie has through its exploitation of the world market given a cosmopolitan character to production and consumption in every country ... The bourgeoisie, by the rapid improvement of all instruments of production, by the immensely facili-tated means of communication, draws all, even the most barbarian, nations into civilisation ... It compels all nations, on pain of extinction, to adopt the

bourgeois mode of production; it compels them to introduce what it calls civilisation into their midst, i.e. to become bourgeois themselves. In one word, it creates a world after its own image. (Mark and Engels 1977: 37–8)

Thus, for Marx globalisation is ultimately a product of the dynamism of the capitalist mode of production, which itself is a product of historically specific relations of production. These relations are based on the separation of labour from direct access to the means of production – that is, on the removal of producers from the land. This ongoing process was particularly common in England from the seventeenth century, and continues throughout the world to this day. With this removal, labourers are forced to find paid employment in order to be able to buy commodities, which enables them to feed and clothe themselves and their families, and enables their capitalist employers to make a profit through paying a wage lower than the value of the commodities produced by labour. The removal of the producers from the land simultaneously generalises production for the market. When labour has direct access to land, it consumes goods produced on that land (and sells its surplus); when labour ceases to have access to land, it consumes goods bought through the market mechanism. Displacement of labour from the land – or the commodification of labour power – thus simultaneously generalises commodity production. Market societies do not arise spontaneously or naturally; rather, they are the product of political and social processes (Polanyi 1944).

At the same time, this generalisation of commodity production leads to competition between units of production, as each unit attempts to sell its goods at the most competitive rate in the marketplace. If goods are too expensive, then a particular production unit will go bankrupt. Potentially uncompetitive producers can lower costs by cutting wages or increasing the intensity of work (extracting absolute surplus value), but this process eventually comes up against physical limits – wages can only be cut so far, and people can only work so hard. So, an alternative strategy is for capital to invest in new technology, which increases labour productivity (and therefore increases the extraction of relative surplus value). This investment in new technology is a never-ending process, as specific capitals always face the danger of being undercut by innovative competitors. States may protect specific capitals from competition, but ultimately capital accumulation is an ongoing, dynamic and never-ending process. This accumulation is uneven and unequal, and potentially uncontrollable, and it is a process that is not, and never has been, confined to national borders. In the quotations above, Marx was clearly wrong in his belief that the global expansion of capitalism would lead to similar processes of capitalist development throughout the globe; instead there emerged an unequal international division of labour. But he was clearly correct that the dynamism of capitalism paved the way for what we now call globalisation.

At the same time, the 'freeing' of labour from the land also led to a further separation.[7] In feudal society, the regulation of peasant labour with access to land was the task of the 'state'. There was no economy or civil society separate from the state: the state was the economy. Peasants worked the land to feed themselves, but states also ensured that landlords received a rent in the form of goods, labour or money-rent. With the emergence of capitalism, the state did not directly regulate the relationship between employer (capitalist) and employee (worker), as this was a purely 'economic' matter. The modern state – the creation of a separate political sphere – is thus also the product of capitalist social relations. The separate economic sphere (the market) is thus no longer directly regulated by the political sphere. Indeed, the very separation of these spheres is accomplished by the rise of capitalist social relations. We therefore have a potentially global market existing side by side with national states. States and globalisation, therefore, do not exist in opposition to each other; the expansion of one does not lead to a weakening of the other, since both are the product of capitalist social relations. Moreover, states are not irrelevant, nor merely instruments of capitalist domination. They serve a number of functions for capital, including the protection of private property rights, the provision of infrastructure, the protection for industries, as well as broader functions of repression and the provision of social legitimation. Some states – above all the US state – have also actively promoted processes of globalisation, as we will see in later chapters.

Understanding the relationship between capitalism and globalisation is essential, because we need to understand how specific processes of globalisation relate to wider social and political structures. We will then be in a better position to understand that these processes have not simply 'come from nowhere', and that they are a product of particular agents, embedded in particular places, based on particular power relations (and therefore relations of conflict). Having said that, recognising the global character of capitalism from the outset does not tell us what is distinctive about the current period of contemporary (neoliberal) globalisation, or how this came about, and these tasks will be undertaken in Chapter 5. But what should be clear by now is that, in claiming that globalisation has either come from nowhere, or is the product of new technologies, globalisation theory fails convincingly to address US hegemony and neoliberal capitalism, and is thus in some respects complicit with both.

GLOBALISATION AS REALITY, GLOBALISATION AS IDEOLOGY

My main argument in this chapter has been that globalisation theory conflates globalisation as outcome (something that needs to be explained) with globalisation as agent (something that does the explaining). The result is that globalisation easily slips from being a concrete analysis – globalisation as reality – to become a political project. Focusing on political economy, James Cypher (cited in Dowd 2000: 170) usefully distinguishes between globalisation as tendency and globalisation as ideology:

> As an objective tendency, globalization implies a deepening and strengthening of trade, financial markets and production systems across national boundaries. Propelling this tendency we find broad institutional changes occurring, strengthening the integration of the circuits of trade, finance and production. Globalization implies a greater degree of convergence in markets and institutions, and a greater degree of homogenisation of dysfunctional movements such as economic crises which quickly shift across national borders … As an ideology, globalization implies both the *inevitability* and *desirability* of the above described tendencies toward integration and the *denial* of the existence of dysfunctional movements arising from this tendency.

The approach suggested in this chapter, and taken up in the rest of the book, is to argue that globalising outcomes have intensified in recent years, and that these need to be explained in terms of specific agents who have promoted them. Indeed, many of the changes in the global order since the 1970s have been the product of particular nation-states, and of political projects within those states. And these projects have essentially been neoliberal in character, whether in the form of neoliberal fundamentalism in the 1980s, the Third Way of the 1990s, or the neoconservatism of the Bush II administration (Kiely 2005: Chs 2 and 4). This project is above all committed to market expansion through trade, investment and financial liberalisation, and to the universal (cosmopolitan) expansion of liberal democratic politics.

Globalisation is therefore linked to the (neo)liberal internationalists' project of the expansion of free-market democracies. This is regarded as a progressive aspiration, as it will enhance the 'goods' of globalisation, such as economic growth, poverty alleviation and universal human rights (through market efficiency and humanitarian intervention), while reducing the 'bads', such as environmental destruction and global terrorism (through multilateral cooperation and the promotion of peaceful, liberal states).

My argument in the chapters that follow therefore suggests that, despite some differences, there is fundamental continuity in the expansion of neoliberal capitalism from the early 1980s to the present. But because I also want to address the issue of the 'outcomes' of globalisation, I suggest that these have not been as benign as implied by various advocates of globalisation. Neither is it the case that bad outcomes have been caused by insufficient globalisation. Instead, the argument will be made that neoliberal globalisation is intrinsically hierarchical and exploitative. Of course, we should not expect anything else from capitalism, whatever social gains may be made under this system. However, I will also argue that, in many respects, neoliberal globalisation constitutes a backward step from the gains made in the post-war period – and that, therefore, whatever the prospects for socialist alternatives to capitalism, it is simply illegitimate for globalisation theorists such as Giddens to take neoliberal capitalism for granted on the grounds that there is no alternative to it. This is a debatable point, which I return to in Chapter 7. But Giddens makes the leap from acceptance of capitalism to unsustainable arguments about its capacities to deliver a better world.

There is a close parallel between the perspective offered in this chapter and Karl Polanyi's critique of the laissez-faire ideology of free-market economics. I will return to Polanyi in the concluding chapter, but I want briefly to outline his argument concerning the relationship between 'states' and 'markets' here – not least because it gives some insight into the relationship between the US state and contemporary globalisation. Polanyi, like Marx before him, argued that there is no such thing as the free market as such. Instead, the market economy is created by a process of disembedding the 'economy' from social regulation. Markets exist in all societies, but it is only in the market economy (capitalism) that the market becomes the overriding principle of production and distribution. Key to this process is the creation of the 'fictitious commodities' of land, labour and money. These commodities are defined as fictitious by Polanyi on the grounds that they are not naturally commodities, but become so through specific social and political processes. Thus, following Marx, Polanyi argued that labour power and land only become commodities when labourers are separated from direct access to land. This has the effect of converting increasing areas of production into commodities, and thus creating the free-market economy. It is for this reason that Polanyi (1944: 141) argued that '(l)aissez faire was planned'. The creation of a market economy therefore occurs through a process of disembedding, so that economy is separated from polity and society. Such a separation is never complete, however, as 'economy' always relies on regulation by polity, and the free market has a number of destructive effects precisely because it is based on a severing of the market from social regulation. These include inequality, exploitation, alienation, and accumulation without end.

I return to these issues in later chapters, but what should be clear is how this approach provides us with a potentially useful starting point for understanding globalisation. For the current era of globalisation is about a new stage of increased disembedding, involving the expansion of commodity production and distribution. However, contra Giddens, this process has not simply come 'from nowhere', but needs to be seen in terms of a political project closely tied to neoliberalism. This has implications for our understanding of global politics (whereby some nation-states and international institutions are directly part of the neoliberal project, while others play a wider policing role), the global economy (whereby trade, production and finance have in some respects become more closely, though hierarchically, integrated) and global culture (whereby the promotion of 'universal' human rights exists alongside the increased domination of the commodity). Globalisation is also, however, a contested process, so that, for example, institutions of global governance are not simply reducible to the neoliberal project, even if they are seriously implicated in it.

3
Globalisation and Politics I: State Sovereignty, Imperialism and Cosmopolitanism

One of the most important areas of contention in the globalisation debate relates to the questions of the nation-state, international institutions and global governance. The post-war period has seen a proliferation of international institutions and agreements, or an increased role for already established ones. This can be seen in the cases of the United Nations, the Bretton Woods institutions, regional agreements, the World Trade Organisation and the International Criminal Court, and in the increase in the number and the reach of international summits.

The growth in the significance of such institutions of governance is said to constitute a significant 'break' from existing modes of international political interaction, which was based on the nation-state system, empires and colonialism. For those independent states that existed at the time, international relations were said to be premised on the sovereignty of states. This notion of state sovereignty dates back to 1648, but it was actually only generalised as a principle in the era after the Second World War, when the former colonies began to win their independence, a process that was supported by the US. But it has been claimed by some globalisation theorists (see Chapter 2) that recent changes associated with political globalisation have undermined state sovereignty, and indeed may eventually lead to the end of the nation-state. In its place, some argue that we now have a system of global governance, and for some 'cosmopolitan' theorists this represents a potentially welcome development. Most Marxists, on the other hand, argue that the current global order is still composed of nation-states, and that the international state system and the uneven nature of capitalist development mean that the world order is still based on relations that can be characterised as imperialist.

This chapter examines these issues, relating them to globalisation through detailed discussion of the development of state sovereignty and the international institutions of 'global governance'. The chapter engages particularly with the theories of cosmopolitanism and Marxism, relating them to the question of US hegemony. I start by examining state sovereignty, and question the idea that 1648 represents the starting point for understanding the modern state system. Rather than undermining states, I argue that globalisation is actually associated with the (still incomplete) universalisation of the system of nation-states. Having said that, there is a need to recognise that there has been a considerable increase in the number and role of international institutions, especially since 1945, and this is discussed in the second section. In the third section I examine some of the debates around global governance, and focus on whether these have led to – or at least opened up the possibility of – the promotion of genuinely multilateral governance, beyond the system of nation-states. I examine competing approaches that attempt to understand the nature of global governance, and pay particular attention to the possibility of dialogue between cosmopolitan and open Marxist approaches. The discussion is then developed further in Chapter 4.

THE MODERN STATE SYSTEM

Standard realist accounts of international relations argue that the world order is anarchical, as it is composed of nation-states all exercising their self-interest. The world order may change, in that some states may climb the hierarchy of the international order while others fall. But the international order itself is characterised essentially by a permanent state of anarchy. This system had its origins in the Treaty of Westphalia of 1648, which ended the Thirty Years War in Europe. From this point on (if not before), the international order was based on modern, sovereign nation-states.

This view can be challenged in a number of ways. For the moment, the focus will be on the question of the origins and development of supposedly modern states. Some Marxists have argued that the modern international system of nation-states actually developed at a later date than 1648 (Wood 1991; Teschke 2003; Lacher 2003). The essential argument is that a specifically *capitalist* sovereignty only emerged in the nineteenth century, and this specific form of sovereignty was based on the development of impersonal public authorities – modern states – that recognised the sovereignty of other (European) states. Existing alongside these modern states were capitalist market economies, under which commodity production was generalised, thus replacing the dominance of production for direct consumption.

To understand the distinction between the sovereignty of 1648 and capitalist sovereignty, we first need to understand the distinction between feudalism and capitalism. Feudal Europe emerged out of the collapse of the Carolingian Empire around the turn of the tenth century (Teschke 2003: 84–6), which covered much of what are now France, Germany, Austria, Italy and north-east Spain. The result of this breakdown was the fragmentation of power, and the development of overlapping forms of sovereignty based on personal rule or patrimonial power (Anderson 1974; Weber 1978). The feudal political order was thus based on a number of overlapping systems of authority, and political power and the means of violence were distributed among a variety of dominant classes. The exercise of force was crucial to the extraction of a surplus from the peasantry. In feudal society, peasants retained access to land, their principal means of livelihood, and political power was the instrument by which peasants were compelled to give up a surplus, which could take the form of labour, goods or rent. The ability to extract surplus thus depended on access to political power, which facilitated extra-economic compulsion. Expansion in this era largely took a territorial form, and was designed to increase the number of peasants (and therefore surplus) that came under the jurisdiction of a particular lord.

However, lords held land as a 'fief' from an overlord. Fiefs were granted in return for military and administrative services. Property rights were therefore dependent on certain obligations to higher lords, and ultimately this system of obligation was directed up towards the king. As bearers of arms, lords could carry out feuds, which 'straddled the boundaries between the private and the public, the domestic and the international, the legitimate and the criminal recourse to arms' (Teschke 2004: 17). This order ensured that, as the means of violence were distributed (upwards and downwards) among a variety of lords, medieval 'international' politics were prone to violence and territorial acquisition. The acquisition of land was central to increasing finance, as this was ultimately derived from the exploitation of peasant labour. *Political accumulation* (Brenner 1986) was the driving force in feudal society, and geopolitics was based on territorial competition for increased territory which would enhance access to the exploitation of peasant labour.

However, feudal society was more complex than this, and the existence of different kinds of lordship in the Carolingian Empire crucially influenced later developments. First, banal lordship was based on the king's royal power, and entailed direct taxation of the peasantry (or at least taxation through the king's counts). Second, there was domestic lordship, based on absolute power over serfs. Third, there was landlordship, based on land ownership, tenant freedom and limited rights of service. At the height of the Empire, the first two kinds of lordship existed side by side. Local lords therefore extracted rents in both labour and kind from serfs who worked on their manor, while the king taxed free peasants. Potential territorial conflict between competing lords was partly moderated by the king's protection of the free peasantry, who were an important source of revenue for the king. But crucially, internal conflict was moderated by outward expansion through conquest, and the consequent redistribution of land acquired through wars of annexation (Teschke 2003: 69–73).

These opportunities for territorial acquisition gave the Empire some stability. But this was undermined by the expansion of Vikings, Hungarians and Saracens into the Carolingian Empire, which weakened territorial jurisdiction, imperial authority and ruling-class solidarity. The result was an increase in attempts to extract surplus from peasantries, the usurping of public offices in order to maintain control of the peasantry and to offset lost income opportunities, and open conflict between regional lords and overlords. The centralised authority of the Empire was gradually broken up and decentralised. Political units were decentralised, local fiefs and local taxes were developed, and free peasants became serfs. The period from 950 to 1150 was one of great violence, territorial competition, and military innovation. Localised banal lordship required heavy military backing in the context of heightened competition over land, labour and other feudal privileges.

From the eleventh to the fourteenth centuries, feudal Europe recovered, and underwent a new period of expansion, fuelled by population growth, reclamation of arable land, and increased exploitation of serf labour. The increase in lords' incomes further stimulated demand and laid the basis for urban revival and long-term trade (Hilton 1976: 145–58). The growth in trade was still embedded however, in predominantly feudal social relations, under which production for use dominated. As a result, there was little incentive to increase productivity. However, there was significant regional variation, which is crucial for understanding the transition to capitalism in England.

In France, political power was fragmented. The king and princes tried to regain power from the lowliest of lords, known as the castellans. The authority of the king was quite weak, and competition emerged between different sections of the ruling class, particularly over taxation of the peasantry. This conflict within the ruling class gave some space for the peasantry to resist successfully: they shook off the bonds of serfdom, some labour rents were turned into money rents, and by the fourteenth century peasants had de facto property rights. Rents became fixed, which – reinforced by peasant appeals to the royal courts, which were supported by the king, who benefited from free peasants paying tax to him rather than rent to landlords – undermined the income of the castellans. This development meant that, by the fourteenth century, independent lords had effectively disappeared, the peasants had independent property rights (subject to royal taxation), and the nobility's income was mainly acquired through service to the king. This eventually led to the emergence of the absolutist state, in which the feudal lord–peasant rent regime was replaced by the absolutist king–peasant tax regime. Absolutism did not lead to modern, capitalist sovereignty based on a market economy and a bureaucratic, impersonal state that monopolised the means of violence. Instead, production was still mainly for consumption, and peasant taxation was used to finance consumption and military spending. The long-term tension between punitive taxation and increased military spending eventually led to the French Revolution of 1789 (Comninel 1987). State sovereignty was based on proprietary kingship and personal domination. The aristocracy were incorporated into the state as office-holders, which gave them access to new privileges. In particular, the means of violence were personalised by the king, but also awarded to patrimonial officers through the sale of army posts. Foreign policy was carried out, not in the 'national interest', but in the name of the king. Accumulation continued to take place through war and marriage between dynasties, and trade was politically enforced through the sale of monopoly trading charters to merchants. War was essentially fought over dynastic territorial claims and exclusive trading routes. The Westphalian system of 1648 was essentially, then, a treaty between absolutist, personalised states, not modern, capitalist states.

In England, on the other hand, (and, from 1707, Great Britain) social development took a radically different direction. After 1066, Anglo-Saxon landowners were dispossessed or killed, and land was redistributed to William the Conqueror and his leading warriors.

These barons held estates in the service of the king, and the king in turn presided over a centralised state and exercised unquestioned sovereignty. Private feuding in the context of parcellised sovereignties was thereby minimised, institutions were established for peacefully settling land disputes, and peasants were turned into serfs. England therefore maintained a system of lords exploiting serfs on their manors, alongside a king who taxed freeholding peasants. The English system of a centralised state, powerful ruling class and serfdom contrasted sharply with the decentralised state, divided ruling class and independent peasantry of France. This contrast was sharpened further by the reaction to the crises of the fourteenth and fifteenth centuries. While in France, lords turned against each other to retain income, in England lords attempted to recover income by increasing rents, despite a fall in the population. Peasants successfully resisted attempts to increase the rate of exploitation, and as a result serfdom ended (Hilton 1973). But instead of the establishment of freeholding peasants based on owner-occupation, the English peasantry were gradually removed from the land through enclosure. Landlords then leased the land out to tenants who employed wage labour. Surplus was thus extracted less by direct coercion, as in France, and more by the success of tenants in selling products in a competitive marketplace. A growing number of English tenancies were basically economic in nature, with rents fixed not by legal obligation but by market conditions. In other words, there was a market for leases, and thus competition in the market for consumers and access to land (Brenner 1976). Agricultural producers therefore became increasingly market-dependent for their access to land, with the result that 'advantage in access to the land itself would go to those who could produce competitively and pay good rents by increasing their own productivity' (Wood 2002: 100–1). The most competitive farmers therefore had potential access to more land, while the less competitive faced the danger of losing direct access. French peasants thus had the potential to specialise and increase production for the market, but they generally did not respond to this market opportunity. In England, on the other hand, variable economic rents meant that peasants were *compelled* to do so – otherwise they would not be able to pay their rent and would therefore risk losing their lease (Wood 2002: 102).

The (long, slow) process of peasant differentiation, in which some peasants were displaced from the land and became wage labourers, was reinforced by the emergence of a strong state that facilitated, rather than restricted, this market imperative (Marx 1976: Ch. 27; Corrigan and Sayer 1985). In the long run, the English social structure based on landlords leasing to capitalist farmers, who in turn increasingly employed wage labourers, facilitated the movement from agrarian to industrial capitalism. This was due to the increase in productivity that fed a rising non-agricultural population, the emergence of a labour force displaced from the land, and the competitive accumulation of capital which eventually gave rise to industrial development (Hobsbawm 1962: 47).

The long-term result of these processes was the establishment of a specifically *capitalist* sovereignty (Rosenberg 1994), based on a market economy of generalised commodity production, and a political state that had a monopoly over the means of violence. Surplus extraction now took place through 'purely economic' relations (the market), but the state still (indirectly) guaranteed capitalist social relations through its defence of the system of private property, of contracts, and of violence. British capitalist development paved the way for new geopolitical relations. From the late seventeenth century, British politics was based on parliamentary sovereignty and a constitutional monarch. Foreign policy was now directed by parliament and separated from dynastic interests. Britain played the role of balancing power relations in Europe, which was still dominated by territorial accumulation. Rivalries persisted, and Britain became involved in a number of wars, maintaining territorial ambitions outside of Europe, albeit for commercial gain. In the long run, Britain benefited most from European rivalries, as its productive, market-led, economy ensured that it alone could afford military, and especially naval, expansion. On the other hand, other absolutist states faced ongoing fiscal crises and peasant revolt.

Capitalism was thus 'born into' a European state system, which it then transformed but did not displace (Teschke 2004: 45; Lacher 2003). By the nineteenth century, European powers and the US were effectively forced to promote capitalist development in order to defend and promote their interests. Capitalism was thus often promoted by pre-existing states, which intervened to promote 'market economies', and often protected themselves against foreign competition, particularly from the already highly productive British economy (Chang 2002). Thus, it was not until the nineteenth and twentieth centuries that geopolitics based on capitalist sovereignty emerged. However, the unevenness of the emergence of sovereign states and market economies was most clearly apparent in the continued territorial expansion of the dominant capitalist powers in Europe (Wood 2003: 119–30). It was only after the Second World War, when colonies slowly won their independence, that we can identify a system of sovereign, capitalist nation-states, which existed alongside an increasing number of international institutions. The promotion of sovereign states and the capitalist market took place in the context of US leadership of the 'free world', and indeed both state sovereignty and capitalist expansion were encouraged by the US, albeit so long as such states were its allies. Indeed, given that much of the world remained communist until recently, perhaps we should consider 1989 as the key date on which capitalist sovereignty was (almost) universalised. Ironically, just as the capitalist-led nation-state system had become universalised in the international order, many globalisation theorists began referring to the hollowing out of the nation-state.

THE NATION-STATE AND GLOBAL GOVERNANCE

The fate of the nation-state is often linked to the rise of contemporary globalisation. As we saw in Chapter 2, much of the debate focuses on the ways in which global flows or international institutions may undermine the authority of the nation-state. But a further point has been developed, which can be related to the idea of the rise of a global consciousness based on the rights of 'distant strangers', regardless of nation-state affiliation. This *cosmopolitan* perspective has seen a significant resurgence in recent years, although it is not necessarily linked to contemporary globalisation. For example, US President Woodrow Wilson established his 'Fourteen Points' for national self-determination after the end of the First World War, and even Lenin championed the right of nations to self-determination. Lenin was fully aware that this principle was not an accurate reflection of the actual behaviour of imperial nation-states, which had constantly colonised overseas territories, but he saw it as a useful tool in the mobilisation of people oppressed by colonialism to establish independence. On the other hand, Wilson hoped to establish a principle of collective security through the League of Nations, which aimed to provide some protection if the self-determination of (some) nations was threatened by hostile aggressors. In practice, however, the League was relatively powerless. The US Congress successfully resisted US membership, and the conflicts between European states undermined any commitment to multilateral agreement. This culminated in the rise of Hitler and the Second World War. However, after the war the United Nations was established, and this helped to set the agenda for a new era of (limited) global governance, albeit one where the US was clearly 'first among equals'.

The principle of self-determination for nations implies the need for some policing of this system, in order to protect those nations under threat from aggressor states. This means some limitation on the principle in the first place, as states agree to some policing by international systems of governance. Even more important, the primacy of state sovereignty can be questioned in cases where those same states exercise systematic human rights abuses within their own territory. Indeed, this was a point powerfully made in the eighteenth century by the leading philosopher of cosmopolitanism, Immanuel Kant (Kant, 1983). Thus, the United Nations was committed to the principle of the right of nations to self-determination, but was also committed to the rights of individuals, and the two principles could potentially contradict each other. If the right of the individual took precedence over the principle of self-determination, then the sovereignty of the nation-state would be questioned. This debate has become particularly acute, both since the end of the Cold War and after the terrorist attacks on the US in September 2001, as we shall see in the next chapter.

The establishment of the UN was thus an important development in the exercising of the principle of governance alongside the nation-state system. The UN is composed of an enormous number of agencies that have played an important role in the affairs of nation-states, particularly those former colonies that won their independence in the post-war period. These include UNESCO (Educational Scientific and Cultural Organisation), UNHCR (High Commission for Refugees) and UNICEF (Children's Fund). Moreover, wider social, economic and political change since the establishment of the UN, and especially since the 1970s, has provided further impetus to the expansion of global governance. This includes the expansion of the global economy, which has meant, for example, increased regional agreements between states (such as the North American Free Trade Agreement), newly established regional institutions such as the European Union, an enhanced role for the IMF since 1982, and the formation of the World Trade Organisation in 1995 (see Chapter 5). These developments have been further reinforced by the recognition that some problems operate beyond the interests of particular nation-states – a principle most clearly established in the case of environmental regulation. Finally, they are not only restricted to the growth of formal, governmental institutions of governance. Indeed, one can recognise the development of a transnational or global civil society, made up of international NGOs that lobby these same formal institutions and attempt to mobilise public opinion around specific issues, such as debt relief. It could be argued that the rise of 'anti-globalisation' protest movements is part of this emerging global civil society, based on the transnationalisation of social movement organisations.

In some respects, then, there has been a global transformation in the character of politics in recent years. In 1900, there were 37 international government organisations and 176 international non-government organisations. By 1996, there were 1,830 international government organisations and 38,243 international non-government organisations (Held and McGrew 2002: 6–7). But does this quantitative increase amount to a qualitative transformation? This debate is discussed in detail in the next section, through an examination of competing theoretical perspectives on global governance. But some immediate comments need to be made, and these relate to the continued significance of the nation-state. In some respects, the principle of state sovereignty has always been limited. As we saw in the first section of this chapter, capitalist sovereignty is based on a territorial state and a generalised commodity-producing market economy, the latter never having been completely embedded in the former (Lacher 2003). Moreover, in much of the nineteenth and twentieth centuries, most of today's states were colonies. Even the most powerful state during the nineteenth century, Britain, did not enjoy full sovereignty or the total exercise of power over other states – a point that became slowly clear to a backward political class as competitors eroded British hegemony. Even the most powerful nation-states were therefore influenced by international affairs over which they had limited control. On the other hand, in the era of so-called global governance, we should not make the mistake of thinking that new international institutions have completely undermined the power of states. The UN has never been able to exercise governance entirely beyond the interests of specific states, as the UN Security Council gives five nations (US, UK, Russia, France and China) the right to exercise a veto power. In the Cold War period the power of the Security Council was almost always undermined by US–Soviet conflict. One-member-one-vote does exist in the UN General Assembly, but this body has no meaningful power. Deadlock at the Security Council can in theory lead to an emergency debate at the General Assembly, but this practice has not been exercised since the 1950s, when the US successfully lobbied for a debate on the Korean War. Interestingly, it could technically have been exercised in the build-up to war with Iraq in 2003, potentially causing massive embarrassment to both the US and Britain, whose governments both seemed intent on going to war with or without UN approval. That it did not – and indeed that it was not even seriously considered – perhaps tells us something about the nature of power relations at the United Nations.

I will return to the Bush administration in the next chapter. What should be clear from this brief discussion is that it is a mistake to argue that globalisation means the end of the nation-state. Nation-states have never been fully sovereign, and in the current period it has often been these same states (or some of them) that have promoted pro-globalisation policies, as well as undermining the principles of multilateral global governance. Indeed, one of the main characteristics of contemporary globalisation is actually not the erosion, but the *universalisation*, of the nation-state system. The nation-state system and global governance are therefore not opposites, but part of a greater whole.

DEBATING GLOBAL GOVERNANCE

There is widespread agreement that the last 50 years have seen a large increase in the number of international institutions, both governmental and non-governmental. The disagreement concerns the significance and political implications of the growth of these institutions. For some, these institutions could potentially lead to the growth of genuinely multilateral global governance, above and beyond the interests of specific nation states. Others are far more sceptical. This section reviews the debate, focusing on the following areas: neo-liberalism and liberal internationalism; cosmopolitanism; communitarianism and localism; realism; and Marxism.

Neoliberalism and liberal internationalism

Neoliberal approaches to global governance are ambiguous, since they contend both that markets are self-adjusting, with no need for public institutions to regulate the free market and that there *is* a need for the state in order to provide law and order, and some public goods such as defence. Public goods are goods that cannot be consumed by one individual without others also enjoying them. The classic example in neoliberal thought is that of street lighting – one individual alone cannot pay for this service, as it will lead to others using it for free. In order to overcome this problem of free riders, the state has to provide some public goods. There is, however, an important debate over whether public goods can be objectively defined, or whether the definition in part reflects the values of a particular society at a given time – for example, is health a public good, as the health of one individual may well have implications for the rest of society?

This is not a purely academic debate, as the definition of a public good has implications for the extent to which a state intervenes in the so-called free market, and this brings us back to the question of global governance. For, despite their anti-state rhetoric, neoliberals have continually relied on public intervention to protect market transactions. For instance, the debt crisis of 1982 was regulated by the IMF, and this public institution continues to play a crucial role in lending to countries (and bailing out creditors) in financial difficulty. Moreover, along with the World Bank, it is an institution that promotes 'free-market' policies. Critics have argued that the main purpose of this lending is not to protect the interests of debtors – especially the poor in indebted countries – but to protect creditors from the prospect of failed repayment and bankruptcy (see Chapter 5).

Market forces, then, are imposed on the weak, while the rich have the protection of public institutions. Indeed, there is no such thing as the free market, as markets are always regulated by the state, and so the key question concerns the form of regulation. The expansion of neoliberalism over the last 20 years has not occurred because of the natural behaviour of markets, but because mechanisms of regulation have promoted such expansion. Thus, the increase in financial flows has occurred because states – above all the US – have liberalised and deregulated controls on the movement of money. Public institutions such as the IMF and the Bank of International Settlements, as well as nation-states, continue to regulate these movements, but the trend has been for regulation to be market-expanding rather than market-restricting. Free trade has (selectively) increased because of a reduction in tariffs in most sectors of the international economy, and this has been agreed by states at meetings of the General Agreement on Tariffs and Trade (GATT), and, since 1995, the WTO.

Thus, despite claims to the contrary, neoliberalism does rely on international and national institutions in order to expand the realm of the market. What is important here is that a great deal of the regulation of the last 20 years has promoted such market expansion, and that for neoliberals this is a desirable outcome. They argue that the expansion of markets will lead to rapid growth, as each country specialises in producing those goods in which they have a comparative advantage. This specialisation occurs through the principle of open competition, according to which barriers to trade are eliminated, or at least severely reduced. Through such specialisation growth will occur, and eventually developing countries will catch up with the advanced countries. Thus, insofar as global governance promotes market expansion, it is seen as a desirable outcome. Just as states should limit intervention into the 'free market', so institutions of global governance must also play a 'minimalist' role.

This leads us to consider the related perspective of liberal internationalism, which itself can be related to the question of US hegemony (Deudney and Ikenberry 1999). In this approach, US hegemony is regarded as being a force for good, and there is no inherent conflict between the US's promotion of its national interest and the interests of international order. This argument can be traced back to the establishment and expansion of the US in the eighteenth and nineteenth centuries, but its implementation beyond national borders is often linked to President Wilson. In response to the First World War, he wanted to restructure Europe, avoid conflict that might again involve the US, and promote international cooperation through the League of Nations. His vision was undermined by continued European instability, the Bolshevik Revolution in Russia, and domestic opposition within the United States. US promotion of a liberal international order was revived during and after the Second World War, with the establishment of the UN and Bretton Woods institutions, and support for the independence aspirations of anti-colonial movements. This liberalism was undermined by the concrete agreement made at Bretton Woods, the undemocratic nature of the Security Council, and the intensification of the Cold War, particularly in the context of conflicts in different parts of the developing world. But it was revived after the Cold War with talk of a new world order, and especially of the idea that the US could act for the 'global good'. This 'new world order' was quickly undermined by the failure of intervention in Somalia in 1993, but by the late 1990s the idea of a benevolent hegemonic power acting for the global good was revived. The Clinton administration accepted – albeit selectively – that such benevolence could only be guaranteed through cooperation in a multilateral environment, and globalisation theory argued that the context of globalisation facilitated the genuine promotion of liberal internationalism, or even cosmopolitanism. Insofar as US hegemony continued, it could therefore be exercised in a more benevolent fashion. Whether or not the Clinton administration represented a benevolent hegemon is a matter for debate, but certainly the Bush administration interpreted the idea of benevolence in a more openly unilateralist way, as we will see.

Cosmopolitanism

Influenced by Kant, contemporary cosmopolitan 'is concerned to disclose the cultural, legal and ethical basis of political order in a world where political communities and states matter, but not only and exclusively ... [It] should be understood as the capacity to mediate between national cultures, communities of fate and alternative styles of life.' (Held 2003: 167–8) For cosmopolitanism to become a reality, at the very least there is a need for the institutions of global governance (and nation-states) to be properly reconstructed and democratised. There needs to be an expansion of international law so that all states are subject to the rule of law. Although not without its problems, the recently created International Criminal Court is regarded as a potential enforcer of the cosmopolitan principle of the international rule of law. International institutions need to be democratised, so that the United Nations General Assembly has more power, and veto power and permanent membership of the Security Council is abolished. Regional bodies such as the European Union also need to be democratised. This global democratisation also needs to be accompanied by an expansion of democracy at national and local levels.

The more radical cosmopolitans also argue that democratisation should not only be about institutional change. Liberal democrats have an essentially limited conception of democracy, based on formal procedures leading to the election of a government. A more substantive approach to democracy is needed, which includes more participatory mechanisms at all levels, as well as a radical redistribution of resources at local, national, and above all global levels. This would include regulations restricting market mechanisms, rather than simply enhancing them, and so they would be concerned with social and collective as well as individual rights (see Chapter 6). This would involve policies such as an increase in the amount, and improvement in the quality of, aid to poorer countries; increased controls on capital, including on the movement of money; and possibly some investment priorities set by public institutions, as well as increased social and environmental regulation. This version of cosmopolitanism is thus a kind of globalised social democracy.

However, one of the most controversial issues associated with cosmopolitanism is its approach to state sovereignty. Cosmopolitans do not see this principle as so important that it can override all others, as this can lead to an undermining of the rights of individuals within sovereign states. The restructuring of democracy involves the promotion of 'a model of political organization in which citizens, wherever they are located in the world, have a voice, input and political representation in international affairs, in parallel with and independently of their own governments' (Archibugi and Held 1995: 13). This approach can therefore rationalise a number of more contentious positions, such as support for neoliberal policies or the promotion of humanitarian military intervention. Seen in this light, cosmopolitanism has a wide range of political colours, as we will see.

Critics argue that there are two main problems with the cosmopolitan approach: feasibility and desirability. The first of these relates to the extent to which existing institutions are not multilateral at all, but actually dominated by certain states. Indeed, in some respects these institutions can enhance such domination. Much of the recent expansion of institutions of 'global governance' is not associated with a movement towards greater global democracy, but actually involves the expansion of market forces and the power of some states over others. So, for instance, the WTO may have a principle of one member one vote, but this is meaningless in the context of massive discrepancies in global resources. If, for example, the US does not abide by a WTO decision, threatened sanctions against it are of relatively little significance. However, if the US takes a developing country through the dispute settlement mechanisms of the WTO and wins its case, the effects on that developing country of US retaliation are potentially catastrophic. Moreover, dispute settlement takes time, and can therefore be very expensive, disproportionately affecting poorer countries. In addition, decision-making at the WTO is often carried out by major powers in closed meetings, and, given that the

WTO expands free-market principles with only limited attention to the relative competitive capacities of individual countries, it actually undermines the development potential of later developers (see Chapter 5). For all these reasons, critics argue that global governance is not genuinely multilateral, and that it in fact expands the power of special interests – be they dominant states (realism) or both states and capital (Marxism).

Cosmopolitanism is aware of these difficulties, but insists that there are more hopeful signs of progressive social and political change. This is because of the complexity and plurality of a multi-layered system of global governance, which means that not all international institutions can be reduced to the power of dominant states or capital. It is also clear that, precisely because some issues are of global importance, no one nation state can impose its will entirely separately from every other nation. Global problems such as environmental destruction and terrorism require global solutions, and therefore global cooperation. There has also been an increase in the number of international conventions and agreements on human rights, and promotion of an international criminal court, which, despite their limitations, show that there is some basis for international agreement on universal principles. Moreover, governance also involves some processes of dialogue with transnational civil society, which is composed of international NGOs that can pressurise existing institutions into implementing more progressive social policies. For instance, the campaign around Jubilee 2000 in the late 1990s had the effect of forcing the issue of debt relief for the poorest countries onto the agendas of the G7 nations, the World Bank and the IMF. Like theorists of 'global transformations', cosmopolitans of all shades argue that there is some room for optimism because of the increased intensity of global interconnectedness, even if such optimism has been undermined since 2001.

The other question that needs to be addressed is that of desirability. Cosmopolitanism clearly involves some commitment to universal principles; indeed, as I noted above, state sovereignty can be questioned in this approach if specific states are not conforming to these principles. Critics argue that this carries its own dangers, as it fails to address the question of who sets the 'universal' norms. If it is an unaccountable hegemonic power, then this cosmopolitanism can easily become an ideological justification for the exercise of power-politics. While Marxists and realists again link this to the dominance of states and/or capital, relativists argue that universalism is impossible, and that what is needed is the restriction of globalisation in favour of localisation.

Communitarianism and localisation

Communitarian approaches to international relations contend that local and national diversity should be celebrated, and that cosmopolitan universalism is likely to lead to the dominance of the most powerful states over weaker states. There are no universal values, because norms and ideals can only exist within particular localities and cultures. Although we all have identities that may cross borders, our most important identities are political and bounded, and are therefore linked to the nation-state. For some – though by no means all – communitarians, state sovereignty therefore trumps other values, including human rights, which are too easily used by the powerful to justify their continued dominance of the international order (Chandler 2002).

Though not identical, the localisation approach draws on some of these arguments and often applies them to an explicitly environmental and anti-globalisation politics. Although there are important differences, the focus of this approach is on grassroots movements, and a bottom-up approach to politics. Like cosmopolitanism, localism challenges state sovereignty, but in this case in the name of greater local rather than global power. Burnheim (1995) advocates the principle of demarchy, in which governance would be based on what he calls communities of fate. These communities would be self-governing, and tend to exercise the principle of subsidiarity, in which 'all decisions should be made at the lowest level of governing authority competent to deal with them' (IFG 2002: 107). For some deep ecologists, this principle can only be exercised in bioregions, where boundaries are said to be created by natural divisions.

Such decentralised systems of governance will exercise the principle of self-determination, and so the issue of universal values does not arise. But the problem of course, is that it does arise. What if one locality has far more resources than another? Or, what if one locality imposes its will on another? What if inequality and oppression are particularly great in specific localities? One prominent international NGO, the International Forum on Globalisation (IFG 2002) accepts that these are important issues, and calls for systems of global governance to redistribute wealth from richer to poorer areas. It envisages the bypassing or elimination of pro-free-market institutions like the IMF, World Bank and WTO, and the creation of democratic institutions through the United Nations. These reforms are not so far removed from the principles of cosmopolitanism. This may not be a bad thing, but it certainly undermines the principle of self-determination for localities. Localisation, in other words, implies that there must be some global governance to guarantee this commitment, even if this means some watering down of localist principles and practices. Thus, even those most suspicious of globalisation and cosmopolitanism are forced to recognise that institutions of global governance are necessary, but that they need to be more accountable to localities and regions, and that therefore they are not intrinsically imperialist.[1] One clear implication is that the universal principles espoused by cosmopolitanism do not *necessarily* lead to the exercise of power-politics. Nevertheless, there is a need to separate the current reality of power-politics from a commitment to universalism, and so a critique of cosmopolitanism should be made at the level of practice (Marxism or realism) rather than principle (relativism).

Realism

Realist accounts of international relations are sceptical of normative approaches such as cosmopolitanism. The realist argument is that we have to take the world as it is, rather than how we would like it to be, and that this world is made up of competing, self-interested nation-states. International relations are based on the struggle for power between these states, and security and peace can only be guaranteed by the maintenance of a precarious balance of power. The need for international order is therefore paramount, and it can only be maintained by hegemonic states. In practice, this currently means that order is maintained by US hegemony (although in the absence of other balancing forces, this may present some dangers).

Global governance is therefore neither feasible nor desirable. Democratisation of the foreign policy of each state is said to render it vulnerable to the irrational whims and desires of an ill-informed mass of people, and is therefore potentially far more dangerous than existing practices. Moreover, it is unlikely to take place anyway, as talk of global democracy will always be biased towards some states: thus, 'global democratisation' will in practice favour US interests. There is no global will above and beyond the interests of competing nation-states. Global governance is thus little more than an extension of the interests of these states, and of the hegemonic state in particular.

There are enormous problems with the realist perspective. The existence of sovereign states tends to be taken for granted, and there is little analysis of how these states are influenced by social and political forces in civil society. Moreover, realism assumes the existence of nation-states prior to the existence of an international system, when in fact the two exist at one and the same time. This has at least two major implications. First, it is an individualist myth that a single person exists outside of society, and a similar argument can be made regarding the relationship between an individual nation-state, and the international state system. Most nation-states did not first enter an unregulated international system, and then pursue their national interest; rather, they emerged out of an already established international system of nation-states. It is therefore a mistake to dichotomise the nation-state and the international system, including in the current era of globalisation. A second, related point follows – namely, that the power of some states over others cannot simply be taken for granted, as it is in realist theory. This tells us little about the rise and fall of particular powers, other than the fact that such movement occurs in a never-changing, anarchical international system of national states. Indeed, in assuming a never changing international order based on the state-system, realism ultimately fails to provide us with a theory of the transformation of the international order. Even more seriously for a theory that sees the state as central to its analysis, it therefore fails to provide us with a theory of the state, assuming that all systems of territorial authority are basically the same – a position challenged earlier in this chapter.

Moreover, realism can also easily conflate (supposed) analysis with apology, as hegemonic states are deemed to be necessary providers of international order. Many rogue states have been led by dictatorships that terrorise their own populations, but it is equally true that the hegemonic state in the international system has often been guilty of showing a similar contempt for international rules and norms. The effect of states should not be measured purely in relation to domestic populations, but also in respect of the wider international system of nation-states. Insofar as realism theorises this relationship, it tends to be through an ahistorical notion of anarchy that can only be alleviated by a hegemonic state and a balance of power. The theory thus assumes that, in this respect, the hegemonic power preserves order. But this may be at great cost – and indeed the hegemonic power may well undermine order.

However, for all its weaknesses, realism at least accepts that states continue to be major political actors in the international order, that the US is by far the most powerful state, and that the real world of international politics is subversive of the aspiration for global governance – a point also emphasised by Marxism.

Marxism

Marxist approaches to contemporary international relations emphasise how the rule of capital, and of nation-states promoting 'their' capital, undermines any trend towards global governance. Beyond this point, there are many disagreements among contemporary Marxists as to how to theorise the international system. This is probably because of the legacy of classical Marxism, which, unfortunately is treated by some Marxists as the gospel truth to this day. In this section, I will briefly examine classical Marxist theories of imperialism, assessing the relevance of these accounts to an understanding of contemporary global capitalism.

As is well known, Marx was sometimes an apologist for colonialism, because he believed it would hasten the development of capitalism in the colonies. Although Marx was anti-capitalist, he believed that capitalism was progressive compared to pre-capitalist societies, and so the spread of capitalism into the colonies was welcomed, even if it was unfortunate.[2] Capitalism was progressive because it developed the productive forces and created a working class. Development of the productive forces expanded the total wealth by increasing the social surplus product, which potentially meant that people would not have to work so much, and could live off the surplus product. However, this potential could not be realised in capitalist society because a dominant class (the bourgeoisie) continued to live off the social surplus product at the expense of the producing class (the proletariat). However, capitalism created its own gravedigger because the working class would, through its cooperative and unifying role in the process of production, eventually overthrow capitalism and create a society (socialism) in which everybody lived off the social surplus product. This process would occur globally, as what we would now call a transnational capitalist class exploited a transnational proletariat, and so nation-states and national differences would gradually be eroded by the dynamic, expansionary but exploitative nature of capitalism.

There are problems with this account that relate to the nature of the goods produced in capitalist society, the optimism concerning working-class revolution, and the fact that socialist revolutions have taken place in peasant-based societies where the social surplus product was relatively underdeveloped, with disastrous consequences for the building of socialism.[3] What is more important for our purposes is to recognise that capitalism was regarded by Marx as progressive, compared to previous modes of production in history. Indeed, for all its shortcomings, I think Marx was correct in this view. On the other hand, in apologising for colonialism, Marx often assumed that the international expansion of capitalism – imperialism – would lead to a similarly dynamic capitalism in the colonies. In this respect Marx was wrong, and indeed he appeared to recognise this in much of his work (see Kiely 1995: Ch. 2). The expansion of capitalism did not lead to a simple replication of an 'English model' in the colonies, or in other parts of the world. Indeed, colonial powers ensured that this would not occur. Instead, many colonies and independent countries were integrated into an international division of labour, mainly as producers of low-value primary products. Clearly, societies did not follow similar stages of development, and uneven development – between and within countries – was the norm.

These debates were taken up later by classical Marxist theories of imperialism. Marx's optimism concerning the disappearance of national differences was undermined by the intensification of rivalries between imperialist powers, as shown for example in the late-nineteenth-century scramble for Africa and the First World War. Capitalist expansion, or imperialism, had led to a dual process of nationalisation and internationalisation. The nationalisation of state capitals did not mean taking the private sector into public hands, but an increased role for states in promoting their capitals at the expense of others. Internationally, this was reflected in intensified competition, which included territorial conquest, and uneven development. For two of the major Marxist theorists of imperialism, Lenin and Bukharin, this competition culminated in the devastation of the First World War. These theories are problematic, and Lenin's argument (Lenin 1975) that imperialism was the highest stage of capitalism is unconvincing. Most capital flows actually went to other imperialist countries (though in different forms from today), and there was actually limited capital accumulation in the colonies – indeed, this was a reason why they were 'left behind' in the world economy (Emmanuel 1974; Phillips 1987). Ultimately, late-nineteenth-century imperialism was a product of a relatively early period of capitalist expansion. This did indeed involve inter-imperialist rivalry, as states undertook protectionist policies at home and territorial, exclusivist policies abroad, designed partly to ensure 'catch up' with Britain, whose productive superiority meant that it could support free trade abroad. There was thus some considerable continuity with earlier periods of territorial expansion, albeit now in a capitalist framework and extending beyond Europe. In this early period of capitalist expansion, imperial power embraced the world 'less by the universality of its economic imperatives than by the same coercive force that had always determined relations between colonial masters and subject territories' (Wood 2003: 125). Under US hegemony, capitalist expansion by the mid-to-late twentieth century increasingly took more directly economic forms – albeit not completely independent of the state and in an international system where the principle of state sovereignty had massively expanded. It is partly for this reason that some Marxists now prefer to use the term 'globalisation' or 'transnational capitalism' rather than imperialism.

Nonetheless, whatever the weaknesses of classical theories, they maintained a strong hold over Marxist theory throughout the twentieth century. After the first World War and the Bolshevik Revolution in Russia, these theories of imperialism came to be dominated by the cruder interpretations of the Stalin-dominated Third Communist International. From the late 1920s, it was argued that imperialism was a reactionary force, because it held back the progressive development of capitalism in the colonies and semi-colonies. Lenin and Bukharin had not theorised in any depth the effects of imperialism on the developing world, and were more interested in how competition between imperialist powers led to war. Stalin and his cronies were unambiguously anti-imperialist, and recommended support to all forces, including national bourgeoisies, that supposedly opposed imperialism. In the process, analysis based on class struggle between capitalists and workers was eroded, and replaced by a conception of the world in which there were imperialist and anti-imperialist nations. This analysis remained very influential within Marxist circles after the Second World War, even after the crimes of Stalin gradually eroded the appeal of official Communism.

Today, classical Marxism influences three theories: those of super-imperialism, inter-imperialist rivalry and ultra-imperialism. Super-imperialism refers to the unquestioned hegemony of the United States in the capitalist world after the Second World War. Clearly, there were no (capitalist) challengers to the US at this time, and so some writers argued that US leadership had changed the nature of imperialism. This leadership included military as well as economic hegemony, and an enhanced role in policing the world to protect it from the 'communist threat', and to preserve the expansion of an increasingly internationalised capital. The post-war era saw a massive increase in the growth of multinational companies, and US hegemony played a key role in policing the profits of this expansion (Baran and Sweezy 1966). For underdevelopment theory, the effect on the developing world was disastrous (Frank 1969). There were many wars, where the superpowers usually backed opposing sides, and the 'space' for capitalist development was increasingly undermined by the control of investment and trade by western, especially US, companies. Capitalist expansion and imperialism did not involve the promotion of a dynamic capitalism in the developing world; it did not even involve an unevenly developing capitalism; rather, it led to the development of underdevelopment, in which established powers grew by underdeveloping weaker powers. But in fact these claims were unconvincing. The East Asian region began to develop rapidly from the 1960s, and its defeat in its war in Vietnam undermined the US's hegemony, both militarily and economically. From 1975 onwards, the US was increasingly reluctant to commit itself to ground-troop interventions in the developing world. This was further reinforced by the Iranian revolution in 1979, and the forced withdrawal from Lebanon in the early 1980s. Interventions continued, but (under Reagan) these were usually illegal or covert, or (under Clinton) were basically wars fought from the sky rather than on the ground. Economic hegemony was undermined by the massive cost of the war in Vietnam, which paved the way for the devaluation of the dollar, discussed in the next chapter. For some Marxists, this led to a new era of imperialism based on a return to inter-imperialist rivalry. This was reflected in the rise of competition, especially from Germany and Japan, and their leadership of alternative areas of capital accumulation – the European Union and Pacific Asia. However, continued US military hegemony, the collapse of the Soviet Union, US success in getting countries to liberalise trade and especially the movement of money (which has been a major factor in financing US trade and budget deficits), plus an economic boom in the 1990s, led to a renewal of analyses based on the super-imperialism of US hegemony.

These two principal analyses – of inter-imperialist rivalry and super-imperialism – are not mutually exclusive. The argument of the former is that the main conflict in the world today is between major capitalist powers, and that in fact the wars of the 1990s were really proxies for these rivalries[4] (Callinicos et al. 1994; Callinicos 2003). Rather than stressing inter-imperialist rivalry, the super-imperialism thesis emphasises the successes of the US in exercising its hegemony in this competitive environment (Gowan 1999; Hudson 2003). But despite this difference, both perspectives share the view that global governance is simply an ideological screen that attempts to cover up the exercise of power in the world system (Chandler 2000; Gowan 2001; Baxter 2003). Although they may disagree on the mechanisms and implications, Marxists agree that there is no prospect for democratic, multilateral, global governance. Thus, Gowan (2001) points out that the US successfully removed the Secretary General of the United Nations, despite the fact that every other country wanted Boutros Ghali to remain in post. The US also successfully eroded the Articles of Agreement of the IMF, and won further liberalisation of capital accounts in East Asian states in 1997–8. It has also ignored the formation of the International Criminal Court, arms reduction treaties and international treaties that attempt to control environmental degradation. For this approach, then, global governance amounts to the exercise of entrenched power, whether that of the US state, or of competing capitals and their states.

However, there is another Marxist approach that also has its roots in the Marxist debates that led up to the First World War. This is associated with the work of Karl Kautsky, and his concept of ultra-imperialism. He argued that capitalist competition need not give rise to war, as international capitalism requires mechanisms of cooperation as well as competition. Obviously, this argument looked unconvincing in the wake of two world wars; but Kautsky's contention was not that war would not take place, it was just that it need not *necessarily* occur. Moreover, the world has changed substantially since Lenin's day, and it could be argued that international capitalism – or at least relations between the leading capitalist states – is in many ways structured more closely along Kautskyan lines. Immediately before the First World War, rivalries took place in the context of relatively closed national capitalisms and colonies. Those sceptical that globalisation constitutes a new reality have rightly argued that trade-GDP ratios were not substantially lower in 1913 than in the current era (see Chapter 2), but there were still important differences between then and now. Money and traded goods did flow between countries, but tariff rates among the 'advanced' countries were high (except in Britain), trade with colonies was generally based on an exclusive system of imperial preferences, and above all the internationalisation of productive capital was extremely limited. In the current era, firms that originate in one country are likely to compete with a wide range of companies from other countries in a number of 'national economies', which renders a very different picture from the pre-1914 period. Indeed, after the First World War and into the 1930s, world trade actually declined amid protectionism and competitive devaluations.

The Bretton Woods agreement of 1944 was designed to promote a capitalist system of global governance which explicitly avoided the economic problems – competitive devaluations and trade contraction – of the first half of the twentieth century. The US was clearly the leading power, but other major capitalist powers were prepared to submit to US leadership in return for military protection in the Cold War, aid in the form of the Marshall Plan, favourable access to the US market, and US foreign investment, the last of which was reciprocated by transnational investment in the US from the 1970s onwards (see Chapter 5). In a sense, then, the post-war order was organised along the lines of ultra-imperialism, albeit with the US as the unquestioned leader (Bromley 2003). Competition continued, and in many ways intensified, taking the form of disputes at trade talks, limited protectionism, and some devaluations – but not war. Of course, wars persisted, particularly in the developing world. But insofar as these local and national conflicts were internationalised, they were wars between the two rival blocs – communism and capitalism – organised in the Warsaw Pact and the North Atlantic Treaty Organisation (NATO), and not between rival capitalist powers. A pact between capitalist competitors in NATO would, on the other hand, have been unthinkable before 1945.

This analysis also has implications for how we think about imperialism and anti-imperialism. It is plainly unconvincing to reduce the bloody wars of the 1990s to simple proxies for inter-imperialist rivalries and/or the projection of US power. There may be disagreements between powers over the conduct and principles of war, but there is also considerable cooperation. Indeed, there is a tendency in such accounts to divide the world into an imperialist and anti-imperialist bloc, and to support the latter against the rivalries and big power projections of the former. But this is a particularly one-sided account of imperialism – it would be absurd to reduce the Gulf War of 1991 to the supposed rivalries between Germany and

Japan, on the one hand, and the US on the other. Some account of the 'sub-imperialist' ambitions of Saddam Hussein's regime, and its territorial ambitions in Kuwait, is also necessary. The ignoring of such factors betrays a commitment to an old-fashioned Stalinist anti-imperialism, in which the world is divided into imperialist and anti-imperialist blocs, with Saddam (when fighting the US, but not when he enjoyed its support) in the latter camp. Contemporary anti-imperialism often reduces the developing world to a theatre in which rival imperialisms play out their expansionary ambitions. In fact, parts of the developing world remain areas where bloody, violent processes of primitive accumulation, state formation and inter-state conflict persist.[5] Certainly these processes have been influenced by the actions of powerful states, but they are not reducible to them – indeed, 'blowback' implies that the movements that the US has supported in the past cannot be fully controlled (Johnson 2002).[6] Similarly, it is completely reductionist to argue that imperialism automatically leads to underdevelopment in the periphery. This will depend on specific relationships between imperialist states and local states, and between class forces and forms of resistance. Certainly, the promotion of neoliberalism is not conducive to the promotion of sustained capitalist growth and development in the periphery, but even this does not necessarily mean unchecked underdevelopment.

Thus, simplistic Leninist updates for the twenty-first century are themselves guilty of a kind of methodological imperialism, which denies any agency – or even relevance – to the developing world. On the other hand, recognition of the weaknesses of contemporary anti-imperialist analyses does not necessarily mean endorsement of 'post-imperial' interventions in the developing world. Martin Shaw has argued that

> [t]he global system of power is centred on a post-imperial, internationalised Western state-conglomerate, which harnesses – although not unproblematically – the legitimate global layer of institutions to its own purposes, and responds to the contradictions of quasi-imperial power elsewhere. Global power networks are best understood, therefore, as frameworks in which the dominant West negotiates its relationships with the other major and minor state centres (Shaw 2002: 335–6).

This argument has the undoubted strength that it recognises agency in the developing world, and that such agency can have reactionary intent. But the notion of a western state conglomerate – what Shaw elsewhere calls a global state (Shaw 2000) – is under-theorised. First, the reference to the 'not unproblematic' nature of western intervention requires further consideration. Second, and related to this point, western intervention is regarded as reactive to events in the 'minor state centres', which takes the argument about agency too far in the other direction. The puppets of anti-imperialism become the only pro-active agents in Shaw's account, which again begs a number of questions about western domination.[7]

Where, then, does this leave the Marxist position on global governance? I would suggest that the Leninist-Bukharinite position is based on an outmoded anti-imperialism, and an overly instrumentalist account of global governance. On the other hand, it would be foolish to ignore the unequal context of global governance, or the ways in which states and capitals subvert the potential for genuine global democratisation. The cosmopolitan perspective argues that global governance is contested, and that progressives should support further democratisation within this contest. Marxists rightly argue that this is too optimistic about the prospects for democratisation, as it ignores the structured inequalities that pervade both the system of nation-states and 'global civil society'. But at the same time, all but the most dogmatic Marxist would accept that, even in an international capitalist system, some social and political arrangements are better than others. Marxists have accepted this point at the domestic level – social democracy is preferable to fascism, for example – and I see no reason why a similar point cannot apply internationally as well.[8] Nation states may ultimately be capitalist states, but they are also sites of struggle. International institutions may be dominated by the most powerful capitalist states, but they too are sites of struggle[9] (Bartholomew and Breakspear 2003). This point is not made to champion cosmopolitan over national politics, as though the two could be separated. Rather, it is made in order to problematise any simplistic separation of national and cosmopolitan politics.

This chapter has outlined the broad debates on the relationship between state sovereignty, global governance and globalisation. It has problematised the idea that globalisation constitutes a radical break from an era of state sovereignty, and indeed has argued that a specifically capitalist sovereignty has only been universalised in the post-1945 period. It has also argued that there is a tension between the principle of state sovereignty and the cosmopolitan idea of universal human rights that may provide some grounds for 'humanitarian intervention'. But we have also seen that the universalisation of state sovereignty has not meant the necessary expansion of cosmopolitan democracy, and that systems of 'global governance' remain seriously compromised by the hierarchical nation-state system – and possibly even by contemporary, US-led imperialism. These issues – and their full implications – are addressed further in the next chapter.

4
Globalisation and Politics II: International Relations and the Post-9/11 World

The terrorist attacks in the United States on 11 September 2001 had a significant impact on the conduct of international relations. In particular, they enhanced the unilateralist stance of the administration of George W. Bush. This is sometimes presented as the start of a substantial break in the conduct of US foreign policy (Kaldor 2002). There is even sometimes nostalgia for previous US administrations. Much of the rest of this book will challenge this argument, showing how the US has behaved in unilateralist ways in the past – a point that even applies to the Clinton administration. Nevertheless, 9/11 and the prior 'election' of Bush intensified the unilateralist agenda and paved the way for a more overt exercise of US state power. This was clearest in the cases of war in Afghanistan (although this did command wider international support), and, most controversially, the war in Iraq in 2003. This chapter develops the general themes discussed in the previous one, and applies them to an understanding of international relations since 2001. It does so by focusing particularly on the invasion of Iraq in 2003, its wider implications, and how these relate to the questions of imperialism and cosmopolitanism.

FROM 9/11 TO WAR IN IRAQ

Before 11 September the foreign policy of the Bush administration was ambiguous. For example, Bush claimed that US-led intervention in the former Yugoslavia was Clinton's war.[1] But at the same time many top advisers within the new administration had called for a far more active and aggressive approach by the US in world affairs, and they were hopeful that Bush was 'their man'.[2] Inspired by the highly questionable practices of the Reagan administrations of the 1980s, the right-wing think-tank Project for the New American Century was established in 1997. Its founding statement was signed by prominent members of the Bush team like Paul Wolfowitz, Donald Rumsfeld and Vice President Cheney. The statement embraced the idea that US strategic power was paramount, that there was a need for greater military spending, that 'economic and political freedom' should be promoted abroad, and above all there was a need 'to accept responsibility for America's unique role in preserving and extending an international order friendly to our security, our prosperity and our principles' (Project for the New American Century 1997). The following year, in an open letter to President Clinton, the Project called for the removal of Saddam Hussein's regime from power. The letter also argued that there were sufficient UN resolutions to justify this approach, and that '(i)n any case, American policy cannot continue to be crippled by a misguided insistence on unanimity in the UN Security Council' (Project for the New American Century 1998). In 2000, the Project argued that there was a need for substantial military presence in the Gulf, and that this issue transcended 'the issue of the regime of Saddam Hussein', and must be linked to a broad project to democratise the whole of the Middle East (Project for the New American Century 2000). Clinton and the so-called US liberal elite promoted complacency among the US electorate, which was reflected in liberal decadence at home and a confused foreign policy that did not sufficiently embrace the country's dominant role in the international order (Kagan and Kristol 2000a, 2000b). What was needed was a far more belligerent US foreign policy; but, crucially, the US would be first among a system of liberal democratic nation-states. Although the realist wing of neoconservatism was more sceptical, this world-view amounted to advocacy of the unilateral, US-led promotion of liberal democracy throughout the world, which was deemed to be good for both the US and the world (Wolfowitz 2000).

The influence of US neoconservatives increased enormously after the atrocities of 9/11. After the quick removal of the Taliban regime in Afghanistan and the (temporary) dispersal of al Qaeda forces, Bush made his infamous 'axis of evil' speech in January 2002. The terrorist threat was linked to the opposition to rogue states that were said to back terrorists and undermine international stability. Iran, North Korea and above all Iraq were initially targeted, and Libya, Syria and Cuba quickly followed. In June 2002 Bush first outlined the strategy of pre-emptive action, which upheld the right of the United States to strike against potential and actual enemies *before* these countries or terrorist groups acquired significant weapons. The unilateralism of the administration was made clear in its National Security Strategy:

While the United States will constantly strive to enlist the support of the international community, we will not hesitate to act alone, if necessary, to exercise our right of self-defence by acting pre-emptively. (National Security Strategy 2002)

In the build-up to war with Iraq, there was some conflict in the Bush administration between unilateralists around Cheney and Rumsfeld, who were prepared to bypass the UN, and multilateralists, led by Colin Powell (and in Britain by Tony Blair). However, multilateralism was always conditional and qualified. After winning agreement for the return of US inspectors, Powell's 'victory' was qualified by remarks by Cheney that there was no doubt Saddam had breached US resolutions and had Weapons of Mass Destruction (see Coates and Krieger 2004: 31–2). Moreover, in the build up to the passing of UN Resolution 1441, it was clear that US multilateralism was conditional. Colin Powell himself stated on 4 September 2002:

The President made it clear today that he has every intention of consulting widely ... with our friends and allies and with the UN. He at the same time made it clear that we preserve all our options to do what we believe is necessary to deal with this problem ... We cannot allow the international community to be thwarted in this effort to require Iraq to comply. (quoted in Coates and Krieger 2004: 33)

Immediately after Resolution 1441 was passed, on 8 November 2002, there began a propaganda battle in which the US and British governments continued to pre-judge the outcome of inspections, and even made efforts to undermine Chief Weapons Inspector Hans Blix. Blix himself was critical of Iraq's non-compliance with inspectors in his first report to the UN, which further fuelled Washington's impatience. On 5 February 2003, Powell addressed the UN with 'evidence' of Iraqi links to al Qaeda, and of the country's possession of chemical and ballistic missiles, and programmes for the development of nuclear weapons. Except by those already converted to the case for war, this evidence was treated with scepticism at the time, and became a major embarrassment after the war (though for some time Tony Blair continued to 'believe', in much the same way that James Stewart believed in the existence of Harvey the rabbit). Certainly, the majority of the Security Council remained unconvinced of the case for war, but Powell's basic message was that, given this 'evidence', the UN would become irrelevant if it did not act. When it became clear that even a 'moral majority' could not be won at the Security Council, despite promises of considerable amounts of aid to some of the poorer member countries, the argument was retrospectively made that there was no need for a second resolution. This despite the fact that, in Britain at least, Blair had explicitly promised the House of Commons that 1441 was not 'an automatic trigger point' and that 'paragraph 12 of the resolution makes it clear that it is not' (quoted in Coates and Krieger 2004: 57). It also begs the question of why Blair put so much effort into winning a second resolution. A green light was given to Blair when Jacques Chirac stated that France would veto any Security Council resolution that supported war. The British government then selectively interpreted Chirac's statement to mean that whatever happened France would veto war; and so bypassing the UN – and war – was justified. Many Labour politicians used the Chirac statement – even implying that war could have been avoided if not for Chirac's stubborn behaviour; or they simply claimed that support for Resolution 1441 meant support for war (conveniently ignoring Blair's statements to the contrary).

Previous resolutions such as 678 authorised the use of force against Iraq in the context of the 1990 invasion of Kuwait, but this was ended by 687, which agreed a ceasefire and made the Security Council responsible for enforcing implementation. Resolution 1441 did talk of serious consequences for Iraq if it violated its obligations concerning disarmament, but these consequences were to be considered in the context of a report by the UN weapons inspectors. The actions of the US and British governments ensured that war occurred before inspections could be fully carried out and a report presented. Some Labour politicians claimed that chief UN weapons inspector Hans Blix had been sufficiently critical in preliminary reports to the UN for war to be justified, but in fact Blix was highly critical of the decision to go to war, and argued that the US had planned war irrespective of the outcome of the weapons inspections. Moreover, it was quite clear that the Blair government itself was searching for reasons for war almost as frantically as the Bush administration. In the face of public disquiet about the build-up to war, a dossier was published in September 2002 (HM Government 2002: 6, 163), which alleged that Saddam had weapons of mass destruction, 'some capable of deployment within 45 minutes'; that Iraq was seeking quantities of uranium from an African country; and that it was hiding missiles with a range beyond the prescribed 650km. The dossier led to a degree of panic about the 45-minute claim at the time of publication, and the misinterpretation of the weapons by the press (they assumed this referred to WMD and not battlefield weapons) was not corrected by the government. But the dossier still failed to convince, although the 45-minute claim did come back to haunt the government after the war, when a dispute with the BBC led to allegations of 'sexing up' by the government, and the suicide of a civil servant who had spoken to a BBC reporter. But this sideshow, in relation to the decision to go to war was far less important than the publication of a second dossier in February 2003, some of which was quickly shown to be plagiarised from an academic article. This caused some considerable embarrassment to the government and forced a grudging apology – but no resignations.[3]

It is clear, then, that both the US and British governments were committed to war with Iraq. What is perhaps of wider interest, particularly for our understanding of globalisation, is that the war coalition was based on an alliance between US unilateralists and a British government that claimed allegiance to multilateralism, and even to the principles of cosmopolitan democracy. If Bush is 'anti-globalisation' and Blair is 'pro-globalisation', how was such an alliance possible? In some respects, of course, the alliance reflected the messy world of real politics, and Blair's (misguided) view that by entering an alliance with Bush he could have some influence over him and (presumably) curtail the latter's worst unilateralist tendencies. But entering such an alliance – and indeed Blair's claim to have exercised some influence on Bush – implies that there was sufficient common ground in the first place. We therefore need to understand where such common ground existed.

The starting point is that both the neoconservatives and Blair's Third Way support the expansion of liberal democracy in the developing world. This may be no more than rhetoric, and neoconservatives have been more than prepared to support authoritarian regimes when it suited US interests – including, to some extent, Saddam Hussein. But they do believe that US hegemony is good for the whole world, and they are basically prepared to utilise hard power in order to achieve this aim. In his speech to the US Congress on 18 July 2003, Blair made the following statements:

> Ours are not western values. They are the universal values of the human spirit ... What you can bequeath to this anxious world is the light of liberty ... Why America? ... [B]ecause destiny puts you in this place in history, in this moment in time, and the task is yours to do. And ... our job is to be there with

you. You are not going to be alone. We'll be with you in this fight for liberty. (quoted in Coates and Krieger 2004: 9)

Clearly, Blair is committed to the idea that the national interest of the US and the universal interest of humanity is inseparable – an argument with deep roots in British Labourism,[4] old and new (Coates and Krieger 2004: Ch. 6). As we have already seen, this argument is not a new one, and can be traced back at least as far as the liberal internationalism of Woodrow Wilson. But crucially, as we have seen, this belief is also central to neoconservative thinking. When President Bush (National Security Strategy 2002: 3) argues that '[t]he United States ... [has] unparalleled responsibilities, obligation and opportunity', he is merely echoing a long tradition in US foreign policy. The same point applies to Condoleezza Rice's assertion that the US has unrivalled power and 'is on the right side of history' (Rice 2000: 47). For those who believe that there is an inseparable link between US national interest and universal, global interest, the complaint made by former British cabinet minister Robin Cook that the war in Iraq was about the expansion of US hegemony is irrelevant. What therefore links Blair and Bush is the belief that US hegemony and the global good are inseparable. Blair therefore saw his support for the US-led war against Iraq as fully consistent with his underlying political philosophy, and on its eve talked of a 'Third Way war' (Blair 2003).

The case made for this link is closely related to the neoconservatism of the Project for the New American Century, which argues that freedom, the free market and liberal democratic states are universal goods, and that the US must play a role in their promotion (Kristol 2000). The definition of freedom is contested, but in this case it means certain individual freedoms such as freedom of speech and movement, and above all the right to own private property and compete in a free market. Thus, both Bush and Blair remain committed to the expansion of neoliberal globalisation. Quite typically, for example, Chapter 6 of the 2002 National Security Strategy of the United States was titled 'Ignite a new era of economic growth through free markets and free trade'. In this context of globalising market expansion, liberal democracy is regarded as the best type of government, partly because it allows for such market expansion, but also because it is associated with government which is neither authoritarian nor dictatorial. It is for this reason that many critics of Bush (and to an extent Blair) supported the war against Saddam Hussein – a point I will return to below. According to Bush and Blair, then, US hegemony expands human rights and democracy (see also Chapter 6). Moreover, in the process of such expansion, the threat of war, terrorism and instability is undermined, as liberal-democratic states are more likely to negotiate and compromise, rather than go to war with each other. In opposing individuals and groups hostile to democracy and freedom, US hegemony therefore serves to promote a democratic peace. It is therefore the duty of freedom-loving peoples to support the US-led war against terror and rogue states, even if this must involve some considerable historical amnesia about the country's allies – including bin Laden and Saddam Hussein – in its recent past.

Robert Cooper, a former adviser to Tony Blair, has argued that the world can be divided into three kinds of state (Cooper 2002). Post-modern states are basically advanced liberal democracies, committed to peace and compromise and beyond the power-politics of the old state system. Modern states, such as China, are relatively stable but are still committed to competitive expansion. Finally, pre-modern states are failed states and sources of instability. It is the duty of the post-modern states to intervene in the pre-modern states in order to preserve order, even if this means the promotion of double standards and colonial power. Interestingly, Cooper is hesitant over the nature of the US state, and it is not clear whether he would categorise it as modern or post-modern. Indeed, Robert Kagan (2002) has criticised Cooper for failing to recognise that the rejection of power-politics by 'post-modern' states rests on the continued exercise of benign power-politics by the United States.[5] Nevertheless, despite these differences, it could be argued that, given the right direction by someone like Tony Blair, the US would fit the role of the post-modern hegemonic state. In this way, the Third Way acts as a kind of bridge between 'European cosmopolitanism' and 'US neoconservatism'. Indeed, Cooper is a far from isolated figure, and another link between the Clinton–Blair Third Way and neoconservatism is provided by Philip Bobbit. He argues that the Clinton years constituted a sea change in international relations, as the principle of national sovereignty was challenged and intervention justified on the basis of defence of human rights, anti-terrorism, and in order to block nuclear proliferation. The long-term goal of such interventions was incorporation into the liberal sphere through the extension of the market state (Bobbit 2002: 228). This state is defined as a constitutional adaptation to contemporary political changes, which together effectively comprise what is often described as globalisation. Bobbit does not share Cooper's ambivalence about the US state, arguing that 'it is simply not in the same position as other states, and therefore should not be shamed by charges of hypocrisy when it fails to adopt the regimes that it urges on others' (Bobbit 2002: 691). Certainly these arguments link Blair, Bush II and Clinton, the last of whom was a very prominent cheerleader for the war in Iraq. They also suggest that liberal internationalism, supposed cosmopolitanism and neoconservatism are not necessarily mutually exclusive.

THE IRAQ WAR: WIDER IMPLICATIONS

What, then, are we to make of the arguments concerning hegemony and intervention, both in relation to the Iraq war and more generally? Specifically in relation to the Bush administration, a number of points can be made. While there are significant continuities between Bush and previous presidencies, particularly over conceptions of the relationship between US national interest and the global interest, what was different about Bush was the way in which this leadership role was justified. In effect, the supposedly special role of the US was used to ignore dissenting voices, both within and beyond the US. US leadership and its manifest destiny were regarded as articles of faith, requiring little reasoned justification, and therefore justifying unilateralism. There was no need to promote multilateralism because 'American values are universal' (Rice 2000: 49), and the US leads a 'benevolent empire' (Kagan 1998; 2003). But this is mere assertion dressed up as argument, and easily leads to double standards. Thus, in addressing the UN, Bush made the case for military intervention against Iraq on the basis that 'a regime that has lost its legitimacy will also lose its power' (quoted in Reus-Smit 2004: 155). But, as Reus-Smit argues, '[o]ne might well ask why the Bush administration comprehends the importance of international legitimacy for Iraqi power, but fails to understand its importance with respect to American power' (Reus-Smit 2004: 155). Much the same point can be made against those liberal imperialists, like Cooper (2002) and Ignatieff (2003), who argued that double standards are an unfortunate but necessary practice in an imperfect world. But this argument is simply an assertion that, within the international state system, might is right. This argument is rightly rejected for states in terms of their relations with domestic populations, but not for states in relation to each other. Moreover, given the practising of double standards, it is hardly a surprise when this is met with resistance by other states and peoples throughout the world. Such resistance may not have progressive means or ends, but the practice of double standards certainly provides a recruiting ground for terrorism and other forms of resistance to US power. Seen in this light, the attempt to portray such resistance under the blanket term 'evil' is symptomatic of the unquestioned belief that the US must represent the global good. In unconvincingly contrasting the Hobbesian US with Kantian Europe, Kagan and Cooper are essentially arguing that good rests on the exercise of power, rather than power resting on the exercise of good. But if this is so, then it is hardly surprising that people resist US hegemony. Thus, if this hegemony represents cosmopolitanism – as Tony Blair, for one, believes – then it is a highly selective cosmopolitanism. This view is reinforced by the non-cooperation of the Bush administration in arms limitations, the International Criminal Court, and by its breaches of the Geneva Convention and non-compliance with the Kyoto agreement.

Specifically in relation to the war in Iraq, the case was made that Iraq was in possession of weapons of mass destruction and had links with al Qaeda, both claims now having been discredited.[6] The argument that the war was good because it rid the world of an evil dictator is more convincing, but the post-war situation – within both Iraq and the Middle East region – suggests that the world is a far more dangerous place, while it ignores the deaths caused by the war (the coalition has made no attempt even to count the number of Iraqi deaths[7]), the continued questionable alliances made in the war on terror,[8] and their long-term consequences (see further below). These factors suggest that while the removal of Saddam is the one desirable consequence of the war, removing an evil dictator was not the main motive for the war: as Monbiot argues, the US state 'is not morally consistent, it is strategically consistent' (Monbiot 2003a). Given this strategic consistency and moral inconsistency, Monbiot rightly concludes that 'the wrong reasons, consistently applied lead, at the global level, to the wrong results'.

The Bush regime therefore hardly counts as a benign hegemonic power. It could of course be argued that the problem lies not with US hegemony itself, but with the way the Bush administration has projected this hegemony. This is an argument made by a number of liberal critics of the Bush government, who are committed to the multilateral route to preserving hegemony. Thus, cooperation represents the best way forward for preserving what is usually a benign hegemony (Nye 1990; 2002). This view advocates a multilateral route both on its own merits and as the best way of securing prolonged US hegemony. While it undoubtedly captures the break that Bush made from the Clinton presidency, especially after 9/11, there is still some need for caution, as it also exaggerates Bush's break from previous governments. First, previous US administrations, including the 'globalist' Clinton presidency, have behaved unilaterally. It was Clinton's second term that saw the sanctions regime most stringently implemented, air-strikes intensified, and international organisations bypassed – most notoriously in the case of the illegal bombing of Sudan in 1998 – as well as air-strikes in Iraq and Afghanistan. Clinton's second Secretary of State, Madeleine Albright, once infuriated Colin Powell by asking him '[w]hat's the point of having this superb military that you are always talking about if we can't use it?' (quoted in Dorrien 2004: 225–6) Even Bush's supposedly novel strategy of pre-emptive war can be traced back to Cold War strategic discussions in the 1950s. Moreover, the US has a long history of self-interested interventions throughout the world, and few of these have been made to promote democracy. Indeed, most have been anti-democratic, some have been declared illegal under international law, and some members of the Bush team have been implicated in the past in illegal activities – most notably John Negroponte and Elliot Abrams. The much admired Reagan administration was on friendly terms with Saddam's regime, and supported resistance movements in Afghanistan, among them the forerunners to al Qaeda. It could be argued that these policies were in the past, and a product of the necessary power-politics of the Cold War. But history cannot simply be ignored; not least because of the consequences of questionable alliances for future scenarios. Current US policy is critical of human rights in Saddam's Iraq but not in Turkmenistan, Saudi Arabia, Israel and the Occupied Territories, Pakistan or Uzbekistan. To argue once again that such double standards are necessary – better to have US hypocrisy than Saddam's dictatorship – is an evasion of politics, because the likelihood is that current questionable alliances will have dire consequences in the future, just as past alliances have done. To ignore such alliances is to condemn the world to ongoing processes of constant war, not least against past and present US allies. Certainly the commitment to an independent Palestinian state – a concession perhaps granted to Tony Blair in the run-up to war in Iraq – was quickly abandoned when Bush met Ariel Sharon after Saddam Hussein's removal from power. Indeed, neoconservatives – particularly their Christian fundamentalist contingent – have close ties with the Israeli right, and regard the current territorial boundaries of the state of Israel as largely nonnegotiable.[9] This failure to resolve the Israel–Palestine conflict – indeed, the effective support of Israel in it – is not conducive to the pursuit of peace in the region. More generally, the commitment to global neoliberalism has exacerbated problems of inequality and marginalisation, and is therefore unlikely to enhance the prospects for a peaceful and prosperous future for the world.

Liberal notions of democratic peace should therefore be seen in this light. It is true that liberal democracies in the advanced capitalist countries are less likely to go to war with each other today than in the past. But this so-called 'liberal peace' is itself a product of a history of bloody conflict, and the idea that such peace can be simply imposed on 'pre-modern states' ignores the ways in which the advanced powers have generated bloody conflict in those parts of the world. It also ignores ongoing processes of state formation and territorial conflict in relatively new states. Cooper's division of the world into post-modern, modern and pre-modern states has a simplistic appeal, but it is purely descriptive, and tells us nothing about the (violent) histories of state formation that have led to such a division. It also betrays a simplistic linearity in which the virtues of the advanced can quickly be imposed upon the backward. This is a version of modernisation theory, in which countries are said to be poor simply because they are insufficiently globalised (see Chapter 5). Quick-fix solutions such as the illiberal imposition of liberal democracy are thus likely to exacerbate such problems, no matter how well-intentioned they may be – and we would do well to remember that past interventions have been justified by recourse to support for freedom and democracy. Indeed, these have often been based on the idea that intervention in the past was ill-intentioned or misguided, but that we have got it right 'this time'. These points are not made to support a blanket anti-interventionist position, but they do warn against easy solutions, liberal follies and messianic rhetoric.

Moreover, no US administration has really been committed to genuinely democratic principles of multilateral global governance. All post-war US governments have upheld the belief in the desirability of US hegemony, even if some have regarded multilateral negotiation as more important than others. It could of course be argued that because the US is a liberal democracy it has a greater right than others to exercise world leadership. But if democracy is to be valued, then it cannot be selective: it must apply to states not only in relation to their domestic populations, but also in relation to the international system of nation-states.[10] In this international system, the US has a poor record in terms of democratic principles, as we have seen. Singer usefully makes the point:

> Advocates of democracy should see something wrong with the idea of a nation fewer than 300 million people dominating a planet with more than six billion inhabitants. That's less than 5 per cent of the population ruling over the remainder – more than 95 per cent – without their consent. (Singer 2004: 191)

It may of course be utopian to espouse the cause of global democracy, even if, as cosmopolitan democrats point out, a similar argument was used in the past to argue against democracy within nation-states. But surely it is wishful thinking to expect the world's population to acquiesce passively to such a patently undemocratic international system. This is not to romanticise much of the 'anti-imperialist' resistance to current US global domination, much of which is reactionary. Terrorism should be condemned, and indeed efforts should be made to counter terrorist attacks. But it is absurd to dismiss *all* resistance to the US as the actions of terrorist minorities, whose actions are completely beyond explanation. Only the most ardent wishful thinking about 'US destiny' and the most dangerous amnesia about history – such as that shared by George Bush and Tony Blair – can reduce global politics to simplistic struggles between good and evil.[11] This is hardly surprising, as it reflects a long tradition of liberal thought justifying illiberal measures against 'illiberal people'. John Stuart Mill argued that 'despotism is a legitimate mode of government in dealing with barbarians, provided the end be their improvement and the means justified by actually effecting that end' (Mill 1974: 69). In the 'war on terror', terrorism has been reduced to a totally inexplicable, polymorphous mass. As a result, '[w]ithout defined shape or determinate roots, its mantle can be cast over *any* form of resistance to sovereign power' (Gregory 2004: 140).

Before we return to the specifics of the Iraq war, one final point should be made, which brings us back to the question of US hegemony – and to an understanding of globalisation. Bush and the neoconservatives have attempted to develop a strategy of 'US first' without any meaningful global dialogue. Insofar as the US government has committed itself to multilateral principles, it is largely on the country's terms – thus, on the eve of war the UN was expected to carry out the US's wishes or risk becoming an irrelevance. But this begs the question not only of the desirability of such 'unilateral multilateralism' (J. Anderson 2003), but its *feasibility*. The idea that the US can lead without any challenge rests on the belief that US power, especially military power, is alone sufficient to secure dominance.[12] This may be reinforced by notions of 'US destiny', 'divine right' or even soft, cultural power, but it is ultimately backed up by US resources, which ensure total domination through 'unashamedly laying down the rules and being prepared to use them' (Krauthammer 1990: 33; 2002/3). Indeed, many neoconservatives outside the Bush administration have criticised its foreign policy for not being sufficiently belligerent. Kaplan and Kristol (2003: 98–9; Kaplan 2003) were unconvinced that the administration, including their allies such as Rumsfeld, Cheney and Wolfowitz, had the stomach for a long-term occupation, or for invasion of other 'enemy states'.[13] The former were therefore critical of the latter's support for 'Iraqification' in the face of continued insurgency, arguing that this should be met with overwhelming military force (Kristol and Kagan 2003). Indeed, perhaps the most open advocate of US empire,[14] Max Boot, argues that 'blowback' can only be avoided by a massive expansion of US overseas commitments. For him, the international cause of 9/11 was not US support for Islamic militancy against the USSR, but rather the withdrawal of the US from Afghanistan in 1989 once the communists had been defeated (Boot 2003a). Boot (2003b) advocates a mixture of liberal imperialism ('Wilsonian internationalism') and conservative realism ('US unilateralism'), backed up by a massive expansion in US military spending, amounting roughly to a 25 per cent increase *every year*. This amounts to a call for massive expansion of US overseas commitments, but it is difficult to see how this can be compatible with the preservation of a system of state sovereignty, or any idea of liberal or perpetual peace (see chapter 6).[15]

THE IRAQ WAR AND US IMPERIALISM

Neoconservative realist arguments for US domination through military resources are not so far removed from Marxist theories of 'super-imperialism', which similarly argue that such resources are sufficient to ensure US domination – though of course they draw very different political conclusions (Gowan 2001: 89). But against Krauthammer's neoconservative realism *and* Gowan's theory of US super-imperialism, it could be argued that military power alone is insufficient to secure hegemony. Indeed, some Marxist theorists of transnational capitalism argue that military intervention may actually be *dysfunctional* from the viewpoint of a novel transnational capitalism that has 'outgrown' the nation-state system, including the dominance of the single hegemonic state (Hardt 2002; N. Harris 2003; Negri 2003; J. Harris 2003). For these theorists, transnational capitalist expansion is best secured through 'the dull compulsion of economic relations', and therefore the expansion of global capital through trade, investment and financial liberalisation. More traditional Marxists like Callinicos, who is keen to defend the relevance of Lenin and Bukharin's analyses for the current epoch, tend to argue that military expansion does ultimately represent the interests of capital, and of US capital in particular. Both arguments, however, tend to miss the wider picture, and measure state action by the extent to which it follows a (functional or dysfunctional) logic for capital. Both are therefore guilty of economism, with theories of transnational capitalism exaggerating the 'globality' of capitalism and the decline of the nation-state system, and classical theories of imperialism collapsing the state and capital into one (see Kiely 2004/5). More fruitfully, we need to recognise that the Bush doctrine is a political project in its own right, but also that this impacts on wider international relations in a variety of different ways. The recognition of an internal relationship between the 'market economy' and the 'political sphere' does not mean that the latter should somehow be reduced to the former.

How then do we situate the Bush doctrine and US hegemony within wider international relations? The Bush doctrine is an attempt to reinvigorate US hegemony in the post-Cold War world, partly in response to the perceived vacillations of the Bush Sr and Clinton presidencies. This does involve the exercise of US military power, and even a commitment to the (attempted) expansion of US principles of liberal democracy and free enterprise throughout the world. The hope is that this expansion will lay the basis for the defeat of terrorist networks and rogue states, and thus for promotion of liberal peace under US leadership. This is not mere rhetoric, designed as a cover for US economic interests, even if such interests may gain from the policy. The Bush administration, like previous US governments, is convinced that this doctrine does serve the 'global good', even, if at times, others have to be forced to see the world this way. But this is the great weakness of the doctrine, because it essentially has to rely on military might in order to secure hegemony, and this alone cannot succeed for any lengthy period of time; it is bound to meet resistance throughout the world, which in turn forces the US back to negotiate with institutions – such as the UN – that it previously dismissed.

Contrary to the interpretations of classical Marxist theories of imperialism, the relationship between military and economic power is far from straightforward. Moreover, neoconservative strategy is not simply an ideological screen for US economic interests, not least because – given ongoing political instability in areas where the US has intervened, especially post-9/11 – it is a strategy that is unlikely to work. The neoconservatives – and Tony Blair – may have naively believed that the strategy could work, and that therefore US economic interests could be served, but this strategy was also carried out in order to undertake regime change as part of a wider geopolitical vision. More generally, among the leading capitalist states there is a growing interdependence, which makes the revival of inter-imperialist rivalry both unlikely and counterproductive. This is especially reflected in Europe's and Japan's reliance on the US market and the US's reliance on capital inflows to finance its long-running trade deficit (and, under Bush, its renewed budget deficit). Contrary to theories of transnational capitalism, the current era of globalisation is one in which the nation-state system remains central, and the US retains some degree of economic, as well as unprecedented military, hegemony. The current order is therefore one of economic multi-polarity and interdependence alongside military uni-polarity, which is very different from the pre-1914 world order,[16] and indeed the post-1945 world order (see Chapter 5).

How then should we contextualise the Bush doctrine in terms of US hegemony in the Middle East? One common explanation is that the wars in both Afghanistan and Iraq were concerned with securing access to oil supplies. The usual argument is that the US wanted to secure oil pipelines through Afghanistan, while Iraq is potentially the second-largest supplier of oil in the world today. Historically, the US has not been as reliant on Middle East oil as other major capitalist countries, but this dependence is increasing as domestic production declines and consumption increases. Moreover, as a strategic commodity, control over oil supplies gives the US a certain leverage over its (actual and potential) competitors. Although it was mainly committed to finding ways of increasing domestic energy efficiency, the National Economic Policy Development Group Report of 2001 (better known as the Cheney Report) accepted that the US would become increasingly dependent on oil imports, which in turn meant dependence on 'foreign powers that do not always have America's interests at heart' (NEPDG 2001: x). This meant that '[e]nergy security must be a priority of US trade and foreign policy' (NEPDG 2001: xv; see also Klare 2004). Clearly, such statements can be linked to neoconservative support for US-led power-politics, and the removal of over-ambitious tyrants like Saddam Hussein. But the question of US hegemony is wider than the question of oil, and US control of Iraqi oil supplies provides only some leverage over other countries. If the objective is to secure access to cheap oil, then war is a very expensive way of gaining Iraqi supplies.[17] Moreover, if the price of oil fell too much then this could have disastrous consequences for US oil magnates, not least those working in Bush's cabinet. If the objective is to restrict competitor access to Middle East oil, then war is again a limited strategy. The international oil industry is too complex and interdependent for a strategy of restricting supplies to competitors to work. This argument repeats the errors of those Marxist fundamentalists who continue to try to mechanically apply the theories of imperialism of Lenin and Bukharin to a changed world.

Having said that, oil is not irrelevant, and it has played an historically important role in the promotion of US hegemony in the region. As the main transnational oil companies lost direct control of oil supplies in the region in the early 1970s, US hegemony increasingly relied on close connections to politically independent allies, and in particular Saudi Arabia and Iran. In the case of the latter, this was undermined by the revolution in 1979, and the growth of what was perceived by the US right to be an 'Islamic threat'. New but unreliable alliances were formed, including one with the secular regime of Saddam Hussein's Iraq. The US and Britain both provided intelligence and weapons to his regime in the 1980s, along with more prominent (and generous) allies such as the Soviet Union and France. The oil price rises helped to fuel Saddam's own imperialist ambitions in the region, and he declared war on Iran in 1980. Despite western and Soviet assistance, the war was a disaster for Saddam. Desperate for increased oil revenues to finance post-war reconstruction, Saddam invaded Kuwait in 1990. Saddam accused Kuwait of cheating on its agreed OPEC quotas, and thereby undermining agreed oil prices, and of stealing oil from the shared Rumaila oilfield. He also thought that the US would turn a blind eye to the annexation – an assumption based on the US's effective support for Iraq in the Iran–Iraq war. In fact, after some initial ambiguity, the US strongly opposed the invasion and went to war to remove Iraq from Kuwait. In 1991, after an uprising by

Iraqis against Saddam's regime, the US withdrew, leaving Iraqis to the mercy of a brutal dictatorship. The US withdrawal was based on a fear of the creation of an Islamic (or, less likely, communist) state, which would be even worse (from the US's viewpoint) than Saddam's Baath regime. In this sense, the 2003 war was both a return to unfinished business and an important break with the post-1991 status quo. But there was also continuity, in that the longer-term exercise of hegemony remained the most important factor in explaining the two wars. The US led the war effort in 1991 not because of oil per se, but as part of its exercising of hegemony in a strategically vital region for global capitalism (Bromley 1991). The war was fought in defence of US allies (Kuwait and Saudi Arabia), who were major contributors to global oil supplies. But the need for these supplies was not exclusive to the US, which has in fact not in the past been overly dependent on Middle East oil – although, as we have seen, this is likely to change in the near future. But oil has been crucial for global capitalism, and for the US's post-war role as the hegemonic power policing the world order. Moreover, there was also a more direct link between Middle East oil revenues and US capital, as such revenues were generally deposited into global financial markets, rather than used for productive and social investment within the Middle East region. Since the early 1980s, these markets have overwhelmingly concentrated their investments within the US, financing budget and trade deficits and helping to preserve US hegemony.

For all these reasons, then, the wars can be linked to the exercise of US power. They *do* represent the expansion of US military hegemony, and even of US corporate investment *in Iraq*. However, it is unlikely that this latest war will lead to an era of generalised colonial annexation, and access to Iraqi oil supplies is unlikely to deprive competitors of access to oil from other sources. Moreover, even if it were possible, the denial of such access could have negative side-effects for the US, not least in relation to continued access to the overseas investment that helps to finance its twin deficits. We thus arrive back at a theory of imperialism that (in some respects) is closer to Kautsky than to Lenin. Moreover, contemporary theories influenced by Lenin tend to downplay the nature of reactionary regimes in the developing world. As I argued above, despite the continued reality of US and other imperialisms, the world is not reducible to these phenomena. Indeed, Saddam's regime was clearly one that had its own imperial ambitions in the region. These came into conflict with the far more powerful US state, with its own imperial interests; but this does not nullify the fact that Saddam's regime was both repressive and imperialist. These points return us to wider questions of anti-imperialism, state sovereignty and cosmopolitan human rights.

This chapter and the preceding one covered three main issues, and I want to bring these together in this conclusion. In particular, the links between state sovereignty, imperialism and anti-imperialism, and cosmopolitanism, discussed in the previous chapter, require further consideration. The first issue addressed was the question of state sovereignty, and I argued, contrary to realism, that a specifically *capitalist* sovereignty emerged from the long history of state formation and primitive accumulation, generalised in western Europe only as recently as the nineteenth century, and globally only after the Second World War. But we can go further than this, because it can be argued that such processes continue to this day. Given that these processes were violent and unstable in Europe, it is not surprising that such instability and violence has repeated itself in parts of the former 'Third World'. This violence has been further complicated by the intervention of major powers, through colonialism, the Cold War and contemporary 'humanitarian military intervention'. The second major issue was that of the relationship between state sovereignty and international institutions. I showed how state sovereignty had become more universalised in the world, but at the same time international institutions had become more significant. This leads to the problematic argument that the latter has led to the marginalisation of the former. Sometimes this argument is based on a rigid dichotomy between a realist system of nation-states, from 1648 to 'globalisation', and the current, post-Westphalian era. I suggested in the first section that the characterisation of a Westphalian era of state sovereignty was problematic, and that the notion of a clear break with this era is equally problematic. Nevertheless, the rise of international institutions is an issue that required theoretical reflection, and this task was undertaken through consideration of a number of perspectives on 'global governance', with particular attention paid to cosmopolitanism and Marxism.

These strands must now be brought together to address some difficult – and uncomfortable – questions. If we accept that, in Europe, state formation and the primitive accumulation of capital was violent, and that parts of the periphery are repeating these bloody processes (though with no predetermined outcomes), then there are a number of possible political implications. One is that the so-called failed states of the periphery are simply states that are undergoing inevitable historical transitions, and that the end result may (or may not) be a progressive one. Dominant interpretations of failed and rogue states therefore lack historical awareness, not least of the bloody history of their own states. Moreover, it could be argued that western imperialist intervention has simply made matters worse, and therefore that there can be no intervention in the developing world. Intervention can thus be opposed on grounds of historical inevitability and anti-imperialism. Let us leave aside anti-imperialism for the moment, and focus on historical inevitability, which does beg a number of questions. If we support such a linear account of history, so that some nation-states (in formation) are at a lower stage of history, and that the lives of many people in those states are simply necessary sacrifices in the onward march of progress, then we have a politics of indifference, in which the suffering of such people is an unfortunate necessity. Of course, most anti-interventionists do not make their case in terms of historical necessity, but instead refer to the self-interest of major powers or the (under-theorised) expansion of capitalism. But both positions do face the problem of insensitivity to the sufferings of people living under highly authoritarian states. This brings us back to the cosmopolitan perspective, which supports forms of intervention that can protect the rights of individuals, over and above the sovereignty of nation-states. The question then becomes: What kind of intervention? Most contemporary cosmopolitans have strongly opposed the wars of the Bush administration (Archibugi 2003; Held 2004), but (one-sided) cosmopolitanism has become a guiding principle of Blair's commitment to humanitarian wars in the age of globalisation. This cosmopolitanism, however, suffers from effective indifference to the inevitable deaths of innocents in wars which, given the inevitability of such deaths, cannot be excused by reference to 'higher motives' than those of the deposed dictators.[18] Moreover, double standards and military might are experienced by many of the world's population, not as the promotion of human rights, but as the imperialist exercise of power. This is all the more visible in the light of the unilateralism of the Bush administration. Moreover, cosmopolitanism itself can suffer from a linear approach (ironically, given its eighteenth-century origins) based on a broad acceptance of the rigid Westphalia–globalisation dichotomy that this chapter has rejected. As a result, it too easily lends itself to notions of globalisation as progressive and state-centrism as reactionary (see, for example, Kaldor 2003). This first step can then move on to

Blair's self-defined cosmopolitanism, and ultimately to a defence of US hegemony in the name of human rights and against failed (pre-modern) states. In other words, cosmopolitanism can easily lead to justifications for the exercise of power by the dominant states. And when it is further linked to the globalisation of neoliberalism, it becomes the latest phase of capitalist imperialism.

These issues also relate to questions of 'difference'. Post-colonial critiques of liberalism and Marxism, and by implication cosmopolitanism, emphasise the ways in which 'universal' theories tend towards an authoritarian homogenisation of societies, cultures and polities that do not 'fit' the requirements of the theory in question. But the problem with post-colonialism is that it too can lead to 'indifference', so that acts of violence, persecution and so on are tolerated in the name of 'difference'. Thus, in our discussion, crude relativist arguments could be used to justify slavery or political persecution in the name of 'anti-imperialism'. Arguments along these lines have been made by Saddam Hussein and Robert Mugabe, among others. Much has been made of this 'instrumental relativism' by liberal imperialists who supported the war in Iraq. However, the approach to difference taken here is slightly different, and the focus is less on cultural particularity and more on social specificity. In other words, in the absence of wider social and political change, notions of 'universal standards' are unlikely to have the desired results, precisely because universal standards ignore such specificity in the first place. This focus on social specificity does not mean accepting the rhetoric of a Mugabe, Milošević or Saddam; but neither does it mean minimising the unequal social and political contexts that militate against the quick-fix solutions offered by liberal imperialists. This is not an argument for blanket relativism; nor against universalism (see Chapter 6); nor indeed for total opposition to all forms of intervention in the developing world. Crude relativist arguments are guilty of absolutising difference and, insofar as they assume that dominant norms are shared by all within specific nation-states, of bad sociology. However, this accusation applies equally to liberalism, which tends to assume that human behaviour can be reduced to the rational individual of liberal thought, except when this is 'held back' by rogue states or terrorists. Thus, in the case of post-intervention Iraq, the population has been represented as being divided into 'good' and 'evil' Iraqis (and outsiders), the former said to be clamouring for western-style free markets and liberal democracy, the latter simply promoting nihilism. But while it is the case that much of the opposition to the occupation in Iraq may be reactionary, it is equally true that 'good Iraqis' have increasingly opposed the occupation, and even shown some sympathy for some (though not all) insurgent groups within Iraq. The misplaced optimism of the interventionists is rooted in liberal claims to universalism outside specific historical and social contexts, and thus fails to recognise the limitations of 'humanitarian intervention' and nation-building, and the fact that, in many cases, certain forms of intervention make things worse. Indeed, US neoconservatism is more guilty of liberal optimism than US liberalism, even if the former is more willing to compromise its liberalism than the latter, in terms of promoting the means to the desired ends.

If this attention to context sounds like a recipe for indifference, then apologists for the war in Iraq would do well to remember the rhetoric of those pro-war politicians who argued that there was simply no time to delay intervention. Such a war was 'sold' – at least to those who wanted to believe – at a time when US annual military spending remains significantly higher than the finance required to eliminate the extremes of global poverty (Pogge 2002: 2). There are over 1 billion people in the world who have no access to clean water, and one-third of the world's population have no access to essential medicines. Every year 2 million children die as a result of hunger. The causes of these specific manifestations of poverty are complex, and the question of whether neoliberal, 'pro-globalisation' policies are good for the poor is addressed in the next chapter (where I give a negative answer). Nevertheless, one final point can immediately be made. Britain's commitment to increased aid is well documented, but the actual amounts of aid still fall well short of the UN target of 0.7 per cent of GNP. The average was 0.31 per cent from 2000 to 2002, which meant a shortfall on the UN target of £9.5 billion. In contrast, after just one year, the British war and occupation in Iraq cost $5 billion (*Independent*, 28 July 2004). Given the human rights rhetoric deployed in support of war, we are entitled to ask the question addressed by a *New Statesman* leader during the war in Iraq: '[W]here are the strict deadlines, the inspectors, the urgent meetings in the Azores, the announcements of exhausted patience?' For cosmopolitanism to have any real meaning, it must be suspicious of, and ultimately challenge, the cosmopolitan rhetoric of imperialist states.

5

The Global Economy: US Hegemony from Bretton Woods to Neoliberalism

This chapter examines the emergence of the contemporary global economy, and critically examines the arguments made by advocates of 'economic globalisation'. It first provides a brief outline of the post-war international settlement at Bretton Woods, and its effective breakdown in the early 1970s. The focus in this section is on the key role that the US played in stimulating post-war recovery, but also how this partly undermined US hegemony and led to the effective collapse of the post-war settlement. This shift also led to the weakening of the viability of 'national capitalist' development, and the beginning of pro-globalisation economic policies, which would have a wider global impact in the 1980s. The first section thus focuses on the broad context in which contemporary economic globalisation emerged, as well as making some reference to agencies that promoted globalisation. The chapter then examines neoliberalism in the 1980s, the Third Way in the 1990s, and neoconservatism in the early 2000s, all of which, despite important differences, argue that increased 'globalisation' is good for every country and person in the world economy. This second section therefore focuses on both agency and outcome in the globalisation debate. Finally, through an examination of trade, production and financial flows, I suggest that, globalisation has in fact been associated with increased inequality in the world economy, and that it has not alleviated poverty or uneven development. This final section therefore suggests that the outcome is not as benign as the ideologists of globalisation suggest.

FROM BRETTON WOODS TO NEOLIBERALISM

US hegemony and the Bretton Woods agreement

The world economy between the wars was characterised by depression, a breakdown in world trade, and competitive currency devaluations. These factors helped to undermine liberal capitalism, particularly in Germany and Russia, and facilitated war. Towards the end of the Second World War, a meeting was held in Bretton Woods in the United States. The purpose of this meeting was to provide the basis for a more secure post-war world order, which would avoid the disasters of the 1930s. In the political sphere, the US would join the new United Nations, and in the economic sphere, there was to be a commitment to (managed) free trade. For free trade to be advanced, there would have to be an internationally acceptable currency to pay for internationally traded goods. At the same time, if some countries faced persistent trade deficits, they would not be able to pay for their imports. The problem, then, would be that international trade could break down, since one country's imports are another country's exports. Therefore, an institution would be needed to 'tide countries over' through the provision of loans when they faced such deficits. This institution was the International Monetary Fund (IMF). At the same time, the US was committed to rebuilding war-damaged economies in Europe and Japan, and the promotion of 'development' in the colonies. The US gave political support to the end of Empire and the move to independence in what came to be known as the 'Third World', and economic support through the provision of aid. Aid therefore became a major vehicle for development, and this was to be dispensed partly through the second economic institution that came out of the Bretton Woods agreement – the International Bank for Reconstruction and Development, better known as the World Bank (Brett 1985).

The post-war settlement at Bretton Woods therefore appears to be one based on US generosity. Money was to be made available for 'development' and reconstruction, support was to be given to countries facing balance of payments difficulties, and the US supported independence for the colonial world. This generosity should not be dismissed out of hand, and some European liberals would do well to remember how the US supported the end of European empires. The European powers were too weak to challenge this view, especially as nationalist movements in the colonies were successfully resisting colonial rule. The period from the mid 1940s through to the mid 1970s and beyond was one of independence for a whole host of former colonies, including India in 1947, Ghana in 1958 and Jamaica in 1962.

On the other hand, the agreement at Bretton Woods was not as generous as may first appear. The US needed some reconstruction, in part as a market for its own mass-produced goods that could only realise a profit through massive production and sales. Marshall

Aid to Europe was partly implemented for this reason – and aid to the Third World was far less generous, and usually tied to US commercial, military or political interests. The second, related reason for US generosity was fear of the spread of communism, which could potentially undermine those sought-for markets, but above all represented a challenge to the 'US way of life' (see Chapter 6). In other words, aid was substantially a political vehicle that was used to boost US interests in the context of the ideological division between capitalism and communism. Communist states were in many respects repressive and authoritarian, but this was also true of many countries in the (developing) capitalist world, and the US and its allies were more than happy to support some brutal dictators of their own, as well as intervening in many countries during the Cold War era.

Furthermore, it was more immediately clear at the Bretton Woods negotiations themselves that the US was not committed to an altruistic set of policies. The key British delegate, John Maynard Keynes, had very specific expectations of the role of the World Bank and IMF. He argued that these should operate in the context of a new, specially created international money, which he called the 'bancor'. This currency would facilitate international transactions, and the IMF would operate as a central bank. It would then automatically recycle money from countries with balance of payments surpluses to those with deficits, thus effectively acting as a redistribution mechanism at an international level, as money would automatically flow from surplus to deficit countries. For Keynes, this mechanism represented the common interest, as it would mean that deficit countries would not have to cut imports and living standards to restore equilibrium, and surplus countries would not lose important export markets. In addition, Keynes argued that the World Bank should be provided with large sums of money to facilitate the rapid growth and development of the colonies. He therefore envisaged an international market economy based on genuinely transnational governance, which would be above the interests of particular nation-states.

However, representatives from the US rejected these proposals. Instead, the dollar was to be the international means of payment, the IMF and World Bank were to have relatively small amounts of money, and voting power within these institutions would be dominated by the most powerful capitalist countries, above all the US. Due to the low levels of finance committed to the World Bank, aid levels through the Bank were low, and the burden of restructuring deficit countries would be faced largely by these countries. In the case of the World

Bank, loans would be charged at higher rates of interest than Keynes envisaged, and even in the case of concessional loans (that is, long-term aid), there would still be interest charges. Having the dollar as the main reserve currency potentially gave the US enormous power, as it could in theory run payments deficits with the rest of the world without penalty, as the dollar was also its own domestic currency. It could effectively print money to relieve any payments deficits. However, it was initially agreed that the value of the dollar should be fixed against the value of gold, and that all other currencies would be fixed against the dollar. Some managed devaluations would occur, but the basic principle was a commitment to fixed exchange rates.

At Bretton Woods, there was also a proposal for an International Trade Organisation, which would help to facilitate free trade. This was rejected, however, mainly because of pressure from US farmers, who benefited from a system of government protection for agriculture. Instead, a more informal General Agreement on Tariffs and Trade (GATT) was established, in which trade talks between various government ministers would periodically take place over a number of years. The various rounds of GATT talks, from the 1940s to the early 1990s, showed some commitment to free trade, mainly through the reduction of tariffs. There were some double standards in this commitment, however, and many developing countries felt discriminated against through 'advanced' country protection of its own agriculture and clothing – the two areas where the developing world in general enjoyed some export successes. On the other hand, the GATT did allow for some protection for weaker economies from the potentially devastating effects of cheap imports from more established competitors, and this provided considerable leeway for European and Japanese recovery after the war, and indeed some development in the Third World. The basic development strategy in the developing world was one that promoted industry through state protection from foreign competition, usually through a mixture of high tariffs, import controls, currency controls and subsidies. This strategy of import-substitution industrialisation was not without its problems, but it did at least provide some 'space' for national development, a space which had been similarly granted to earlier capitalist industrialisers (Chang 2002). In the 'advanced' capitalist countries too there was some 'space' for progressive reform. Controls on the movement of capital facilitated expansionist economic policies that guaranteed high rates of employment and substantial increases in state spending on social welfare. Fordist manufacturing techniques, based on capital-intensive technology and hierarchical methods of work organisation, were unevenly introduced throughout the First World, and this facilitated high rates of productivity, thus allowing for substantial wage increases and therefore mass consumption (Harvey 1989: Ch. 8).

The post-war international order was based on a long-term commitment to free trade, in which trade would be largely paid for in international dollars. There was some space for the management of national economies, through state-managed capitalist development, which led to some industrial development in the developing world, and indeed close to full employment and welfare states in the First World. From the 1950s to the late 1960s, there were considerable advances in terms of economic growth, increased trade and output, and wider social improvement, including in the developing world. For these reasons, some have called this the Golden Age of capitalism (Glyn et al. 1990). By the late 1960s, however, there were considerable strains in the system, and by the early 1970s it had effectively collapsed.

The breakdown of Bretton Woods

There are a whole host of reasons for the breakdown of the post-war agreement, but we need only focus, for our purposes, on the narrowly economic ones (although some wider analysis is unavoidable). These reasons are closely linked, and they relate to declining US hegemony, the changing role of the dollar, intensified competition, and the internationalisation of production and finance. After the war, the US was the uncontested power in the capitalist world. The dollar was the only national currency that could act as an international currency. Dollars therefore flowed out of the US, in the form of US Marshall Aid to Europe, and later through very high rates of military spending in Korea (1950s) and Vietnam (1960s), and increasing rates of direct foreign investment. In this way a potential liquidity shortage was averted, and between 1950 and 1958 global foreign exchange reserves increased by nearly $7 billion (Glyn et al. 1990: 69–70). This expansion enabled some countries to buy US goods on favourable terms, including the purchase of capital as well as consumer goods, which helped to facilitate their long-term recovery. While this was clearly a system which benefited some of the US's potential competitors, there was also some benefit to the US, as it could run balance of payments deficits on its overseas accounts without having to 'balance the books' through deflating its economy.

It should be clear, then, that the US dollar deficit was essential to the post-war economic recovery, providing war-damaged economies with much needed money to finance reconstruction. However, in the long-term the competitive strength of the US economy was undermined. There was a basic contradiction between the dollar as the national currency of the US and the dollar as the international currency. Its value relative to other currencies rested on the viability of the US economy, for if this became so weakened that it could not compete, or if the US government adopted inflationary policies, which increasing its balance of payments deficit, its foreign exchange reserves would disappear and it would have to devalue. The basic problem, then, was that the supply of US dollars to the rest of the world depended on the US deficit, while the stability of the dollar depended on the US economy returning to surplus.

These problems cut across a number of competing, and largely incompatible, interests. From the viewpoint of the US, the deficit guaranteed military supremacy, but also reflected a decline in US productive power located in the 'home economy', while at the same time guaranteeing expanded consumption without normal balance of payments constraints (because of the role of the dollar). From the viewpoint of Europe and Japan, their surpluses meant that their foreign exchange reserves were constantly expanding, but these surpluses were mostly held in dollars. Devaluation would wipe out the value of some of these savings, but if the US deficit continued, there was the problem of growing inflation. In either case, the problem manifested itself as a dollar glut, in which excess dollars in the international economy were increasingly worthless. As the US's competitors no longer needed as many dollars to buy US goods, so dollars stockpiled in European banks. The Eurodollar currency market developed from the 1950s, and it was basically composed of deposits that fell outside the control of normal domestic banking regulations. These Eurodollars reflected the erosion of US competitiveness, as these dollars would have returned to the US as payment for goods, had it been able to sell more goods. Transnational companies based in the US also took advantage of this market to finance foreign investment in Europe and elsewhere (Kiely 2005: Ch. 3).

By 1971, in order to counter declining competitiveness, the US decided to sever the link between the dollar and gold. Two years later, fixed exchange rates across the world had effectively ended, and the values of currencies would now be decided by international financial markets. This paved the way for the deregulation of financial markets, which came to dominate the era of globalisation from the 1980s. In the 1970s there was a massive glut of Eurodollars held in European banks. These increased with the oil price rises of 1973–74, when oil producers deposited their oil windfall profits in European and North American banks. Faced with increased import bills (in the case of oil importers), or the potential for substantially enhanced development (oil exporters), richer developing countries increasingly borrowed money from these banks at low rates of interest (poorer developing countries were not sufficiently credit-worthy, and so relied on government aid). Some of these loans were undoubtedly wasted on useless projects, or simply went into the hands of corrupt dictators, but much was also used for longer-term productive purposes. The problem was that these projects would take time to make a profit and/or earn foreign exchange, which was needed to pay back the debt (Kiely 2005: Ch. 3). This became an increasingly important issue from the late 1970s, as more and more debt had a short-term payback period, and interest rates increased. From 1980 to 1982, some countries began to default on the interest payments on their debt, until in 1982 Mexico threatened default and other high-debt Latin American countries followed. This was potentially a major problem for the creditors, as they had committed so much capital to Latin America that wholesale default threatened banks with widespread bankruptcy. A way had to be found to police this debt crisis, and it was the IMF that took on this job and paved the way for neoliberalism in the developing world.

Meanwhile, in the First World, there was a major economic recession in the mid 1970s, and both inflation and unemployment soared. From the late 1970s and early 1980s, this paved the way for a neoliberal restructuring in the developed world. Associated principally with Margaret Thatcher in Britain and Ronald Reagan in the US, this led to a set of policies designed to curb inflation through control of the money supply, and to bring down unemployment through a reduction in the power of trade unions, who were supposedly responsible for winning wages that were so high that they priced other workers out of jobs. In practice, this led to a policy of high interest rates and cuts, or lower increases, in state spending, which had devastating consequences for economic expansion and employment, as well as for indebted Third World countries. These policies were applied inconsistently, and the deregulation of the economy made it very difficult to control the supply of money, as liberalised financial companies found new ways of expanding credit.

In the US the Reagan administration abandoned efforts to roll back the state, and instead cut taxes for the rich while massively expanding military spending, leading to enormous budget deficits. The US thus now actively competed for global investment, and used high interest rates as an inducement to financial investors searching for high returns on their investments. This policy starved other countries of investment funds and led to the debt crisis, as interest rates soared. This laid the basis for a sea change in government policy, in both First and Third Worlds, involving above all a general commitment to expanding the private sector and cutting the state sector, discussed in the next section.

The contemporary, neoliberal globalisation of the economy can therefore be traced back to the 1970s and the growing crisis of global capitalism. This was reflected in slower rates of growth, high inflation, and intensified social struggles across the world. It was also, crucially, associated with the threatened decline of US hegemony, and the decision to sever the gold–dollar link and the fixed exchange rate system. This laid the basis for the liberalisation of finance and important changes in US economic policy, which led to increased bank lending to the developing world in the 1970s and the debt crisis in the 1980s. Globalisation thus did not arrive literally from nowhere, as Giddens has claimed (see Chapter 2). It was a product of the transition from neo-Keynesian to neoliberal capitalism in the 1970s and early 1980s – a transition in which the actions of the US state were central. In the 1980s and 1990s, globalisation was further extended – a process in which the US-dominated international financial institutions played a central role, as we will now see.

NEOLIBERALISM, THE THIRD WAY AND NEOCONSERVATISM

Control of inflation and the debt crisis helped to set the agenda for a new – or more precisely, a revived – political project in the 1980s. Associated with Ronald Reagan and Margaret Thatcher, but also with the IMF as the regulator of the debt crisis, this project came to be known as neoliberalism. The basic contention of this approach was that states should leave economies to the efficiencies of market forces. State-led development was deemed to be inefficient, not only in the communist world, but in the post-war capitalist world. States should be rolled back through processes of privatisation, deregulation and liberalisation. The freeing of market forces from state restrictions would lead to rapid growth and improved living standards for all.

This may involve considerable inequality, but it was better to have 'efficient inequality' than 'inefficient equality', as the poor would still be better off in a situation of high growth/high inequality than in one of low growth/low inequality.

The 1980s debt crisis and neoliberalism

The IMF's policing of the debt crisis from 1982 onwards was more or less in accordance with the ideology of neoliberalism. As we have seen, the debt crisis was a crisis for the debtor countries because they were not earning sufficient foreign exchange in order to meet their debt (or interest) payment obligations. For the creditors, the debt crisis was a crisis because they faced the prospect of never recovering their debts, or even interest payments on their debts, which could undermine confidence in the international banking system. The way out of this problem was to ensure that debtor countries were granted sufficient new money to meet their short-term obligations to creditors, while at the same time restructuring their economies so that their balance of payments deficits would be restored to surpluses, thus earning sufficient foreign exchange to meet longer-term obligations. The problem was that while it made sense for all banks to provide new loans, it made no sense for one individual bank to do so, since other banks might not follow suit: what was rational for the international banking system was irrational for each individual bank. An institutional mechanism was therefore required that ensured that interest payment obligations would be met, in both the short and long term. This task was carried out by the IMF, which after years of relative neglect became a major actor on the international stage. It loaned money to countries, and approved policy changes by states that acted as a green light to new, but now highly restricted, rounds of bank lending.

However, to win access to new loans, countries now faced the prospect of adhering to certain conditions. This conditionality also applied to the World Bank, which from 1981 became an institution increasingly committed to neoliberal ideas, and which pursued 'structural adjustment' loans that reflected this commitment. The basic assumption of neoliberalism was that the debt crisis was not caused by unfavourable international circumstances – such as declining demand for Third World exports, or higher interest rates – but by policy errors internal to their national economies (World Bank 1981). This applied not only to the globally high debts owed by Latin American and East Asian countries, but also to the comparatively smaller debts of poorer countries, especially in Africa and parts of Asia, where actual debt levels were internationally insignificant, but which were a major burden for the countries themselves. Failure to meet debt obligations reflected a balance of payments deficit, which in turn was caused by importing too much and not exporting enough. Another way of putting this – though not strictly the same thing – was that indebted countries were consuming too much and not producing enough. What was needed, then, was a set of policies to either increase production and exports, or decrease consumption and imports. Contrary to Keynes's wishes, the burden of adjustment therefore fell largely on the deficit countries. There were new loans by the IMF, and some debt relief, both of which effectively meant that some public money was being used to police the debt crisis; but the amount of money was too small to alleviate the devastating effects of adjustment on the deficit countries – or more accurately, on some people in the deficit countries. In the short term this led to a set of policies that essentially cut consumption and/or imports. This included state expenditure on essentials like health, education and food subsidies. New bank loans to 'bad debtors' declined enormously and so, in an unsympathetic international environment, there was little alternative to making drastic cuts in order to return a balance of payments surplus. For most of the 1980s, substantial debt relief was not on the agenda, and the consequences of default by individual countries were likely to be even worse than the consequences of not meeting debt obligations. Nevertheless, creditors wanted a guaranteed return on their loans, and IMF programmes were designed less to meet the needs of debtors than they were to ensure that creditors' interests were served. The results of such cuts were devastating, and sacrifices were forced on the very people who had hardly benefited at all from the original loans. Indeed, as creditors demanded that countries meet their interest payment obligations, the rich in those same countries often exported their own money into the US to take advantage of the very same high interest rates that had aggravated the debt in the first place.

For neoliberals, the development reversals of the 1980s were regarded as an unavoidable sacrifice, caused not by the adjustment itself but by the policies that made adjustment necessary. In the longer run, more efficient policies would lead to countries producing more and exporting more. Although adjustment varied from country to country, and continues to do so 20 years later, it was united by a broad commitment to pro-free-market policies. The essential rationale for structural adjustment policies is that countries have not produced or exported enough because there has been too much state intervention in the economy. This intervention is inefficient because it leads to the protection of inefficient producers from competition, both within the domestic economy and in international trade. Import-substitution industrialisation is thus regarded as one example of inefficient government policy. For neoliberals, tariffs, overvalued currencies and import controls protect high-cost domestic producers from foreign competition, while subsidies work in a similar way, in that they discriminate between domestic producers without the discipline of market competition, and also encourage corruption. High tax rates are also said to crowd out private investors and thus lower investment levels. The result of too much government is therefore deemed to be the protection of high-cost, inefficient producers, operating in closed national economies sealed off from the opportunities of the world market.

The solution to this set of problems was a set of 'structural adjustment' policies that encouraged the promotion of market forces. In practice this means a basic triumvirate of policies: privatisation, deregulation and liberalisation. Privatisation of former state companies is said to lead to the enhancement of competition, and therefore efficiency. Deregulation, often seen as a second-best option to privatisation, involves the trimming of the state sector and the introduction of competitive practices that make this sector run along lines similar to those of the private sphere. Liberalisation is a policy of openness to international trade and investment, so that countries can grow through increased exports and foreign investment. In the 1990s it also included liberalisation of the capital account, which meant that individuals could now easily move money from their domestic currency to a foreign currency. This certainly occurred before adjustment – though it was often illegal, and usually more difficult to practice – but adjustment has made it easier. This practice is said to be conducive to growth, as it increases a country's access to foreign savings (McKinnon 1973; Shaw 1973).

In the 1990s the debt crisis officially ended, as the Latin American debtors received substantial amounts of foreign capital flows, combined with debt relief. Debtors therefore no longer faced the prospect of financial collapse. However, as a crisis of development, the debt crisis continued. The poorest countries continued to face massive debt service burdens, and economic growth and social development continued to stagnate for many – including in the higher-growth

Latin American countries. The much-trumpeted debt relief for Heavily Indebted Poor Countries (HIPC) initiative, introduced in 1996 and extended in 1999, has had little impact for the majority of countries that qualify for relief. Moreover, the post-communist countries saw massive reversals of living standards as the IMF promoted a policy of shock therapy, in which it was assumed that Eastern Europe and West Asia could quickly attract mobile foreign capital, and therefore rapidly develop. Instead, open competition intensified massive social disruption, and in some cases the development of unproductive, import-based gangster economies. Moreover, the capital flows to Latin America and East Asia proved to be unstable and volatile, as we will see.

Neoliberalism modified: the Third Way and neoconservatism

By the early 1990s it was clear that the optimistic expectations of neoliberalism had not been fulfilled. Low growth rates and poor social development persisted. Nevertheless, neoliberals insisted that embracing the world market continued to be the best policy option, and for a while pointed to the success of East Asia to back up this claim (World Bank 1993). What was needed was some 'tinkering' with the free market, to ensure that it was implemented more effectively. This paved the way for a movement away from the straightforward neoliberalism of the Washington consensus to a new, post-Washington consensus, which included increased attention to some safety nets for the poorest, as well as the promotion of institutional reforms to enable markets to work more effectively. These included reform of the institutions of 'governance' in order to allow state intervention to be more 'market-friendly'. Projected reforms were intended to make government more accountable and transparent, which in turn would undermine unproductive activity such as corruption, which was said to be derived from the opportunities that arose through government over-regulation (World Bank 1989; 1994). The 1997 World Development Report was perhaps the most sustained effort to theorise the relationship between institutional development and market expansion. The Bank explicitly rejected the increasingly sterile state-versus-market debate, and called for more attention to be paid to the issue of state effectiveness. Crucially, however, such 'effectiveness' was defined in terms of developing rules and institutions that would 'allow the market to flourish' (World Bank 1997: 1). Bad policies were said to include the raising of unexpected taxes on the private sector, the redistribution of economic benefits, and restrictions on the operation of markets, including import restrictions (World Bank 1997: 51). The Bank also embraced more radical concepts such as empowerment, participation and partnerships between aid donors and recipients. While these were potentially radical ideas, the Bank essentially saw empowerment solely in terms of the capacity of individuals to participate in markets. The Bank's explanation for poverty and lack of power was that people lacked access to income-earning activities that were derived from the market (World Bank 1994), and so markets themselves should be expanded. This was also the basic thinking behind the movement from structural adjustment to so-called poverty-reduction strategy papers, where an increased emphasis on poverty reduction remained tied to the idea – and the condition – that this was best achieved through market expansion. It was also central to the Poverty Reduction Growth Facility, which was designed to give the IMF a greater role in the Heavily Indebted Poor Countries Initiative,[1] and which tied limited debt relief to the usual package of neoliberal policies. In all these initiatives, the idea that markets themselves could marginalise some people was thus dismissed from the outset. In the process, participation and empowerment were effectively depoliticised, and the power relations generated by markets were ignored. Similarly, partnership and local 'ownership' of adjustment policies was limited by the need to gain approval for endorsement by the Washington institutions. The post-Washington consensus thus represented only a partial break with neoliberalism (Fine et al. 2001; Porter and Craig 2004).

This search for appropriate institutional support to enable the free market to work effectively closely paralleled the politics of the Third Way, associated primarily with Bill Clinton in the US and Tony Blair in Britain, as well as neoliberal social democrats like former Brazilian President Fernando Henrique Cardoso. Indeed, although this Third Way envisaged greater regulation of markets and a more activist state, in some ways this regulation actually enhanced the power of the free market. Clinton followed through with plans to increase free trade between the US, Canada and Mexico with the passing of the North American Free Trade Agreement (NAFTA) in 1994, and supported the (admittedly already planned) creation of the World Trade Organisation (WTO) in 1995. In 1997, the Clinton administration increasingly pressurised the IMF to make liberalisation of the capital account a condition of IMF membership. The Third Way therefore involved substantial continuity with neoliberalism.

With the arrival of the administration of George W. Bush, there was some initial tension between government and the World Bank and IMF. Following the report of the Meltzer Commission in 2000, which criticised their records on poverty reduction, there was some initial talk of the end of bailouts for indebted countries and their creditors, and a consequent reduction in the role of the World Bank and IMF. Certainly there were protracted negotiations over loans to Argentina, but this was less true in the case of Brazil. There were also tensions over IMF proposals to establish some forms of limited liability for sovereign debtors – a move successfully resisted by the US Treasury. But these conflicts do not represent a radical shift away from neoliberal globalisation. Indeed, in many respects they reflect an administration that wants to control foreign economic policy more directly, but still in ways that are compatible with neoliberalism. This is perhaps most clear in the field of aid and development, with the development of a new policy that dispenses even with the limited and largely rhetorical commitment to partnership and local ownership. This approach was formalised with the announcement of the Millennium Challenge Account (MCA) in March 2002. Aid was to be increased substantially, with a phased-in annual increase of up to $5 billion a year (although such a large amount has been resisted by Congress). This aid is subject to 16 conditions, which essentially conform to the neoliberal formula of open government, respect for civil liberties and market expansion (see www.mca.org). Where the MCA differs from the post-Washington consensus is in its pre-emptive nature. In the past, conditionality was implemented after loans had been dispensed, which at least led to some negotiation, whereas the MCA imposes conditionality *before* aid is dispensed. Under MCA, therefore, aid increasingly takes the form of grants rather than loans, which allows for greater policing of conditionality.[2] This does constitute a significant change in development policy on the part of the US government, but at the same time it remains committed to the promotion of an efficient, free-market economy, introduced through appropriate changes in government. Thus, 'the *form* of the MCA appears novel, [but] its *content* is the same as preceding development agendas' (Soederberg 2004: 281). This policy of pre-empting development therefore closely parallels the security policy of the Bush administration, and it reflects similar attempts to impose political and social stability in order to reduce the threat from terrorist networks and 'failed states'. This linkage of security and development is also closely related to the idea that the expansion of free-market democracies will lead to prosperity and the extension of the liberal zone of peace (National Security Strategy 2002).

Under Bush, trade policy has at times been more openly protectionist than under Clinton, and US relations with the WTO have been more difficult. However, these changes did not mean the end of neoliberal policies, as US inconsistency on trade liberalisation was established practice stretching back to the 1970s and Reaganite 1980s, and Bush continued to pursue a policy of pressurising other countries to liberalise their markets. For the Bush administration, if this could not occur through the WTO, then it could happen through bilateral and/or regional trade agreements. These initiatives were not designed as an alternative to multilateral – or, where they also stalled, regional – trade talks, but instead as an addition to them, designed to hasten free-trade initiatives in the face of obstacles to wider agreements. After the collapse of trade talks at Cancún in 2003, US Trade Representative Robert Zoellick stated that '[w]e are going to keep opening markets one way or another. We are not waiting forever. We are moving elsewhere.' (Cited in Weisbrot and Tucker 2004) Indeed, Bush even won authority to fast-track regional free-trade agreements through Congress.

From the 1980s onwards, there has been an increase in the liberalisation of the world economy. For its advocates, this is regarded as desirable because it promotes a situation in which all participants would win through the exercise of mutual comparative advantage. This argument is based on a very one-sided interpretation of the work of the classical political economist David Ricardo, who argued that, under specific conditions, each country can benefit from free trade, as open competition allows them to specialise in producing those goods and services in which they are most efficient – in other words, which can produce more cheaply than anyone else. Unlike most contemporary advocates, Ricardo argued that for such a win-win situation to occur, certain conditions must be met. For instance, he argued that for free trade to be mutually beneficial, the factors of production (land, labour and capital) must be immobile and that (leaving aside climate conditions) countries must have equal capacities to produce goods. This in turn rested on the assumptions of balanced trade, perfect competition and full employment. This is essentially the same case as that for the economic project of globalisation. Countries have certain capacities, and can produce certain goods and services better than other countries. They can only find out what they are best at producing through open competition, and should then specialise in production in those sectors (see Chapter 2). National economies can therefore best develop by 'going global', rather than focusing on production for the national market first, and the international markets second. For the Third Way, this does allow the state to 'pick some winners', but in a way that enhances rather than restricts the market. Thus, the richer countries can afford higher-paid, skilled jobs, especially in the information technology sector, and it is envisaged that this new economy will provide for most of the jobs in the 'advanced' countries. Developing countries can then attract capital through a comparative advantage in lower wages, which will eventually allow them to climb the ladder towards the developed world (Reich 1983).

Neoliberal, Third Way and neoconservative policies have all promoted liberalisation, deregulation and privatisation. These policies have been promoted by states and international institutions. States have also promoted liberalisation through international and regional trade agreements, such as NAFTA and the WTO. States are therefore active agents of the globalisation process, and not simply its passive victims – though of course some states are far more powerful than others. The US state also promoted the liberalisation of finance – a point I return to below. These processes have been legitimised (or rather, their advocates have tried to legitimise them) through arguments that suggest that everyone – all individuals and countries – can benefit from them. I now will examine this argument in detail.

POVERTY, INEQUALITY AND US HEGEMONY

Global poverty reduction?

On the face of it, the argument that global 'market forces' work to everyone's benefit sounds like wishful thinking, but many of the ideologists of globalisation argue that this process of poverty reduction is already taking place. The World Bank has periodically claimed that those countries that have gone furthest in carrying out structural adjustment polices have been the most successful developers. More recently, it has argued that the number of people living in poverty has fallen from 1.4 billion in 1980 to 1.2 billion in 1998 (World Bank 2002a: 30). Although using a different set of figures, it has also argued that the proportion of people living in poverty fell from 28 per cent in 1987 to 24 per cent in 1998 of the world's population (World Bank 2001: 3). These figures used a poverty measurement based on people living on an income of less than $1 a day. However the 'dollar' in question is not actually a US dollar, but what is called a Purchasing Power Parity (PPP) dollar. The concept of the PPP dollar attempts to find a unit that can account for local differences in living standards and buying power across the globe. This is based on international price comparisons, which are made periodically, and which most recently draw on comparisons initially made in 1985 and 1993. The World Bank claim cited above is actually based on a usually unacknowledged switch from using the 1985 comparison, in 1987, to the 1993 comparison, in 1998. But this shift had the effect of lowering the poverty count in 77 out of 92 countries in which data were available, and these countries contained 82 per cent of the population of the 92 countries (Pogge and Reddy 2002: 7). Therefore, the 'reduced poverty' often cited as an established fact is actually based on two very different headcounts, and these appear to show a downward bias in poverty trends. Poverty may not have been reduced; rather, the way in which it has been counted may be biased towards reduction. In this way, the target of halving world poverty by 2015 may be 'achieved' (though this in itself is highly unlikely) less by a reduction in real poverty than by an effect of the way in which we count poverty. Moreover, PPP is based on a wide basket of consumer goods for international comparison, most of which are not relevant to counting poverty – for instance, cars and airline tickets. A general increase in income – a tendency that predates globalisation – will therefore lead to *some* people increasing their consumption of such goods. This does not mean that the poor do so – but PPP assumes that the increase in income over time is general. Most of the measured fall in poverty in recent years is attributable to changes in India and China, but neither country participated fully in the price comparisons of 1985 and 1993 – China in neither and India only in 1985.

For these and other reasons (see Kiely 2005: Ch. 5), we need to treat claims that absolute poverty has fallen with extreme caution. Moreover, such measures betray an excessively technocratic approach to the question of poverty. Income is only one measure of poverty, and the PPP dollar benchmark is largely arbitrary. Moreover, it tells us nothing about inequality. For neoliberalism, inequality is not an important issue so long as the poor are lifted out of poverty. But if we are to take democracy seriously, then it must involve everybody having the chance to participate equally in both national and global society. Simply lifting people out of absolute poverty does not address the question of relationships of power between individuals and social groups, and it therefore betrays a particularly limited approach to politics and democracy. Inequalities between the richest and poorest, in terms of countries and people, have undoubtedly increased in the era of globalisation, as have inequalities within most countries (Milanovic 2002).

But there is still a need to deal with the question of rapid growth in China and India, especially as these two countries account together for over a third of the world's population. For the World Bank, these two countries are part of a group of 'highly globalised' countries, which are said to have benefited from pro-globalisation policies in recent years. Revisiting the theory of comparative advantage, albeit without Ricardo's qualifications, the Bank argues that a reduction in trade barriers accelerates growth, enhances productivity, creates new jobs and reduces poverty. The good globalisers of recent years are those countries that have increased their ratio of trade to GDP for the years 1977–97 (World Bank 2002b). This measure is said to be a useful approximation of trade openness, and countries like India and China have increased their trade/GDP ratio in recent years. Such measures are also implicit in the far more casual claims made by both neoliberal advocates of American empire and Third Way ideologues that poverty has been reduced through pro-globalisation policies, and that the failure of poverty reduction is due to countries being insufficiently globalised (Lal 2004; Giddens 2002: 73).

Unfortunately for neoliberals, this distinction is useless. Measuring changes in trade/GDP ratios from 1977 to 1997 tells us nothing about trade openness. First, it is quite possible for a country to have a relatively closed economy in some sectors, and still have high trade/GDP ratios because it has successfully broken into export markets, and can therefore also afford substantial imports. Second, measuring the changes from 1977 to 1997 does not tell us anything about openness in the latter year, only the degree of change that has occurred over the 20 years. Indeed, the measurement is biased towards high-growth countries because it excludes countries with high but not increasing trade/GDP ratios from the more globalised category. This includes a number of very poor but relatively open countries dependent on the export of low-value primary commodities (UNCTAD 2002: Pt. 2, Ch. 3). Similarly, the rapid economic growth of China and India pre-dates increased openness, and ignores the fact that, measured in terms of tariffs, these remain relatively closed economies, at least compared to some poorer countries. While their *rate* of opening up was quite high, the amount of openness remains comparatively low.

Much the same argument can be made for the East Asian 'miracle' economies. The rise of South Korea and Taiwan in particular, but also Hong Kong, Singapore, Malaysia and Thailand, is often cited as evidence that pro-globalisation policies can work. Before the Asian financial crisis of 1997–98, these countries were often cited as models of 'market-friendly intervention' for the rest of the world (World Bank 1993). Indeed, structural adjustment and good governance were often justified on the grounds that these were the means by which East Asia managed to develop rapidly. Again, unfortunately for the neoliberals and pro-globalisers, this is not the case. Certainly, these economies exported successfully, and some (especially Malaysia and Singapore) successfully attracted large amounts of foreign investment. But outside the city-states of Hong Kong and Singapore, the miracles took off from the early 1960s in the context of a nationalised banking system, import controls and high tariffs, state planning to favoured industries, and rigid controls over the export of money capital. Controls over the export of money were largely lifted in the early 1990s (though not in Taiwan, and they were quickly re-introduced in Malaysia), and this was certainly one cause of the financial crisis. Clearly, then, East Asia did not develop simply by drawing on the benign effects of global 'market forces'; like earlier developers, in many ways it actually adopted policies that included considerable protection from such forces.

These points undermine some key arguments of the advocates of globalisation. Most obviously, the market-friendly position is unsustainable. But the argument that the rise of East Asia confirms the view that globalisation is a process without direction is also undermined by the financial crisis of the late 1990s, which can be linked to financial liberalisation and US hegemony.[3] The neoliberal case has therefore misinterpreted the 'development successes' of recent years. There have been important gains over the last 40 years, but these cannot be attributed to unambiguously pro-globalisation policies. Moreover, we should remember that these gains have also taken place at considerable cost to some people in the region. South Korea and now China have notoriously high rates of accidents at work; most of the countries in East Asia have had, or still have, repressive political regimes; there has been considerable environmental destruction as rapid industrialisation has taken place. None of these things may have caused the economic miracles, and we should remember that similar costs have occurred elsewhere, without the longer-term social benefits. But we should also remember that rapid growth and social improvements for some have come at considerable social cost to others. It is not sufficient for advocates of growth simply to say that this is a necessary consequence of 'development', a sacrifice made by the present generation for future generations. This growth fetishism (see Chapter 6) has led to too many deaths and sacrifices in the name of a better future, not least under state 'socialism'. Economic growth may be important, but it is not *that important.*

Global inequality

But this problem of sacrifice is all the more troubling for neoliberalism. Some sacrifice may be necessary – the transition from poverty to abundance is far from painless – but uncritical pro-globalisation policies call for short-term sacrifice in the pursuit of long-term gain, while the policies result in too much sacrifice and too little gain. Integrating into the world economy through structural adjustment and trade liberalisation is not a recipe for rapid long-term growth, or for catching up with the 'advanced countries'. Indeed, those countries that have had some success with catch-up have generally not carried out these policies. The underlying reason why they have not is that the global economy is not the benign force that apologists make out. It isn't necessarily completely malign, but neither is it all good. To explain why, we need to take a brief look at trade, productive and financial investment flows, and then use these to criticise the theory of comparative advantage.

If we look at the share of world trade in the late 1990s, we can see that it is highly concentrated. The 'developed' world accounted for around 75 per cent of world trade in 1999, the developing world (including East Asia) 25 per cent (UNCTAD 1999). The share of Africa and Latin America in world trade has fallen in the years of globalisation: Africa's share declined from 4.1 per cent in 1970 to 1.5 per cent in 1995, and Latin America's from 5.5 per cent to 4.4 per cent over the same period (UNCTAD 1998: 183). Asia's share increased, from 8.5 per cent to 21.4 per cent, but as we have seen this was not because of unambiguously open trade policies, still less because of neoliberal policies. Of course, the actual amount of trade has not fallen; rather, Africa's and Latin America's shares are rising less quickly than those of other regions. In 1960, Africa's share of total merchandise exports was 5.6 per cent, and Latin America's 7.5 per cent; by 2002, Africa's share had declined to 2.1 per cent and Latin America's to 5.4 per cent (UNCTAD 2004: 51). In services, concentration was even greater – in 2002, developed countries accounted for 73.2 per cent of the total value of service exports, Central and Eastern Europe 4.2 per cent, and developing countries just 22.6 per cent. Africa's and Latin America's shares have both declined since 1980 (UNCTAD 2004: 61). Advocates of trade liberalisation and globalisation assume that once the correct policies are put in place, both the amount and the share of world trade should increase for the 'backward' areas, because they will specialise in those goods in which they have a comparative advantage. This has clearly not taken place, and trade shares have concentrated despite the liberalisation policies carried out since the early 1980s. Moreover, the rate of growth of international trade has actually been slower in the era of open trade than it was in the era of 'national capitalisms'. From 1950 to 1973, the annual average rate of growth was 1.7 per cent, while from 1973 to 1992 it was 1.1 per cent (Baker et al. 1997: 6). The type of goods exported from the developing world has changed substantially, and manufacturing now accounts for the majority of developing-world exports, but this increase is mainly in low-value, labour-intensive goods, such as clothing and footwear, where there is a significant 'mark up' at the marketing rather than the production stage of the commodity chain.

On the face of it, there seems to be room for greater optimism when we examine foreign investment. The 1990s did see a massive increase in foreign investment, from $59 billion in 1982 to $1.2 trillion in 2000 (although it has fallen substantially since then). This includes substantial increases in the developing world, particularly Latin America and East Asia. Indeed, these flows in the early 1990s were sufficient to turn Latin America around from being a net capital exporter in the 1980s, paying back interest on bad debts, to a net capital importer. But this investment remains highly concentrated. Throughout the 1990s, the developed countries received around two-thirds of total direct foreign investment (DFI), while the capital-scarce developing countries (including East Asia) received one-third (UNCTAD 2002: 5). Moreover, the investment that goes to the developing world is itself highly concentrated, with 10 countries receiving 75 per cent (UNCTAD 2002: 9). Direct foreign investment levels fell in 2001 and 2002. Total DFI for 2001 was $823 billion, of which developed countries received $589 billion and developing countries $209 billion. In 2002 total DFI was $651 billion, with developed countries receiving $460 billion and developing countries $162 billion. Asia and the Pacific received $95 billion, Latin America and the Caribbean $56 billion, and Africa just $11 billion (UNCTAD 2003: 7).

DFI figures do not tell the whole story, and they distort the picture in a number of ways. First, mergers and acquisitions between companies can lead to an increase in DFI figures even though they do not involve any new investment. As most mergers and acquisitions take place between 'First World' companies, this has the effect of exaggerating the concentration of DFI in the developed countries. But DFI figures also increase when countries sell off previously state-run enterprises to foreign capital – once again, this is not new, greenfield investment, but a simple takeover of existing assets. This process has occurred in the developed world, but so too has it occurred on a massive scale, after structural adjustment, in the developing world, especially in Latin America. Indeed, Brazil experienced high rates of FDI in the 1990s, but averaged *lower* rates of fixed capital investment than in the disastrous 1980s. Second, the value of manufacturing imports into the 'advanced' capitalist countries originating from the developing world is low. For the US in 1995, the figure was 7 per cent, for the European Union 4.5 per cent, and for Japan 3.3 per cent (UNCTAD 1999). In other words, in each case over 90 per cent of manufacturing imports came from other 'advanced' countries.

Two final factors confirm the concentrated nature of world investment flows. First, given that the developing world has a higher proportion of the world's population than the developed world, the concentration of DFI is in fact greater than the figures cited above indicate (UNCTAD 2002: 265). Second, as globalisation sceptics remind us (see Chapter 2), DFI only makes up a small proportion of total global capital investment. In 1995, it contributed only about 5.2 per cent of the world's capital investment, and the stock of inward DFI represented just 10.1 per cent of world GDP (Thompson 2000: 109). Thus, big transnational companies like General Motors continue to employ far more people in the US than in any other single country, and in many cases such companies employ and hold more assets in their home country than in all other countries put together. Though there are some exceptions, where companies rely on raw materials (ExxonMobil) or have been particularly successful as global market players (Coca Cola), transnational companies that hold more assets or employ more people beyond their country of origin tend to be those with small domestic markets. Clearly, the hyper-globalisation image of footloose capital dispersing investment throughout the globe is a fallacy. For all these reasons, the argument that globalisation will lead to a global dispersal of capital investment looks to be highly problematic.

US hegemony and global finance

Global financial flows also increased substantially in the 1990s. After the 1980s debt crisis, bank loans became less significant, and following structural adjustment there was an increase in portfolio investment, which basically meant investment in stock markets and in government bonds, and various derivatives. Advocates of deregulated finance argue that these are potentially useful, as they enable capital-scarce developing countries to draw on global sources of savings, and so can be used to finance investment and trade flows. Such flows, like trade and DFI, are extremely concentrated, and largely bypass the poorest countries. But even for those 'emerging markets' that received increased foreign portfolio investment in the 1990s, it was at best a mixed blessing. These financial flows have increased enormously since the breakdown of fixed exchange rates in the early 1970s, but they have not had the desired effects. Indeed, the overwhelming majority of these flows are not designed to increase trade and investment, but are purely speculative. In the late 1990s, the annual value of trade in goods and services was equivalent to four days' trading on foreign exchange markets (Singh 2000: 16). The effect of such speculation is to divert funds away from productive investment, which for all its faults at least has the potential to be used for socially useful purposes. Financial investment remains reliant on the 'real economy' of production and trade, as these are necessary for debts to be repaid, but it is also parasitic upon it.

This parasitism takes a number of forms. First, as we have seen, funds are diverted away from investment in the real economy into what is usually little more than financial speculation. Second, even when funds are not used simply for speculation, such as when money is diverted to hedge against sharp movements in currencies, there is still considerable diversion from production to deal with the uncertainties of a world of flexible exchange rates. Moreover, these funds can become so vast that they encourage further speculation. Third, such funds are often attracted to countries through high interest rates, which have the effect of further choking off productive investment, and therefore undermining expansionary policies that might encourage an increase in employment. Productive investment does at least have the merit of providing some means of economic expansion, and therefore a livelihood for substantial sectors of the population. Indeed, such is the power of financial interests in the current global economy that the decision to withdraw funds held in one currency into another can have a devastating impact on real economies. The East Asian crisis of 1997–98 was just one of a series of financial crises in the 1990s and beyond, which included Mexico in 1994, Russia in 1998, and Brazil and Argentina at the turn of the century. Each of these was facilitated by the rapid removal of 'hot money' that had initially promoted largely speculative investment, and, once removed, had a devastating impact on the real economy (through the build-up of debt, declining share values, and declining national currencies, which further increased dollar-denominated debt). Thus, in five East Asian economies in 1997, there was a reversal of capital flows of $105 billion, the equivalent of 11 per cent of the combined GDP of South Korea, Thailand, Indonesia, Malaysia and the Philippines (Kiely 2005: Ch. 4).

Indeed, it could be argued that, at the global level, the effect of the dominance of financial capital is even more parasitic than this. For above all it is the US that has the most interest in maintaining global financial hegemony, and it is the US that has above all promoted policies to liberalise the movement of finance across borders. Although this can be traced back at least to the 1971 dollar devaluation, the real turning point came in 1981 under Ronald Reagan. As we have seen, his presidency saw the implementation of policies (begun tentatively under President Carter in 1979) based on controlling inflation, high interest rates, tax cuts for the wealthy, and deregulation of capital investment. The US therefore started to compete for greater global capital inflows as it faced increasing budget and trade deficits, exacerbated by Reagan's decision to increase defence spending massively. The US thus went from being the world's main source of liquidity in the 1950s to being the world's main debtor and recipient of foreign capital in the 1980s, and this remains the case to this day. This process was above all facilitated by one of the key legacies of the Bretton Woods agreement – the role of the dollar as the main international currency. As a result, the US is able to finance deficits with the rest of the world by selling government debt securities, secure in the knowledge that there is demand for these dollar bonds. At the same time, to facilitate this process there needs to be active encouragement of the free movement of finance, so that money can move freely into the US. Thus, the country retains a position of hegemony in the world order today, above all because of the globalisation of finance. Indeed, it could be argued that the rest of the world is actually financing the continued military/political hegemony of the US, investing money into the US and thereby financing its deficits. This was certainly the case under Reagan, and to a lesser extent the elder Bush; and while Clinton successfully eliminated the budget deficit, the trade deficit continued to soar. Moreover, the presidency of the younger Bush saw a return to the era of high trade and budget deficits, thus intensifying US dependence on liberal financial flows. By 2003, both trade and budget deficits stood at record levels: since early 2000, the federal budget deficit has grown from 1.8 per cent of GDP to an estimated 3.7 per cent (2003) and 4.3 per cent for 2004 (Brenner 2003: 21). In 2001, the trade deficit was a record $435 billion, which increased to an unprecedented $489 billion by 2003 (Monthly Review 2003: 8). These deficits have been financed by foreigners speculating in the stock market, buying real estate, acquiring firms or setting up new sites, and buying US Treasury bonds. Equity purchases fell by 83 per cent from 2000 to 2002 as share prices fell, and so there has been a sustained movement into buying government bonds. In 2001, 97 per cent of the US current account deficit was financed by foreign purchases of these bonds. From 1992 to 2001, the foreign share of US national debt increased from 17 per cent to 31 per cent (Monthly Review 2003: 10). So long as there is confidence in the US economy and the dollar, these deficits may be manageable, but there is a serious question mark as to whether high trade deficits are sustainable. They are more sustainable for the US than for other countries because of the international role of the dollar, but ongoing deficits are likely to erode this role further.

The continued power – and potential weakness – of the US state is thus central to an understanding of globalisation. Indeed, the US state has been a major agent in the promotion of financial globalisation, and the free-trade policies that indirectly resulted through structural adjustment policies. This of course does not mean that 'globalisation' (either of the economy or more generally) is reducible to the actions of the US, but still less does it mean that globalisation has simply arrived from nowhere and does not involve relationships of hierarchy and power. It also does not mean that the US is fully in control of this process, and the deficits may become so great – particularly with current military commitments – that investors will lose confidence in the dollar, and move into other currencies. But still this potential fragility of US hegemony does not contradict the reality of US power, and its success in promoting capital flows into the US, partly at the expense of other countries, including in the developing world.

The myth of economic globalisation

What should be clear by now is that in the era of globalisation we have not seen a dispersal of capital throughout the globe. Instead, it has tended to concentrate in certain countries and regions, and to bypass others. The questions that follow are: Why does this occur, and what can be done about it? Is it because some countries are insufficiently globalised? In other words, is it the fault of the countries themselves (or, more accurately, some people in those countries) or of the global order of which they are a part? Neoliberalism contends that the answer lies mainly with the countries themselves, just as the 1980s debt crisis was regarded as being a product of the bad policies of the debtors. Some criticism of the richer countries is allowed in this account. In particular, First World governments should level the playing field by practicing what they preach, and endorse free-trade policies in agriculture and other sectors, thereby allowing developing countries to export to potentially lucrative First World markets. Unfortunately, this principle is applied very inconsistently by western leaders, with Jacques Chirac and George W. Bush among the worst offenders (though none can be considered blameless). Neoliberals are rightly critical of these double standards, but they still argue that there is a need for developing countries to open themselves up to foreign competition, in order to eliminate inefficient production and specialise in those areas in which they have a comparative advantage.

Certainly the 'advanced' countries should have a more open policy towards imports from the developing world. It is also true that some developing countries make things worse through bad policies. Having said that, as we saw in the previous chapter, the emergence of 'advanced' capitalist societies was the product of a long history of social struggles, and therefore arguments that reduce 'underdevelopment' to bad policies, as if 'policy' is a simple matter of technical prescription, are guilty of anti-sociological arguments.[4] But perhaps most important of all, *the exercise of blanket free-trade policies is not in the interests of developing countries.* This is not to endorse a case for autarchy, but simply to question a blanket case for more pro-globalisation policies. There has been a generalised pattern of trade, money and investment liberalisation in the developing world in the last 10 to 20 years. For instance, for every year from 1991 to 2002, around 90 to 98 per cent of national regulations covering foreign investment have involved greater liberalisation (UNCTAD

2003: 21). But in that same period there has been an intensification of the concentration of capital in certain parts of the world. The argument that countries need to be more 'globalised' implies that, once liberalisation occurs, there will be an evening up of development between countries; but this has clearly not taken place. As I have argued elsewhere, 'it is not the case ... that some parts of the world are effectively incorporated while others are insufficiently globalised; rather, it is the case that the *actual processes of globalisation that have occurred have been intrinsically uneven, unequal and unstable*' (Kiely 1998a: 11; emphasis in original). Contrary to the claims of neoliberalism, capital does not move from ('high-cost') areas of capital abundance to ('low-cost') areas of capital scarcity. Rather, through a process of cumulative causation, it tends to concentrate in established areas of accumulation. It does so to take advantage of technological development, labour skills, infrastructural development, and close proximity to suppliers and markets. Capital is attracted by the wealth of existing capital, and repelled by the poverty represented by capital scarcity. The concentration of capital is therefore not caused by market imperfections or the absence of competition; instead it is the very process of competitive capital accumulation that leads to such concentration. This means that transnational companies tend to invest most in other advanced economies; and as we have seen, much capital is also invested financially rather than productively (including from the developing world), attracted above all to Wall Street and the main international currency, the dollar. This has enormous implications for strategies that attempt to incorporate 'the periphery' into the liberal core, not only through neoliberal policies but also through state-building by military intervention (I will return to this point in the next chapter).

In terms of the more immediate policies of promoting economic growth in the developing world, this concentration of capital has two related implications. Given the inequality of competition promoted by capital concentration, it is very difficult to break into export markets on the same level as existing producers. And given that pro-globalisation policies of structural adjustment lead to domestic competition with these same established overseas producers, it is these same policies that undermine the construction of developed capitalist economies. Of course it is likely that most countries will find one or two niches in the world market, and their own domestic market, but this hardly means equality of competition. These points were not lost on South Korea and Taiwan, which deliberately went against the grain of market forces in developing domestic industrial capacity, even when the industries concerned were not initially competitive. They also faced favourable open-market conditions in a world economy that was then growing far more rapidly than it is today. Indeed, for all the rhetoric about the efficiency of globalisation, average growth rates for most countries in the world were far higher in the 1960s and 1970s then they were in the 1980s and 1990s. Improvements in living standards were generally also more rapid in the former than the latter period, which reflects the fact that, in both the 'advanced' and 'developing' capitalist countries, some important gains were made in the earlier period, and these have been partly eroded in the era of globalisation (Weisbrot et al. 2002). The two countries that have bucked this trend – though inequality within them has increased – are India and China; but as we have seen, they do not meet the neoliberal criteria of pro-globalisation policies.

Some capital does flow to developing countries, as we have seen. Productive capital does have potentially socially useful effects, such as increasing employment, income, skills and technology. However, for countries to utilise these effectively, they must be regulated by the state; but structural adjustment and pro-globalisation policies generally undermine the capacity of states to undertake this task. Of course, states may not want to carry out the task, and we should not assume that they act for the 'national interest' – too often they act for the interests of the powerful minority ruling classes. But the fact remains that in every case of a transition from 'backward' to 'advanced' capitalism, the state has played a highly active role in regulating capital, forcing capitalists to reinvest and develop new technology, investing in public goods, and so on. These capacities have often been undermined in the last 20 years, with the result that some foreign investment is locked into a vicious downward cycle of low-wage, low-productivity investment – the sweat-shop production so well described in Naomi Klein's *No Logo* (2000). Contrary to the claims of the crudest Third Way apologists (Lloyd 2001), it was not economic growth alone that moved earlier developers out of this cycle, but the struggles for social improvements that forced the state to act in more socially progressive ways. Moreover, as we have seen, it is far from clear that pro-globalisation policies are the most effective means of stimulating growth. The 'globalisation' of the world economy therefore means the expansion of the role of global markets in distributing and allocating resources. But, contrary to the expectations of globalisation's advocates, this market expansion has not led to a dispersal of capital investment throughout the globe. Of course, actual amounts of investment and trade have increased, but not at unprecedentedly higher levels than in previous eras; and the shares of such capital flows have increasingly concentrated. This has led to increasing inequality, and at best a disappointing record of poverty reduction (Kiely 2005: Ch. 5). The countries that have made some advances in poverty reduction are not countries that have carried out markedly pro-globalisation policies.

The need for regulation applies not only at the level of the nation-state, but also to the institutions of global economic governance. However, as we have seen, institutions like the IMF and World Bank have generally not restricted, and instead have usually enhanced, market expansion. This point also applies to the WTO, formed in 1995 to formalise trade agreements previously discussed through the more informal GATT mechanism, and regarded as one of the central achievements of Clinton's 'geo-economic' strategy (although in fact the GATT talks that led to the WTO preceded Clinton's presidency). The WTO is committed to the expansion of tariff reduction in agriculture, clothing and textiles, though to date there has been limited success on these fronts, which partly reflects the successful resistance of the most powerful states. There are also mechanisms for the expansion of patents and copyrights, which mean that purchasers will have to pay a fee for the use of certain protected commodities. This is known as the TRIPS (Trade Related Intellectual Property Rights) agreement. In addition, there is provision for the privatisation of public services through the General Agreement on Trade and Services (GATS).

The case made for the TRIPS agreement is that extra payments or rents are necessary in order to guarantee the recovery of research and development (R&D) expenses. In this way, pharmaceutical companies argue that patents are necessary to help finance R&D into new drugs, some of which will help the poor. But in fact most R&D financing is spent on research into illnesses that affect the comparatively wealthy, and as much is often spent on advertising as on R&D itself. It may well be unrealistic to expect drugs companies to act in an altruistic way and concentrate on developing low-cost, low-profit drugs for the global poor. But it is equally naive simply to wait until the poor can afford the most expensive drugs, as though drug company profits are a simple fact of life, outside the realm of politics. Certainly the TRIPS agreement remains an area of great contention, and has been resisted by some developing-country governments, who want to draw on cheap generic drugs that can help the poor effectively and far more cheaply than the patented drugs. What is undoubtedly needed is the development of public-sector investment in cheap, generic drugs, for market forces lead to money being attracted to existing wealth, and repelled by poverty. The TRIPS agreement further intensifies inequality, undermining the chance for developing countries to develop indigenous technological capacity, thus cementing the concentration of technological capacity in the hands of the already wealthy.

The rationale for the GATS agreement, like structural adjustment programmes in the 1980s and 1990s, is that the private sector is a more effective service-provider than the state. This argument in turn rests on the broader notion that the private sector is more efficient than the public sector, because it allows for competition between innately self-interested human beings. But the assumption that humans are naturally selfish ignores the ways in which humans cooperate in everyday life, including the commitment to the public service ideal. This ideal is assumed to be irrelevant in a world dominated by the free market. We will return to this debate in the last two chapters, but what is clear here is that the free market does not represent the 'universal interest', but rather the entrenched power of a privileged minority.

This chapter has documented the movement from the Bretton Woods era of 1945–71, to the era of globalisation. The former era was committed to free trade and some global governance, but it also made provision for national capitalist development, above all through state expansion, which facilitated (for a while) high growth, full employment and welfare in the 'First World', and 'development' in the 'Third World'. By the late 1960s, this era was coming to a close, as the hegemony of the US dollar on which it rested was undermined. In order to restore competitiveness, the US government abandoned the link to the dollar in 1971, which paved the way for floating exchange rates for the major currencies and the gradual deregulation of finance. In the late 1970s and early 1980s this liberalisation of finance was enhanced by increased government commitment to neoliberal policies, through both government and structural adjustment policies, which emerged from the debt crisis in the developing world and the inflationary crisis in the developed world. Despite the poor record of these policies, the promotion of a 'Third Way' in the 1990s tended to accept the need for globalised markets, and so further expanded free trade and deregulated finance. Under George W. Bush a much greater degree of distrust emerged between the US government and the WTO, further intensified by a number of clashes over trade policy between Europe, the US, Japan and the G20 group of developing countries. But this did not mean a wholesale rejection of free-trade principles – instead, the Bush administration focused more on regional and bilateral free-trade deals, and the selectiveness of its free-trade commitments, while more extensive than the Clinton administration, was far from novel. Furthermore, as we have seen, Bush's policy in terms of development aid has been more unilateralist than previous administrations; but at the same time it is clearly committed to the development of 'market economies' in poorer countries – a policy which, this chapter has suggested, will not work.

For advocates of neo-liberalism, policies that promoted economic globalisation were supposed to be good for economic growth and poverty reduction. Claims were made that poverty levels were indeed falling in the world economy; but these claims were based on questionable data, and ignored the ways in which some countries continued to adopt policies that were not fully compatible with the pro-globalisation agenda. On the whole, the record of economic globalisation is not good. A global free market entrenches inequalities, as capital tends to concentrate in already relatively rich areas, while deregulated finance has increased international instability.

Contemporary globalisation was a product of the economic and social crisis of the 1970s, and of the US decision to liberalise finance as a way to try to restore global competitiveness, initially through a weak dollar policy and then, from the 1980s, through aggressive policies designed to attract capital investment. These included high interest rates which, together with the movement of capital towards the US, had devastating consequences for many countries. Faced with debt and high interest repayments, these countries were only granted access to credit on condition that certain neoliberal policies were adopted, which led to a reorientation away from the home market and towards the world market. In the 1990s, in the context of the rise of the Third Way, a great deal of faith was placed in increasing foreign investment in 'emerging markets'. However, this investment often only amounted to the takeover of assets privatised through structural adjustment policies. Of course, there was also some investment in new plant, but this was generally not on a sufficient scale to increase overall investment rates substantially. Moreover, much of the investment was made up of financial flows into stocks and bonds, attracted by high interest rates that kept growth rates low, and was often liable to rapid withdrawal at the first sign of trouble. The result was a whole series of financial crises that had a severe impact on real economies in Latin America, East Asia and Russia. Perhaps above all, these new flows of investment were highly concentrated, and simply bypassed many parts of the developing world – and indeed were often not used productively at all. The unsurprising result has been an increase in inequality both within and between countries. These outcomes are not the product of 'insufficient globalisation', but in fact reflect the particular form that economic globalisation has taken. Such globalisation is a product of two closely linked factors outlined and discussed in this chapter: those of US hegemony (supported by other states) and neoliberalism. We will return to these economic questions in the concluding chapter.

6

Globalisation, Culture and Rights:
Liberal Internationalism,
Imperialism and Universalism

This chapter addresses questions around the relationship between globalisation, culture and rights, and relates these issues to different ways of talking about 'Americanisation'. The first section examines the theory known as cultural imperialism, which focuses on the Americanisation of popular culture across the world. I then move on to a critique of this account of cultural globalisation, which partly questions the view that we are moving towards a culturally homogeneous global society, but which above all suggests that this debate focuses too narrowly on *consumer* culture. The third section draws on this critique and re-examines the defence of the 'free market', relating such a defence to debates around universalism, rights and difference. It revisits the debates over US hegemony and liberal internationalism that were first discussed in Chapters 3 and 4. This section argues that the US has been inconsistent in its promotion of liberal rights, and further that liberal rights are themselves limited. Following this discussion, in the final section I suggest that the liberal right of sovereign consumers exercising their choice in the free market is based on a one-dimensional view of freedom. In focusing on culture as a way of life (rather than the dissemination of particular products), I suggest that there are important tendencies towards cultural standardisation, which can be linked to liberalism and US hegemony. I will argue that we live in a world increasingly dominated by rationalisation, consumer capitalism and 'growth fetishism'. In this respect we are living in an increasingly standardised world, even though the actual commodities produced and consumed often remain quite different. The freedom of the marketplace thus becomes a form of social tyranny. In making this critique I am careful not to romanticise poverty, so-called 'traditional societies', or 'fundamentalist' responses to US hegemony or consumer capitalism, but at the same time I suggest that a one-sided obsession with economic growth is neither socially nor environmentally sustainable. My discussion in this section focuses on questions of commodification, rationalisation, and what Ritzer (2004) describes as the excessive focus on the need for growth, or 'grobalisation'. I examine the impact of these tendencies, not least for understanding politics in the age of globalisation.

FROM MODERNISATION TO CULTURAL IMPERIALISM

In the 1950s and 1960s, most sociological theories of development argued that Third World societies needed to catch up with the west. Development would be achieved through a process of modernisation, which basically meant the adoption of western technology and values, such as the need for economic growth, meritocracy and entrepreneurship. This approach did not necessarily conform to the reality of western development, and it would be difficult to claim that the US in the 1950s was in any sense a meritocracy. But the ideological role of modernisation theory was important, and it influenced key figures in both First and Third Worlds, who believed that this was the way to 'catch up' with modern, western societies. Various grand theories of development emerged, such as Rostow's theory that all societies pass through similar stages of development on their way to the end-goal of a modern, consumer society, not unlike the US in the 1950s (Rostow 1960). As part of this process of modernisation, it was argued that developing societies should westernise both media practices and cultural values and products. The development of an independent mass media, adopting (supposedly) western values of efficiency, professionalism and cutting-edge technology was seen as an intrinsic part of the modernisation process.

By the 1960s, this conservative view was increasingly rejected in the developing world. Disappointed by the promises of development, and inspired by successful resistance in Vietnam and Cuba, parts of the Third World began to radicalise, questioning the need for development through westernisation. Development was still regarded as necessary, but emphasis was now placed on finding alternative paths, which included the rejection of western 'neo-colonialism'. It was now argued that wholesale contact with the west actually hindered development, and led to an intensification of western domination. Neo-colonialism took place through western transnational domination of specific developing countries, and through western domination of the world economy. For this dependency approach, the end of colonialism had not led to the end of imperialism.

One area in which the west continued to dominate was the media. Contact with the west did not lead to modernisation, but to the continued promotion of westernisation. The western media were therefore agents of cultural imperialism. Through ownership, education, or the diffusion of western values, the media promoted conservative western values that undermined local cultures, and therefore the resources on which the foundations of alternative development strategies could be built. This cultural imperialism could have a directly political effect, as in the case of Chile from 1970 to 1973, when the media played a role in undermining the elected socialist government of Salvador Allende, which was eventually overthrown in a US-backed military coup in 1973. Cultural imperialism was thus a major issue in the developing world in the Cold War era, specifically in the context of US intervention and the widespread belief that cultural flows had a propaganda effect, justifying wider intervention through the promotion of the 'American dream' (Tunstall 1977; Schiller 1979; Seabrook 2004).

In the era of globalisation, the language is couched in terms of the global destroying the local, but the argument is very much the same. Globalisation is said to lead to cultural homogenisation, in which local cultures are destroyed through the homogenising effects of the western media. Indeed, this process is accelerating with the growth of genuinely global media such as satellite television. Thus, Barnet and Cavanagh argue that

> [s]atellites, cables, walkmans, videocassette recorders, CDs, and other marvels of entertainment technology have created the arteries through which modern entertainment conglomerates are homogenizing global culture. With the toppling of the Berlin Wall and the embrace of free market ideologies in former and current communist countries, literally the entire planet is being wired into music, movies, news , television programmes and other cultural products that originate primarily in the film and recording studios of the US. The impact of this homogenization on the rich cultural diversity of communities all around the world is immense, and its contours are beginning to emerge. (Barnet and Cavanagh 2001: 169)

Post-9/11, these critiques are linked to a more overtly propagandistic role for the US culture industries, which are said to be central to the promotion of US imperialism. Sardar and Wyn Davies claim that Hollywood 'has shaped America's self-image and projected the rightness and justification of its will and claim to empire'. They go on to suggest that '[t]he business of show business is the business of colonising all minds and undermining all imaginations' (Sardar and Wyn Davies 2004: 121, 159). The 'soft' cultural power embedded in the US culture industries is thus as central to imperialism as the economic power of the dollar and the hard power of the US military.

The cultural imperialism thesis thus makes the following arguments:

1. Through wider (political, social, economic) forms of domination, the west controls the 'global media';
2. Through this control it leads to the elimination of cultural difference, or, in other words, the (western-dominated) global media industries destroy local cultures;
3. This can have wider political effects, as consumers are seduced by the 'American dream', and are less likely to search for alternatives to Americanisation.

THE CULTURAL IMPERIALISM THESIS: AN ASSESSMENT

Although I want to question the broad argument of the cultural imperialism (CI) thesis, I first want to suggest that it should not be rejected out of hand. Cultural flows are massively unequal, and there is a tendency towards cultural standardisation in the world. The ubiquitous western brands, like Coca Cola, McDonald's and KFC, selling products but also a 'lifestyle', are testimony to this fact. But does this really mean the end of cultural difference, or that consumers of western brands – whether films, television programmes or junk food – are merely passive dupes of westernisation? I want partly to challenge this contention, by looking at three closely related issues: first, the question of the 'sending culture'; second, that of the 'receiving culture'; and third, the relationship between the global and the local. I then want to suggest that some of the fears of cultural homogenisation themselves betray a patronising, romantic, and indeed imperialist approach to local cultures. The force of this critique paves the way for a reconsideration of the role of the free, sovereign consumer, exercising his or her freedom in the marketplace, an issue taken up in the final sections.

The CI thesis can first be faulted for its tendency to homogenise the culture of the 'sending' country. In most cases, this means the US. There is an implicit assumption that all of the cultural products that originate from the US somehow represent the ideology of the dominant forces in US society. But this is clearly not the case, and of course those same forces often come into conflict with the entertainment industry, which is often accused of promoting decadent liberal values. There are many examples of such conflicts, such as George Bush Sr's assertion that he wished American families to be more like *The Waltons* than *The Simpsons*. At its peak, *The Simpsons* was one of the most subversive (and funny) programmes ever to grace our television screens. It was hardly a programme that was guilty of promoting the 'propaganda' of the 'American dream'. The owners of this series are Rupert Murdoch's Fox network, some of whose television coverage could be described as propaganda. This was true in its abysmally crude pro-war coverage of the conflict with Iraq in 2003. However, two points that relate directly to the CI thesis need stressing. First, while the Fox network may be owned and run by US conservatives, not all of its output is conservative, or a simple promotion of the American dream. Matt Groening, creator of *The Simpsons*, ensured full creative control for the makers of that programme. Indeed, in 2003 one episode satirised the gung-ho coverage of the Fox network's news channel, and the latter is rumoured to have withdrawn the threat of a lawsuit only when it realised that the former was owned by the same company.[1] Provided it makes them money, Fox are happy to comply with creative freedom for *The Simpsons*. Second, the effects of the pro-war propaganda cannot be predicted in advance – certainly, its effect in Europe was to harden anti-war sentiments.

Similar points could be made for the popularity of many other US products. The global success of *Nirvana* and hip-hop cannot be regarded as straightforward propagation of the values of the white, middle-class conservative US. Of course, it is crucial to the companies that promote these products that they make a profit, but this only demonstrates that making a profit and challenging those same US conservative values can be compatible. The economics of making money do not uniformly dictate the promotion of a homogenised, conservative US. Indeed, among the main critics of American popular culture is the American right, who tend to regard it as a purveyor of decadent liberal values.

Just as the CI thesis tends to homogenise the sending culture, it tends to make similar assumptions about the receiving culture. In some cases, complaints that cultural imperialism is undermining the nation are made by authoritarian state elites who have little claim to represent the nation, or progressive culture and politics. Resistance to Americanisation dates back to Nazi Germany and the

Soviet Union in the 1930s. Too often, CI theorists take complaints of cultural homogenisation at face value, and conflate the interests of state elites with those of national culture (Tomlinson 1991: Ch. 3). Similarly, CI theorists often assume that the effects on receiving audiences can be predicted. But things are more complicated than that, and audiences construct their own meanings from specific media 'texts'. Many foreign products do not actually sell in sufficient quantities to realise a profit, and 'local' products remain very popular – the Indian film industry, for example. Moreover, those foreign products that do sell have unpredictable effects. Similarly, it is too one-sided to claim that 'global' (or western) destroys 'local'. In many cases, western companies have found that they have had to draw on, rather than destroy, the local. Thus, Music Television (MTV) attempted to promote a globally homogeneous music policy when it first expanded its operations (Negus 1996). However, this was not an economic success, and so it responded by localising its operations, and therefore played more local music alongside its more standardised product. Similarly, McDonald's in India does not sell beef or pork products, but instead sells its 'McVeggie' burger and the 'McAloo Tikki' burger (a potato dish), while pizza chains have toppings such as the 'Peppy Paneer' and 'Chicken Chettinad'. Global companies thus localise in specific settings, and the same point applies to global commodities – that is, they become 'hybridised'. It may be true that corporate executives want to promote a safety-first policy, and promote homogenised, predictable, safe, commercial rubbish. There is certainly a tendency for this to happen – the recent success of disposable, promotional pop shows on British television is just one of many examples. But there are counter-tendencies too, and if companies wish to make money they have to respond to these pressures. This is not to accept that entertainment companies are simply responding to our individual needs as we express them in the marketplace; it is only to question the view that we, or consumers in the Third World, are simply passive dupes.

Indeed, the CI thesis too easily accepts that we – or 'they' in the Third World – are victims, easily subject to the manipulative practices of the culture industries. This criticism all too easily becomes a romantic apology for the supposed authenticity of local cultures, and a call for their decontamination from western commercialism through cultural delinking. This argument is often made by those who implicitly assume that they are 'above' such commercialism, unlike the 'ignorant masses' of the First World, and the 'manipulated masses' of the Third. Unfortunately for such patronising romantics, connections between different cultures are so old that one wonders when 'authentic' culture actually existed. As Marshall Sahlins points out:

> Why are well-meaning Westerners so concerned that the opening of a Colonel Sanders in Beijing means the end of Chinese culture? A fatal Americanization. But we have had Chinese restaurants in America for over a century, and it hasn't made us Chinese. On the contrary, we obliged the Chinese to invent chop suey. What could be more American than that? French fries? (Sahlins (1999: 34)

Such arguments are often linked to the idea of global hybridity, in which global and local interlink in culturally specific ways (Tomlinson 2000: Ch. 4). The idea of hybridity is in many respects useful, as it undermines the argument that there exist pure cultures unaffected by a long history of cultural flows between different regions. At its worst, then, the CI thesis is itself guilty of cultural imperialism, as it assumes that 'local cultures' are pure, static and unchanging, and by implication too weak to resist the homogenising thrust of 'Americanisation'.

But on the other hand, these points beg the question of how contemporary culture itself should be understood. In terms of consumer culture, one possible interpretation is that audience responses to particular cultural goods always take on a resistant quality, which challenges the intentions of the (supposedly) conservative culture industries. This is an argument often associated with cultural theorists such as John Fiske (1989). Another, not unrelated interpretation, is that the western culture industries are simply providing a service, expanding the choices available to rational, sovereign consumers in the marketplace. In both approaches, the assumption is made that we are free to choose, which either ignores or celebrates the wider social context in which such commercial transactions take place. This is the context of the dominance of free-market consumer capitalism. In cultural populist approaches such as that endorsed by Fiske, this largely disappears from the analysis (McGuigan 1992); while in the case of the celebration of consumer culture, we essentially return to the assumption that exercising consumer choice in the marketplace represents the freest choice available to humanity. This argument is close to Giddens' position of global hybridity, in which cultural flows have no direction. But this argument also presupposes the view that the market is the natural arena for social interaction – hardly a politically neutral view (Scott 1997: 6). We thus arrive back at neoliberalism, and the related claim that the 'liberal internationalism' (theoretically) promoted by US hegemony represents freedom. These arguments are considered in detail in the following sections. In the following section I consider the question of liberal internationalism, returning thereafter to the question of culture, and how this relates to ideas of freedom and rights.

NEOLIBERALISM, RIGHTS AND UNIVERSALISM

The critique of cultural imperialism outlined above suggests that it is one-sided, if not mistaken, to view the diffusion of specific cultural products from the 'west' to the 'developing world' as imperialist. My own critique left room for some recognition that while the CI thesis is one-sided, it does at least attempt to recognise the reality of power relations in the world order. I return to this issue in the following section, but first we need to discuss one possible interpretation of the critique of the CI thesis. This is the argument that, rather than imposing products on consumers in the developing world, such diffusion actually allows consumers to express their preferences, choices and therefore *freedom* in the context of a competitive marketplace. In other words, this critique of the CI thesis has much broader implications, as it embraces wider assumptions about human freedom and rights, and their supposed universal applicability. It also, of course, returns us to the questions of neoliberalism and Americanisation.

This section therefore examines the relationship between human rights, freedom and US hegemony in the global order. It starts by briefly defining human rights, and outlining some of the contentious points around the idea. It then moves on to examine how human rights discourse has been linked to the US state's perception of itself, and its hegemonic role in the international order. Particular attention is paid to the Bush administration. As was argued in Chapter 4, in some respects the Project for the New American Century can be considered a liberal cosmopolitan project, even if these principles are exercised through unilateral means and are therefore applied inconsistently. There is thus some overlap with the arguments made in that chapter, but in this case they are related more explicitly to the question of rights.

The idea of human rights can be traced back to ancient Greece, but they were most fully developed from the seventeenth century onwards. Hobbes challenged the idea of the divine right of kings and attempted to ground the state in a social contract between ruler and ruled, whereby the latter have obligations to accept the right to rule of the former, provided that the state provides the right to security for its subjects. The first natural law theorist, John Locke, argued that humans have rights precisely because of their humanity. He argues that the pre-contract state of nature was based on peaceful coexistence in which people engaged in commercial activity and exchange, but that a state was necessary to arbitrate in the case of disputes over property and exchange in the free market. Locke therefore argued in favour of a limited state, in which the state exercised minimal interference in the behaviour of individuals, thus allowing them to exercise their freedom through choices made in the free market. Central to Locke's conception were the natural rights to life, liberty and property. Rights theory has developed substantially since Locke's day, but his argument continues to provide the basis for liberal theories of universal human rights.

The idea of universal rights has been challenged on three related grounds. First, that there is no such thing as natural law, and that rights can only ever be established through states granting civil liberties to individuals. Rights are therefore historically specific and only exist within particular social and political communities. This point is not necessarily an argument against the desirability of human rights, but it is based on a recognition that they must be grounded in social and political realities. Second, the argument is often made that rights are too selective, and that their origins in western, individualist liberal thought means that social, economic and collective rights tend to be ignored. These include the 'positive rights' identified by Berlin (1969), such as the right to a basic income, food, clothing and shelter. 'Negative' freedoms, based on the right to exercise individual autonomy from the state, through ownership of private property, free speech and so on, do not guarantee these rights. Indeed, because of the inequalities associated with ownership of private property – advocated by liberal rights theory – some critics argue that individual rights actually undermine collective rights. These points lead to a third objection, which is that 'universal rights' are nothing of the sort, and that the claim to universalism is actually made to justify western rights over other ideas about rights. This ignores not only the different social context identified by the first criticism, but also the very different cultural values that exist in the world order – a critique we have already come across in Chapter 3, in the context of 'communitarian' and 'local' critiques of cosmopolitanism.

These critiques of universalism are complicated further when we come to examine the international sphere, because this is made up of a world of (sovereign) nation-states. Although globalisation is sometimes associated with the rise of a cosmopolitan, universal human rights regime, this has not led to anything like a global consensus around human rights. This is partly because of the power of the critiques of universal rights (though, as we will see, some of these are problematic), but also because of the difficulty of finding an effective enforcer of global human rights, which again brings us back to the question of US hegemony in the global order.

Since its foundation, the US state has regarded itself as the bastion of liberalism, and quite exceptional in terms of its exercising the liberal principles of liberty, opportunity and democracy. The US thus regards itself as an exceptional state, one that has a special status and is more advanced and freer than the rest of the world. This has led to some considerable suspicion of the rest of the world, which has given rise to the powerful impulse towards isolationism. At the same time, the US state has also regarded itself as a model for the rest of the world, and so has simultaneously promoted engagement with others, so that they may learn from its example. This self-belief is closely linked to the idea of US 'manifest destiny' (Weinberg 1963): that US intervention is designed, in the words of President Wilson in 1916, to 'make the world safe for democracy' (cited in Heffer 1976: 249). Indeed, these beliefs go to the heart of state formation and expansion in the US itself, which was justified on the grounds that it meant extending the area of freedom, and therefore equating US national interest and the universal interest of humanity (Foner 1998: Ch. 4). As US President Polk put it in 1845, 'foreign powers do not seem to appreciate the true character of our government. To enlarge its limits is to extend the dominions of peace' (cited in McGrew 2000: 229). It is not surprising, then, that William Appelman Williams argued that the US has always had an imperial vision based on the idea of 'empire as a way of life' (Williams 1980). In many ways, this is not so different from the British Empire's perception of itself (Howe 2003), but the US is crucially different in one respect. Although the US has engaged in a number of colonial enterprises in its past, it has not developed the kind of territorial empires that existed in Europe until the second half of the twentieth century (Williams 1980). The US has certainly engaged in many bloody interventions, but these have been designed to promote territorial sovereignty (since 1945 at least), albeit through independent states friendly to US interests.

This self-perception depends upon the suppression of many bloody episodes in US history, including the slaughter of native Americans, the annexation of territory in the making of the US, the practice of slavery and ongoing institutionalised discrimination, and civil war. Moreover, American freedom has itself been contested throughout that country's history, and this has included important struggles for labour and social rights by a variety of political and social movements (Foner 1998). Nevertheless, the image of US manifest destiny is an important one, as it has helped to shape US foreign policy since the state's foundation.

Since the Monroe doctrine of 1823, the US has advocated an interventionist policy in its own backyard. After the First World War, President Wilson advocated a far more interventionist role for the US globally, and he envisaged that this would take place through multilateral institutions. To an extent, this ideal was defeated by isolationists in Congress, although this did not prevent continued interventions in Latin America and the Caribbean. However, in the post-war period the US's role as one of the two superpowers was assured. As we saw in Chapters 3 and 4, this was partly due to the country's international commitments, alongside promotion of the related ideals of anti-communism, freedom and universal human rights. The US thus played a central role in the formation of the United Nations, and in the drawing up of the Universal Declaration of Human Rights in 1948. In declaring itself the leader of the free world, the US thereby globalised the idea that it was a desirable model for the rest of the world. The idea of the inseparability of the US national interest and the universal interest was thus also globalised. In practice, this did not stop the US from acting in unaccountable ways or of putting its state interests first (as in the cases of voting power at the Security Council and the agreement at Bretton Woods), but the discourse of universal human rights was not just self-serving rhetoric. Above all, it paved the way for the beginning of the end of colonialism, as independence movements advocated the right of self-determination for sovereign nation–states.

But there were also problems with the discourse of universal rights which were contested on the basis of their selectivity. The state socialist world placed greater emphasis on social and economic rights, emphasising the 'positive' freedoms later identified by Berlin.

Some reference was made to social and economic rights in the UN Declaration, but critics felt that far more emphasis was placed on liberal, individual rights such as freedom of speech and movement, and above all the right to own property. The former colonial world also tended to emphasise a less 'American-centric' definition of rights, which involved allowing the new states to adopt a non-aligned path independent of both capitalism and communism. The basis of this non-alignment was often vague, but the search itself often caused hostility on the part of the US, which often conflated nationalism with communism, a policy which tended to become a self-fulfilling prophecy as US hostility led to some nations being forced to become Soviet allies. The US in turn also gave its support to many authoritarian, but anti-communist regimes, and to insurgents that played a central role in the defeat of communism. Indeed, support was extended to Islamic political movements in Afghanistan, some of which came later to be regarded as 'evil' opponents of freedom and democracy (Mamdani 2004: Ch. 3). The US policy of support for democracy, human rights and the 'free market' thus often became support for only the third of these three principles, which in turn fuelled the suspicion that human rights amounted to the right to own private property. For instance, the Reagan administration, through former US ambassador to the UN Jeanne Kirkpatrick, distinguished between totalitarian and authoritarian regimes (Kirkpatrick 1982). Drawing on Hayek (1960), Kirkpatrick argued that the latter were preferable to the former because they still allowed negative freedoms to operate, while the former did not. Although this was an argument used to justify conservative, 'realist' foreign policy, and particularly the Reaganite policy of intervention through 'low-intensity conflict' (Halliday 1989: Ch. 3), it was also one that attempted to provide some ethical foundations to the policy that were rooted in liberalism. That these foundations were, to say the least, questionable was also true – for example, the only freedoms that Chile under Pinochet allowed was the right to own private property and endorsement of the free market, and the state essentially crushed anyone who got in the way of these rights. While this could be partly explained by the nature of power-politics in the Cold War, it also reflected the one-sided nature of liberal rights.

This was also clear with the end of the Cold War, which presented new challenges and opportunities for US hegemony and universal human rights. On the one hand, the US became the one major superpower in the world, which potentially gave it unrivalled power. Moreover, the collapse of communism intensified the promotion of liberal internationalism, and in particular of the neoliberal direction that the US state had promoted since the Reagan presidency. Furthermore, it was now argued that the end of the Cold War provided fertile ground for the genuine promotion of liberal internationalist values, as the 'new world order' meant that the US no longer had to compromise human rights promotion in the face of a 'communist threat'. In this context it was not surprising that books claiming that there was no alternative to liberal democracy and the free market, and indeed that History had come to an end, became bestsellers (Fukuyama 1992). On the other hand, US hegemony was perceived to be under threat in a number of ways. The rise of East Asia was seen as a particular challenge, especially when combined with the twin deficits faced by the US in the early 1990s. Indeed, the emergence of a powerful economic bloc in East Asia was also accompanied by renewed debates about the universalism of western liberal rights, and the importance of social and economic rights that were supposedly expressed in the idea of 'Asian values' (Bangkok Declaration 1993). There was also fear that new threats were emerging in the South, based on the breakdown of states, growing populations, poverty, lawlessness and the continued threat from rogue states that threatened US interests, and therefore the interests of universal freedom (Kaplan 1994). Perhaps above all, there was a new perceived threat based on the clash between different cultures, particularly between the freedom-loving west and a homogeneous alternative cultural force united by the belief in Islamic religious doctrine (Huntington 1996: 29).

This idea of a clash of civilisations had some influence on US thinking both before and after the attacks in September 2001, although interestingly Huntington's work is at times quite ambiguous. He clearly does see the west as superior to the other cultural formations identified in his book, but at the same time he does not express the same cultural certainties as Fukuyama's 'End of History'. He was at times quite critical of the west's claim to represent universal ideals, and indeed of western power (see Huntington 1996: 310). On the other hand, in homogenising both Islam and the west (and other cultures), he allowed no room for conflict *within* cultures. At one point he even argues that '[t]he underlying problem for the West is not Islamic fundamentalism. It is Islam, a different civilization whose people are convinced of the superiority of their culture and are obsessed with the inferiority of their power.' (Huntington 1996: 217) Interestingly, Huntington then goes on to problematise the west in its dealings with Islam, arguing that western intervention in 'other civilisations' is bound to promote and intensify conflict. It is for this reason that Huntington opposed the war in Iraq, and indeed why prominent neoconservatives have criticised him and others for being right-wing 'anti-Americans' (Kaplan 1998). But Huntington's arguments concerning the dangers of US power tend to be forgotten, and crude interpretations of the clash of civilisations have instead been used to mobilise support for war against 'backward cultures', which reject Huntington's pessimism concerning cultural change and instead argue that US power can be used for cultural, political and economic progress. Conservative uncertainties such as those associated with Robert Kaplan and Huntington therefore question the role of the US state in a uni-polar world.

Whatever the specific disagreements over policy after the Cold War, the US continued to promote the ideal of itself as a model for the rest of the world. Bill Clinton echoed a long line of US presidents when he talked of the need for America to 'continue to lead the world we did so much to make', adding that 'our mission is timeless' (Clinton 1993), while Bush Sr talked of the US's 'unique responsibility' (Bush 1992). The US state found a new mission for itself after Saddam Hussein invaded Kuwait in August 1990, and after the Gulf War of 1991 Bush Sr talked of a 'new world order'. A number of US-led interventions took place against 'rogue' and 'failed' states, including Panama, Iraq, Somalia, Afghanistan, Sudan and Serbia. There were also some significant changes in policy – most important, the US state, as well as institutions such as the World Bank, began to promote democratisation as a crucial policy for the developing world. In the 1950s and 1960s, when modernisation theory dominated US thinking, the argument was made that democracy would follow development as a by-product of economic growth and social and political modernisation. In the 1990s, the argument was made that democratisation and good governance were essential to democracy because they would lead to the promotion of market-friendly policies and therefore freedom, human rights and economic growth. This change in the policy from adjustment in the 1980s to (global) competitiveness in the 1990s was only a change in form, not content, and indeed in many respects neoliberal policies of market expansion intensified (see Chapter 5). In terms of power, Clinton envisaged a complementary policy of 'engagement and enlargement', which entailed using a multilateral approach whenever possible in order to expand market democracies, and deal with the 'zones of war' in the international order. These were largely identified as rogue states, which should be contained in the short term and incorporated into the liberal order in the longer term (Clinton 1994; Litwak 2000). This incorporation could take the form of incentives, such as conditions applied to aid or trade sanctions, but in some cases the use of military power was also deemed to be acceptable. These arguments were linked not only to the idea that free markets would promote growth and prosperity, but also to the idea that liberal democracies were more stable and peaceful, and therefore more conducive to a democratic peace, which was itself sometimes linked to Kant's theory of perpetual, republican peace (Doyle 1983; Russett 1990). Democratisation was therefore accompanied by continued neoliberal policies such as trade liberalisation and privatisation, and if necessary by (selective) humanitarian intervention in the case of failed states. It was these policies that essentially came to be associated with globalisation and the (neo)liberal internationalist project.

For a wide range of globalisation theorists, these post-Cold war developments were welcomed. The Clinton and Blair 'Third Way' was particularly conducive to policies of global engagement through multilateral institutions, the promotion of human rights through intervention, democratisation, and market expansion. Indeed, in terms of rights, state guarantees of positive freedoms become irrelevant, on the grounds that market-friendly policies can ensure that these will be fulfilled without the bureaucracy and hierarchy of state intervention. In this account, globalisation facilitates a progressive, liberal internationalist project with desirable political outcomes. The Bush administration, on the other hand, like many of the fundamentalisms to which it is opposed, represents a 'regressive globalisation' based on the self-interest of US state power (Kaldor et al. 2003; Shaw 2003).

But, as earlier chapters argued, this dichotomy is unsatisfactory, and the linkage of universal rights, globalisation and US hegemony persists, albeit in a more unilateral form. Certainly the neoconservatives in the Bush administration were critical of Bush Sr and Clinton. They grew particularly impatient with the way in which they dealt with multilateral institutions, as well as their (comparative) reluctance fully to utilise hard, military power. Whether or not this is an accurate representation of those presidencies is debatable, and some commentators have argued that Clinton was particularly effective in strengthening US interests against potential competitors (Bacevich 2002). Certainly, as we have seen, the commitment to multilateral rules and to expanding free trade in many ways undermined the development prospects of much of the world – and so the arguments about positive rights will not go away. But more important is the fact that the neoconservative project largely saw itself as continuing the project of liberal internationalist expansion, albeit by different and more openly unilateralist means. This not only paved the way for new certainties in the post-Cold War world, and thus the rejection of Huntington and Robert Kaplan, but reinvigorated the idea that the US state was a force for the global good. Indeed, it was actually more *optimistic* concerning the expansion of liberalism and freedom than its predecessors. Perhaps the most prominent neoconservative thinker and official, Paul Wolfowitz has argued that 'nothing could be less realistic than the version of the "realist" view of foreign policy that dismisses human rights as an important tool of American foreign policy ... what is most impressive is how often promoting democracy has actually advanced American interests (Wolfowitz 2000: 38)' The US's National Security Strategy for 2002 stated that '[t]he United States will use this moment of opportunity to extend the benefits of freedom across the globe ... We will actively work to bring the hope of democracy, development, free markets, and free trade to every corner of the world.' (National Security Strategy 2002) Neoconservatives themselves therefore partially endorse Wilsonian liberal internationalism, albeit in a unilateralist context, and through the use of military power to promote American liberalism abroad (Podhoretz 1999; Kagan and Kristol 2000).

As we saw in Chapter 4, these principles have been applied inconsistently, partly because unilateralism itself involves considerable compromise with democratic principles, and also because neoconservatives themselves are divided on these issues.[2] In particular, there is also a more straightforward 'realist' fear of the rise of rival powers to US dominance, and this is particularly applied to the rise of China, Russia, and 'Arab and Islamic nationalism'.[3] Indeed, in 1992 Paul Wolfowitz and Lewis Libby had argued for preventive policies against potential competitors, an argument treated with considerable hostility at the time (see Bacevich 2002: 44). Thus, even in its idealist, democratic-globalist form, neoconservative foreign policy has combined liberal internationalism with an advocacy of US domination.[4]

But is this as different from Clinton as is sometimes implied? The substance of the Libby–Wolfowitz argument influenced Clintonite policy on rogue states and liberal expansion (Bacevich 2002), and is a major reason why Bobbit admired Clinton's presidency so much (see Chapter 4). Indeed, prior to 9/11, and despite his own criticisms of Clintonite complacency, Wolfowitz himself argued that many had come round to the arguments that he had made in 1992, arguing that many liberal critics now 'seem quite comfortable with the idea of a Pax Americana' (Wolfowitz 2000). Certainly, post-9/11, it was not only neoconservatives who were openly advocating the use of 'hard' power, partly to deter potential rivals.[5] This more open advocacy of military power was one of the reasons why neoconservatives were so critical of Clinton's policy of giving less priority to military spending.[6] Neoconservatives called for renewal of the Reagan Doctrine (Project for the New American Century 2000) and the more overt use of US unilateralism, and hard, military power. This call for a return to Reaganite policies and the promotion of democracy was ironic, for the Reagan administration was hardly sympathetic to the promotion of liberal democracy, and indeed had allied itself with the likes of Saddam Hussein and the forerunners of al Qaeda.

Having said that, before the fiasco of the war and its aftermath in Iraq, neoconservatives were very optimistic about the capacity of the US to promote 'universal' rights and expand democracy in the region. Indeed, neoconservative advocacy of the democratisation of the Middle East is a major source of concern to traditional realists in the Republican Party (Hulsman 2004; Halper and Clarke 2004). But the more idealist neoconservatives did not share these reservations. For example, neoconservative commentator Thomas Barnett divides the world into a 'functioning core' and a 'non-integrating gap', and frames the divide in terms of the degree of states' incorporation into 'globalisation' (Barnett 2003). State Department Director of Policy Planning Richard Haass argues that these divisions mean that the core, functioning states have an obligation to intervene in non-functioning states that have limited rights of sovereignty, a duty that has increased since the attacks on 11 September 2001 (Mazarr 2003: 508). Mazarr, a senior official at the Department of Defence and admirer of Bush's 'idealism', goes as far as suggesting that it represents an idealism worthy of the liberal internationalism of Woodrow Wilson (Mazarr 2003: 509). What is crucial here is the belief that the world can be re-made in the US's own self-image, and therefore, in the process, that human rights, democracy and freedom can be universalised. As two prominent neoconservatives argue, 'democracy is a political choice, an act of will ... History suggests it comes most effectively from the United States.' (Kaplan and Kristol 2003: 108–9) In this argument, liberal cosmopolitan ideals can be unilaterally promoted by the US state, rather than, say, through the United Nations. This takes us back to the arguments of Bush, Rice and Blair outlined in Chapter 4, but as we saw there this reflects a basic contradiction, 'since such principles and ideals are incompatible with the imposed, unelected global dominance of any single nation' (Singer 2004: 192). It is therefore impossible for the US to be both a model for the rest of the world and the global hegemonic power, for if it is a model to be followed by others than at some point in the future it must give up its latter role, something deemed unacceptable by neoconservatives. In this way, liberal democratic expansion is compromised by the more important principle of continued US dominance.[7]

This compromise on the issue of liberal rights is not necessarily an argument against rights per se. The belief that liberal democratic government is most conducive to guaranteeing human rights should not be dismissed out of hand, and a case can be made for universal human rights and the utility of liberal democracy over other political forms. In the case of liberal democracy, for all its limitations it is indeed preferable to dictatorship. Relativist arguments such as those associated with the 'Asian values' debate wrongly assume that cultures are based on consensus and do not change over time. Moreover, claims made by authoritarian leaders that Asian culture demands respect for hierarchy and traditional values beg the question of how we can know this to be the case when people are denied the right to express these (or other) views. Certainly many people in Asia have struggled for democracy, not least because this represents the best political system for people to exercise their cultural values fully (though a distinction should be made between liberal and other forms of democracy). It is therefore no accident that relativist arguments are most commonly made by powerful people with a particular interest in preserving a status quo of which they are the prime beneficiaries. Arguments for cultural relativism should thus be treated with suspicion. A more powerful argument, outlined in Chapters 3 and 4, is that liberal universalism has no basis in the real world, as it ignores the history and specificity of particular social and political formations. But to *describe* or even *explain* such forms does not *justify* them. As Beetham points out:

> It is difficult to see how a liberal society could ever have emerged in the first place except by challenging the validity claims of a paternalist and hierarchical social order; or a democratic polity except by exposing the

distortions or falsehoods underpinning exclusionary forms of politics. (Beetham 1999: 14)

A commitment to universal rights can therefore be defended, and indeed liberal rights have been important as defences against more authoritarian forms of government. But on the other hand, liberal conceptions of rights are limited, as they do not focus on collective rights. Indeed, in defending unequal ownership of private property, it can be argued that liberalism in some respects undermines the rights of others, as it justifies the power of the propertied over the propertyless. For this reason, some liberals argue that the freedom of private property and the 'free market' is more important than political democracy. But this argument sounds remarkably like an ideology intended to defend the interests of the powerful.

How then do these issues relate to the question of US hegemony? A number of conclusions can be drawn. First, US hegemony has historically been committed to liberal internationalism through sovereign states. This has meant the use, at times of unilateral and, at other times, multilateral means. It has also involved some attempts to retreat into isolationism, but international commitments have largely undermined such a policy, at least since 1945.[8] Second, while the US has genuinely supported state sovereignty, US penetration has occurred through economic means, via foreign investment, trade liberalisation and so on; through military means, such as the use and construction of US bases or even direct intervention; and culturally through dissemination of US products. Sovereignty has thus been compromised by the US's attempts to ensure that independent states are its allies. Third, the US state's perception of itself as a defender of the universal good has been easier to justify during multilateral 'moments', but even in the context of rules-based liberalism, this has not meant that a 'level playing field' has been promoted. Indeed, at worst US military interventions have usually undermined democracy and rights, and even when they have not they have involved great cost and very limited, if any, advances in terms of improvements in human rights. Moreover, in terms of economics, rules-based neoliberal expansion effectively takes from developing countries the right to pursue policies that were pursued in earlier periods by the now developed countries: Put differently if Americanisation means advanced capitalist societies developing through neoliberal policies of sovereign states promoting free markets, then *US foreign policy, based on both unilateralist military expansion and multilateral neoliberalism, actually undermines the prospects for the Americanisation of the world.* Fourth, in terms of rights, US-led liberal internationalism has focused on individual and not collective rights, which has led to conflict such as the current debate over so-called Asian values, but implicit in the rhetoric of globalisation theory is the idea that positive rights – insofar as they exist – will be guaranteed so long as sovereign states adopt the correct, market-friendly policies. This can only be guaranteed through state reform, leading to market-friendly policies of good governance; or in the case of failed states, nation-building designed to promote both state sovereignty and market expansion. The neoconservative project that came to prominence under Bush was more prepared to use hard, military power and act unilaterally than previous administrations (though military intervention and unilateralism were far from rare prior to Bush), but the end-goal of 'Americanisation' or liberal expansion through state sovereignty and the free market was the same. But the problem with this view is the assumption that such a model can easily be implemented, and that conflict and liberal democracy are incompatible. In fact, something close to the opposite is true: namely, that state sovereignty and liberal democracy are the outcomes of conflict, as we saw in Chapters 3 and 4. In a sense, the neoconservative position does accept this argument, given that it recognises the need for benign force to overcome dictatorship. But the problem here is the assumption that this force can provide 'quick-fix' solutions that will then lead to the extension of liberal democracy. Neoconservatives make much of the success of nation-building in post-war Japan and West Germany, but crucial to those successes was the existence of domestic social and political forces to lead the democratic transition. The record in Afghanistan and Iraq is very different, and popular forces are in the long term unlikely to enjoy the support of the US. Indeed, despite consistent warnings from the CIA, neoconservatism's project in Iraq was essentially based on a naive belief that Ahmad Chalabi's Iraqi National Congress was a serious social force that could lead the country to liberal democracy. This project was seriously undermined during the occupation, and Chalabi no longer enjoys the significant support of any arm of the US state.[9] In the case of post-intervention Iraq, interventionists have divided the population into 'good' and 'evil' Iraqis (and outsiders), the former said to be clamouring for western-style free markets and liberal democracy, the latter simply promoting nihilism. This argument updates Bernard Lewis's idea that there are good and bad Muslims, the first of whom can become like 'us', while the latter will always remain irrational ('them') (Lewis 1990). But while it is the case that much of the opposition to the occupation in Iraq is indeed reactionary, it is also the case that the 'good Iraqis' have increasingly opposed the occupation, and even shown some sympathy for some (though not all) insurgent groups within Iraq. This reflects the bloody nature of the intervention, as well as the coalition's own human rights abuses and priorities in post-war reconstruction, which fuelled the suspicion that US corporate interests took priority over the needs of Iraqis. The transfer of sovereignty to the Iraq people in late June 2004 took place in the context of the continued presence of 138,000 US and a further 20,000 coalition troops, as well as an estimated 20,000 foreign contractors. All were fully under US control and immune to Iraqi laws. The Coalition Provisional Authority passed a number of 'Bremer orders' (named after CPA head Paul Bremer), which essentially privatised Iraqi assets and gave special preference to US companies[10] (IPS 2004: 33; Juhasz 2004). While such laws probably do not represent a general return to the imperialism of territorial exclusiveness, as theorised by Lenin (see Chapter 3), they are fully consistent with a US-led, neoliberal world order. Just as the expansion of the liberal democratic system of states is compromised by the priority of continued US dominance, so the so-called freedom of the marketplace takes priority over the liberal democracy of the sovereign state.[11]

This final point brings us back to a more general consideration of the question of liberal democracy. Insofar as it relies on the construction of institutionally separate 'economic' and 'political' spheres, and confines formal politics to the latter, liberal democracy is itself a limited form of democracy. It therefore rests on a 'depoliticised politics', in which citizens are entitled to vote and to own private property, but are expected to limit their demands so that there is no excessive 'intervention' in the sphere of 'freedom' – the market economy (Wood 1995). The tension between liberalism and democracy is therefore all too apparent, and, when faced with the alleged trade-off between 'freedom' and 'democracy', neoliberals and indeed neoconservatives opt like Kirkpatrick for the former. The neoconservatives in the Bush administration may therefore be committed to the expansion of 'democracy' to the Middle East and beyond, but it is a limited kind of democracy, and one that can easily be dispensed with in favour of the primacy of 'market expansion' and/or the guarantee of a state allied to the US. Just as the most powerful in Asia may have a vested interest in the supposed exceptionality of Asian values, so the most powerful in the US and elsewhere may have a vested interest in proclaiming the universal virtues of liberalism. The falsehoods, cover-ups and human rights abuses in the war in Iraq are far from being aberrations in the history of US – and western – foreign policy (and are reinforced by the US's recent role in Venezuela and Haiti). Indeed, labour movements have historically often played central roles in the expansion of a democratic public sphere, at least in the western world (Rueschmeyer et al. 1992). These movements have faced a number of political defeats in the 'advanced' capitalist countries, which have facilitated the increased domination of the market and the erosion of liberal democratic procedures. Moreover, in Iraq there has been a limited but significant revival of trade unions since the invasion, but this is hardly likely to be regarded as a positive development, either by US neoconservatives or Islamist forces in Iraq.[12]

Indeed, the spread of liberal democracy to the developing world since the 1980s can be seen in this light. The Trilateral Commission of 1975 was an influential document, arguing that there was some need for concessions to the democratic pressures emanating from within the developing world (Crozier et al. 1975). However, this commission – and US government policy under Carter, Reagan, Bush Sr and Clinton – effectively promoted a limited form of democracy in which the demands of political and social movements would at best be contained, through institutional procedures in which the population chose a government but real power remained in the hands of the propertied minority. At worst, of course this meant continued commitment to authoritarian regimes, as in the Kirkpatrick-influenced Reagan doctrine. This position changed under Clinton, but the limited approach to democratisation did not. As Samuel Huntington, one of the contributors to the Trilateral Commission report, argued, 'in all democracies, private ownership of property remains the basic norm in theory and in fact ... Defining democracy in terms of goals such as economic well-being, social justice and overall socio-economic equity is not ... very useful.' (Huntington 1989: 18) Democratisation has essentially been limited to formal procedures which have left largely intact wider social structures that guarantee high levels of social and political inequality, and have undermined labour and other movements. Indeed, it could further be argued that neoliberal expansion actually *undermines* freedom and human rights, for in the context of structural adjustment, inequalities have often been intensified and, given the influence of the Washington institutions in heavily indebted developing countries, serious questions arise as to the autonomy that democratic states actually enjoy. This does not necessarily mean that processes of democratisation have simply been a 'sham': the end of authoritarian and military dictatorships has been a welcome development. But equally, the limitations are so great that the designations 'low-intensity democracy' or 'polyarchy', are appropriate (Gills et al. 1993: Robinson 1996; Evans 2001). Moreover, the advances in terms of democratisation have been brought about largely through the struggles of social movements, while the forces limiting it have enjoyed the support of the US state – and, of course, some authoritarian states have continued to enjoy US support.

Some commentators have pointed to a close relationship between contemporary neoconservatism and the political philosophy of Leo Strauss (Drury 1997). Strauss argued that the best form of government is an aristocracy disguised as a democracy, which clearly relates to neoconservative methods in achieving their goals (the selective evidence leading to the war in Iraq), but equally to the limited democracy that they perceive to be desirable for the world, including the US itself. Indeed, US neoconservatives regard liberal democracy in the US as something that has been corrupted by excessive liberalism, and that must therefore be constrained by conservative values. There is thus a tension between a messianic liberal foreign policy combined with a suspicion of both liberalism and democracy at home.[13] The former can in some respects be regarded as an attempt to reinvigorate the latter. But neoconservative foreign policy is not simply a means of promoting conservatism within the US.[14] Instead, it must be analysed in its own right, which in turn brings out the tensions between the liberal optimism of neoconservative foreign policy and the conservative pessimism of domestic policy. Moreover, these tensions again point to the selectivity of the commitment of neoconservatism to democracy.

A recent international survey, based on interviews with 36,000 citizens across 47 countries,[15] found that two-thirds of those interviewed disagreed with the idea that their country was 'governed by the will of the people' (World Economic Forum 2003). There is thus a crisis of official politics and liberal democracy throughout the world. In contrast to the neoconservative explanation that this reflects a 'lack of values', the crisis at least partly reflects the fact that genuine democratic development plays a strictly subordinate role to the priority of the 'free market', whose expansion is endorsed by neoconservatives. As we have seen, such expansion means continued and intensified inequality, which in turn undermines social and economic rights – and, in the context of continued uneven development, is one reason why cultural homogenisation has not occurred. But equally, the priority given to market expansion does promote a tendency towards some forms of cultural standardisation, and in the process rests on a one-dimensional view of the ideas of freedom and the 'common good'. These issues are taken up in the next section.

GLOBALISATION, FREEDOM AND CULTURAL STANDARDISATION

As the previous section three made clear, neoliberal cases for globalisation argue that it is desirable because it represents progress, itself linked to the expansion of freedom and the free market. But as we saw, this begs the question of what is meant by progress – a concept that has been used by many thinkers over the last few hundred years, but often without sufficient critical reflection. This section expands on this discussion, and reflects in more detail on the question of progress. As we have seen, too often progress has been used as a shorthand for becoming more like the west. Thus, apologists for colonialism often argued that, as western societies represented the highest stage of civilisation, the colonisation of backward societies was part of a progressive, civilising mission. This crude apology often took an overtly racist form, in which the human species was divided into supposedly superior and inferior races. This led to attempts to justify all kinds of oppressive practices – including slavery and other forms of forced labour, segregation, political repression, and even genocide. While biological racism is usually rejected today, forms of cultural racism are still very influential. These practices can take all kinds of distasteful forms, and are unfortunately not confined to extreme right-wing political parties. For instance, British governments of both left and right have appealed to a cultural racism in which fears are expressed of the dominant culture being 'swamped' by other, 'alien' cultures. These episodes are of less relevance to my immediate concerns, however, than less overt manifestations of cultural arrogance, particularly in the period since 1945.

The idea of development has a long history, which goes back at least as far as the debates over the industrial and commercial revolutions in Europe and beyond. In the post-war period, it was more closely linked to discussion of the poorer parts of the world: what came to be known as the Third World. Led by the US, and inspired by its liberal internationalist project, western nations began to promote a specific idea of development in which the Third World would catch up with the 'advanced' countries. Development thus became the post-war manifestation of the idea of progress. As President Truman stated in 1949 (cited in Escobar 1995: 3):

> More than half the people of the world are living in conditions approaching misery. Their food is inadequate, they are victims of disease. Their economic life is primitive and stagnant. Their poverty is a handicap and a threat both to them and to more prosperous areas. For the first time in history humanity possesses the knowledge and the skill to relieve the suffering of these people ... I believe that we should make available to peace-loving peoples the benefits of our store of technical knowledge in order to help them realize their aspirations for a better life ... What we envisage is a program of development based on the concepts of democratic fair dealing...Greater production is the key to prosperity and peace. And the key to greater production is a wider and more vigorous application of modern scientific and technical knowledge.

Thus, in the postcolonial era, the 'west' was still regarded as the area containing the most advanced, liberal societies – those that had made the most progress; the 'rest' (or at least the non-communist world) could catch up by travelling along a similar path to development as had (supposedly) been followed by the former. This process of liberal internationalist modernisation could be achieved through a combination of economic growth and the adoption of western values, such as individualist entrepreneurship. Before the resurgence of neoliberalism, development was compatible with the adoption of strategies of import-substitution industrialisation (ISI) (see Chapter 5). But from the 1980s onwards, statist ISI strategies were criticised as economically inefficient by the newly converted neoliberals of western and Third World governments, international institutions and so on. Both neoliberals and more radical thinkers argued that development failed, as it did not lead to catch-up or poverty alleviation. In relation to these contentions, it has been argued that globalisation has rendered development centred on the nation-state increasingly irrelevant. The task of the nation-state – development – was now handed over to 'global markets'. The desired result was said to be a global society based on market expansion, individualism, fragmentation and disembeddedness, enhanced risk and opportunity, and consumerism. For globalisation theorists like Giddens, such 'free-floating' phenomena are simply products of modernity, and cannot be tied to a particular location. But, clearly market, expansion, individualism and consumerism are not as placeless as this argument contends (Scott 1997: 9–10). Indeed, they are not so far removed from the older project of western modernisation. Seen in this light, globalisation is in some respects a new form of westernisation, linked to the project of market expansion (see Chapter 2).

These points have enormous implications for how we think about the relationship between globalisation, culture and human rights. While there are strong grounds for rejecting some versions of the cultural imperialism thesis, this does not mean that alternative theories based on a world of directionless cultural flows or disembedded 'free markets' is more satisfactory. Rather than trying to identify complete homogenisation or total fragmentation, we should instead refer to (selective) processes of cultural standardisation. We may consume different consumer goods throughout the world, or give different meanings to similar goods in different places, but more important is the fact of the spread of consumer culture, and with it the increased commodification and rationalisation of the world. In this respect, irrespective of the effects of particular cultural products, globalisation does lead to some processes of cultural standardisation, through the almost exclusive promotion of a (global) society that champions the maximisation of production, economic growth and consumption, regardless of social and environmental consequences. This argument presupposes an account of culture that focuses less on the analysis of particular cultural products, and more on culture as a 'way of life' (Williams 1958). Tomlinson argues accordingly that

> [t]o grasp the order of 'blame' in cultural domination we have to think of capitalism as something wider than the practices of individual capitalist organisations, however large and powerful. This wider view of capitalism as one of the key autonomized institutions of modernity represents it as something within which the routine practices both of ordinary people and of individual capitalist organisations are locked. It is in this wide sense that we can speak of a 'culture' of capitalism. But here the notion of blame is more problematic: it is not individual practices we are blaming, but a contextualising structure: capitalism not just as economic practices but as the central (dominant) position of economic practices within the social ordering of collective existence. (Tomlinson 1991: 168)

The rest of this section will examine these issues through a critique of western-led cultural standardisation, drawing on this wider definition of culture as a way of life. Chapter 5 already questioned the contention that pro-free-market policies were leading to economic convergence between richer and poorer countries and peoples, insisting that, if anything, there was increased divergence. It therefore undermined the argument that 'catch-up' was increasingly *attainable*. Here, the focus will mainly be on whether such 'catch-up' is *desirable* (Sutcliffe 1999). However, in order to address the question of desirability, some further comments on attainability must first be made, which relate to the environmental costs of development. It is unlikely that all societies could develop along similar lines to western societies, because the strain on global resources would be enormous. Moreover, many forms of economic growth are likely to intensify existing problems of global warming, pollution, ozone depletion and the destruction of biodiversity. As long ago as 1928, Gandhi warned:

> God forbid that India should ever take to industrialization after the manner of the West. The economic imperialism of a single tiny island kingdom is today keeping the world in chains. If an entire nation of 300 million took to similar economic exploitation, it would strip the world bare like locusts. (cited in Allen 1992: 389)

Radical environmentalists argue that environmental problems are not simply an unfortunate accident, but are actually an intrinsic part of the problems of the modern world. Western philosophy puts humans above nature, and argues that the former should use the latter for their own purposes. This anthropocentric perspective argues that nature is a resource to be plundered, and used instrumentally for human development. This is reflected in the western obsession with economic growth, and increasing production and consumption. Indeed, progress is often conceptualised in precisely these very narrow terms. The health of a nation is often reduced to quantitative increases in Gross National Product (GNP), despite the fact that this may include severe costs to the environment, and fails to incorporate social costs. Environmentalists have tried to develop accounting methods that more accurately incorporate measurements of sustainability. These include the Adjusted National Product, which subtracts any effects that are detrimental to human capital (such as health considerations), natural capital (such as consumed non-renewable resources), and wider sustainability losses such as species extinction. Other measures include the Genuine Progress Indicator (Redefining Progress 2003), developed in 1995 in the context of the US stock market-and consumer-led boom that came to an end in 2000. This attempts to modify GDP through adding household and voluntary work, and subtracting growth associated with crime, pollution and family breakdown. Using this measure, it was concluded that there was growth in GPI in the US in the 1990s, but not as great as the GDP growth. Other, more official measures (used by the United Nations Development Programme, for instance) attempt to incorporate social development measures such as life expectancy, literacy and infant mortality, as well as the more standard per capita income. These include the Physical Quality of Life Index and, more recently, the Human Development Index. Attempts have also been made to incorporate measures based on degrees of inequality reflecting gender relations (UNDP 1995). These measures are not without their problems, but they do at least point to the shortcomings of focusing exclusively on GDP growth as the measure of human happiness, which in turn also undermines simplistic notions that the 'West' is an ideal model for the rest of the world. It is therefore not only unlikely that developing societies *can* catch up with the west; given these environmental and social considerations, it is also questionable that they *should* try to catch up.[16]

These points relate to the wider question of the desirability of using the 'west', and therefore US led liberal internationalism as a model. For whatever the desirability of some forms of liberal rights, economic liberalism is also associated with increasing inequality and cultural standardisation.[17] Debates concerning cultural standardisation in the era of globalisation are not necessarily new, and many of the most influential critiques can be traced back to nineteenth-century classical sociology. One of the most interesting classical accounts was Max Weber's theory of rationalisation, which has been updated for the global age by George Ritzer. Weber argued that modernity replaced 'traditional' society's religious account of the world with one based on rationalisation. This meant the development of a rational, calculated approach to the world, focused on ends rather than means. Human beings were reduced to calculations, measurements and control. Modern societies therefore focused almost exclusively on work, transformation, progress, the individual, and the acquisition of money. Weber argued that humans became defined by their relationship to things, rather than in their relationships to other human beings. Thus he argued that capitalism is rational 'to the extent that it is organized around capital calculations. That is, if it is ordered in such a way as to make planned use of material goods and personal services as a means of acquisition, so that, when the final balance sheet is drawn, the final revenue ... should exceed the "capital"' (Weber 1978: 334). But the development of formal rationality was not substantively rational, and indeed in some respects constituted a loss for modern societies. For Weber, 'the ultimate and most sublime values have retreated from public life either into the transcendental realm of mystic life or into the brotherliness of direct and human relations' (Weber 1970: 155). This was not a call for a return to an idealised past, but a recognition that the scientific calculation of the modern world could not give meaning to that same world.

Marx's account of alienation in capitalist society is also relevant: indeed, for Marx it was the domination of the market – the sphere of freedom in liberal thought – which meant that humanity lived in an unfree world. In neoliberal, capitalist, consumer societies people are free to choose within an unfree context, from a bewildering array of commodities (Dean 2003). What they cannot choose, however, is the kind of society in which they live, because (so advocates of neoliberal claim) there is no alternative to this commodity-based society. But if there is no alternative, then how can such a society be free? This claim closely parallels the conflation of desirability and inevitability in the globalisation debate, discussed in Chapter 2.

Marx argued that this unfree world could be 're-humanised' through a process of working-class revolution and the creation of a socialist or communist world. Weber, on the other hand, was much more pessimistic. He argued that instrumental rationality had come to dominate the social system. The modern world was ruled by technical, specialised knowledge, in which people acted in accordance with their immediate interests and saw market forces as paramount. There was greater efficiency as more goods were produced, but this was at the cost of a disenchanted world. Beyond a call for the development of an ethic of responsibility, Weber saw little hope of breaking out of this situation. Although he did recognise that some controls could be imposed on bureaucracy, he also argued that modern societies could not avoid the iron cage of rationalisation. The individual rights championed by liberalism thus existed within a distinctly unfree social context.

George Ritzer has updated Weber's theory in his account of contemporary 'McDonaldization'. He argues that the fast-food restaurant is symbolic of wider social change, both in the US and globally. McDonald's represents efficiency, calculability, predictability and control. The McDonald's meal is quick, cheap, predictable and time-saving. There is an almost conveyor-belt mentality, in which the customer orders a set meal and sits down and eats quickly on relatively uncomfortable chairs. The meal is quickly over, and the customer leaves the restaurant quickly. The workforce is strictly controlled by management and technology, and much emphasis is again placed on rapid turnover. Ritzer argues that this rationalisation can be seen in all kinds of sectors of society, including tabloid journalism, lowest-common-denominator television, film sequels, league tables for work in the public sector, standardised shopping malls, and so on.

Following Weber, Ritzer distinguishes between formal and substantive rationality. The modern world is dominated by formal rationality, in which we aspire to satisfy short-term interests, but at the cost of longer-term and wider social interests. Thus, we eat food that is convenient but not good for us; we live in societies based on massive discrepancies in wealth and income, which have enormous social costs; while some of us work far too many hours, others cannot find a job, and so live in a state of poverty; we aspire to buy cars even though roads are dangerous – or, where they are less dangerous, it is only because they are so overcrowded that car transport is too slow to be efficient. Our obsession with expanding wealth knows no limits, but precisely because it is an infinite, never-ending process, it is one that can never satisfy us. Simon Fairlie makes the point effectively when he hypothesises that by the year 2100, average incomes will have increased 18-fold over the century (see Monbiot 2002). This begs the question of what exactly we would spend this money on, and how we could accommodate such expanded consumption. For instance, if there were around 5 billion cars, ten times as much as at present, where would all the new roads be built to accommodate such an increase? Moreover, does increasing consumption lead to an increase in happiness? In the US from 1969 to 1999, average annual work hours increased by 18 per cent for married-couple households, and 28 per cent for single-person households. In surveys, just over two-thirds of workers said that they have to work 'very fast', and over 50 per cent reported recent significant stress levels. Almost two-thirds of workers said that they worked longer hours than they wished (Schor 2001). These figures, which are representative of a general trend, have increased in recent years, as government and business attempt to justify such increased work intensity in terms of the pressures of global market competitiveness. Seen in this light, the free market appears less as a sphere of freedom and more as a constraint, and this seriously compromises the utility of liberal rights.

Ritzer's argument, then, is that the processes of standardisation that emerged in the west in the nineteenth century have increasingly become globalised. The fact that some cultural products, foods, and so on, are available throughout the world is not unimportant, as the cultural imperialism thesis (one-sidedly) reminds us; but far more important is the wider social and cultural context in which these goods are consumed and produced. Cultural globalisation thus represents an increase in rationalisation, bureaucratisation, commodification and alienation. Due to the emphasis placed on quantity and growth in place of meaning, Ritzer describes this process as one of 'grobalisation' (Ritzer 2004).

This approach therefore sees cultural globalisation as leading to a cultural standardisation, and an increasingly disenchanted world. It paints a very pessimistic picture, but unfortunately quite a persuasive one as well. In the era of global rationalisation, different political and social movements have responded, not only to the inequalities generated by global capitalism, but also to the alienation and shallowness of public life. Within this context, such movements have taken a number of forms. Some versions of political Islam emerged in the context of the perceived failure of secular pan-Arab and communist projects; and as we have seen, some movements enjoyed the patronage of the US state through low-intensity conflicts against communism. But equally, these movements grew in popularity even when US support had ended, and this can be linked to the failures – social, political, economic and cultural – of neoliberal globalisation. This does not represent a 'clash of civilisations', but a *political* clash between advocates of neoliberal capitalism[18] and reactionary responses to it (and to US hegemony). For some writers, then, it is a 'clash of fundamentalisms' or a 'clash of barbarisms' (Ali 2002; Achcar 2002).

These clashes are political ones, and therefore by implication they confirm that it is possible for social and political agents to change the world. In contrast, Weber's account tends to present certain rationalising practices and standardising tendencies as iron laws, as though the past agency that created the present society now ceases to operate (Beetham 1985: 268–9; Sayer 1991: 155). In relation to globalisation, it is not the case that global culture leads to unambiguous standardisation; on the contrary, particular places represent specific configurations of global and local cultures (Robertson 1992). This is true not only of particular television programmes, news broadcasts or films, but also of religion, politics, social movements, and so on. These points relate to the wider one made by Giddens that 'late modernity' involves not only an intensification of the disembeddedness of social relations, but also an intensification of the processes of self-reflection on these very same processes (Giddens 1991). We have seen already that Giddens' account may not be sufficiently sensitive to the agency and power relations involved in these processes, and his attempt to 'bring agency back in' is not altogether convincing – we can reflect on globalising processes, but for Giddens we also need to take these as a given. Nevertheless, Giddens' point remains useful, as it reminds us that processes of rationalisation can never be completely sealed off from human intervention, and so the 'cage' can never be made of iron. The rise of 'new social movements' since the 1960s reflects this fact, as they emerged in part to monitor the bureaucratic policing of modern institutions of rationalisation. Indeed, global communications have increased such monitoring, helping to promote the rise of transnational social movements and NGOs.

Giddens thus also reminds us that processes of disembedding are not simply constraining, but can present opportunities as well. This is an important point, for while Weber and others were correct to talk about the downside of modernity, it would be a mistake to present this as an exclusively bad thing. One of the dangers of doing so is a tendency to romanticise pre-modern societies – to champion 'local traditions' ('Asian values') at the expense of global processes. It is one thing to criticise the inequality, greed, environmental degradation and alienation of modern society, but it is quite another to claim that pre-modern societies were somehow better. There is thus a need for caution in celebrating the 'local' preference to globalisation. Majid Rahnema's rejection of development is illustrative of this kind of reactionary politics:

> Vernacular societies had a much more realistic view of things. Not blinkered by the myth of equality, they believed that the good of the community was better served by those of its members it considered to be the wisest, the most virtuous, and hence the most 'authoritative' and experienced persons of the groups – those who commanded everyone's respect and deference.

This statement sounds suspiciously like a defence of ('traditional') dictatorship. Just which societies this refers to is not clear, but pre-capitalist societies certainly had their own inequalities, tyrannies and oppressive practices. Similarly, current regimes and political movements that challenge US imperialism are not necessarily progressive, and all kinds of repressive politics are often justified in the name of 'anti-imperialism'. Global modernity is in need of radical social, political, cultural and economic change, but this does not mean a wholesale rejection of all its manifestations, or a conservative nostalgia for a pre-modern age.

This chapter has examined contemporary debates concerning the relationship between culture, rights and liberal internationalism, and how these relate to Americanisation. I started by arguing that older debates concerning cultural imperialism have their merits, but often tend to betray a patronising tone, in which westerners romanticise other cultures as somehow more authentic than the commercial west. More importantly, they tend to focus on consumer culture, and therefore presuppose a particular social and political context – that of neoliberal capitalism. In this way, cultural diffusion is linked to 'progressive' expansion of (western) modernity through the liberal internationalism advocated by the US. But this liberal expansion has been selective, usually undemocratic, and, in its neoliberal and neoconservative forms in particular, has intensified inequality. Moreover, such expansion is based on a one-dimensional view of freedom, which sees market expansion as paramount. As well as justifying inequality and intensifying uneven development, it also promotes alienation, rationalisation and disenchantment. In this sense, the liberal internationalism associated with US hegemony, and indeed liberal theories of rights, ultimately tend to support social and political developments in which the market 'trumps' politics and liberal democracy. This point applies not only to the 'low-intensity democracies' of the developing world, but also the more established liberal democracies of the west – including perhaps above all, the US itself, although it must be said that Blair's Britain runs it a close second (Marquand 2004; Crouch 2004). Indeed, we must recognise the way in which the liberal internationalist project itself has served to promote global processes that have led to cultural standardisation. If we are to challenge these processes, then 'actually existing globalisation' must itself be challenged. Of course, if we are to find progressive alternatives to current globalisation, then it would be foolish to focus narrowly on consumer culture, or to look for supposedly authentic local cultures or reactionary 'fundamentalisms'. On the contrary, we need to move beyond the aforementioned 'clash of barbarisms and fundamentalisms'. In this respect at least (although there needs to be greater precision over his meaning), Giddens is right to suggest that alternatives are to be found *within* globalisation, not outside it. But these alternatives will constitute a far more radical challenge to neoliberalism, and even capitalism, then Giddens envisages. These issues are taken up in the final chapter.

7

Conclusions: US imperialism, Actually Existing Globalisation, and the Question of Alternatives

GLOBALISATION AND THE CHARACTER OF CONTEMPORARY IMPERIALISM

'Globalisation' refers to the increased interdependence in the world, much of which transcends the boundaries of the nation-state. This is reflected in the growth of international institutions and summits (global governance), increased capital flows (global economy), increased information flows, including the speed of such flows (time–space compression), and growing cultural linkages (global culture). While there are important debates over the amount and form of these flows, even global sceptics would agree that there have been some changes that can be properly described as globalisation. However, globalisation theory draws particular implications from such changes. Perhaps above all, it regards at least some of these changes as both inevitable and desirable. Often these two arguments are conflated, and the inevitability thesis attempts to take the politics out of globalisation, so that it becomes a purely technical process – as natural as the weather (though environmentalists would rightly question this contention). Globalisation's advocates argue that global interdependence is also mutually beneficial, and largely devoid of relations of denomination, except perhaps when subverted by the narrow interests of particular nation-states. So global governance is regarded as an opportunity for all countries to have an equal say in the world order. This may still be imperfect, as in permanent membership of the Security Council and weighted voting at the IMF and World Bank, but the principle of one member one vote (as at the WTO) can lay the basis for genuinely democratic global governance. This is reinforced by the mutual benefits of a free-trade world order in which each country specialises in producing those goods in which they have a comparative advantage.[1] Again, this may be subverted by specific protectionist practices, but in the long run this can be dealt with through institutional reform. Similarly, cultural and information flows provide an opportunity for access to a range of lifestyle choices, and so should be embraced. These may be resisted by parochial fundamentalists, but in the long run the opportunities of globalisation will outweigh the constraints. This, then, is the optimistic thesis concerning globalisation, and is often associated with the 'globalisation theory' of the 1990s, discussed in Chapter 2.

For these theorists, the George W. Bush administration undermined the onward march of globalisation (Held and Koening-Archibugi 2004). Instead of focusing on cosmopolitan principles, Bush promoted a US-first strategy that narrowly focuses on the country's own interests. The rhetoric of globalisation has been replaced by a return to old-fashioned power-politics. So, has globalisation ended? Certainly, the Bush administration has been more unilateralist than Clinton. It has ignored international treaties and institutions, and attempted to carry out protectionist measures in defence of US industry and agriculture. But on the other hand, the idea that Bush represents the end of globalisation downplays the continuities between US administrations, and ignores the realities of 'actually existing globalisation'. It is clearly the case that globalisation was *never* completely independent of the interests of state, or indeed capitalist power. This is true of neoliberalism and neoconservatism in the 1980s, the Third Way and globalisation in the 1990s, and US neoconservatism in the early 2000s. While the Clinton administration gave more active support to the WTO, the fact is that free-trade policies do not promote a level playing field, but best represent the interests of already powerful producers who can benefit from competitive advantage. Moreover, Clinton's commitment to free trade was itself selective, and he continued to provide protection to some US domestic producers. Furthermore, while the Bush administration has been more openly unilateralist in its methods, its aims of (selectively) developing liberal sovereign states (albeit US allies) with efficient market economies was compatible with a whole tradition of US liberal internationalism, and therefore with the globalisation project endorsed by politicians who advocated the global Third Way.

In practice, of course, there is no single liberal internationalist project, and what is crucially different about the current globalisation project is its commitment to 'free markets' without some of the qualifications of earlier periods. In other words, the current liberal internationalist project associated with globalisation is more explicitly neoliberal than say, the (neo-Keynesian) liberal internationalism of the Bretton Woods era, in which there was a commitment to market expansion, but also some basis for 'market-restricting' state regulation. It also follows from this point that, despite significant differences over means, the neoliberal era has witnessed Reagan's neoconservatism, the Washington and post-Washington consensus of the World Bank and IMF, Clinton's Third Way, and Bush's neoconservativism. The Reagan era saw the promotion of state sovereignty, albeit one compromised by the promotion of low-intensity conflict in the Cold War and the promotion of the free market abroad (alongside considerable protection at home). The presidency of the elder George Bush saw the continued promotion of state sovereignty and market expansion, and the use of military power against Iraq through multilateral institutions, especially the UN. The Clinton era saw the extension and expansion of the 'free market', above all through free-trade agreements and the further liberalisation of finance. Clinton's Third Way did involve some regulation of markets beyond that advocated by neoliberalism in the 1980s, and this coincided with a set of policies at the World Bank and IMF that came to be known as the post-Washington consensus. But these policies did not substantially alter the view that market expansion was the best means of producing growth and social development. Alongside these policies, and especially in his second term, Clinton (like Bush Sr) also advocated 'low-intensity democracy' in a post-Cold War context, and was prepared to use military power against rogue states, and in doing so often bypassed the United Nations. Bush Jr has been far more hostile to multilateralism than Clinton, and has more openly pursued a US-first policy. Particularly after the murderous attacks of 9/11, the US pursued a more explicitly US-first policy, and was prepared to use military power whatever the rest of the world thought. Crucial to this world-view is the idea of 'pre-emptive action', whether against mythical threats from Iraq or through the forms of conditionality attached to aid. David Harvey has rightly described this as a movement from consent to coercion, and for this reason some talk about the end of globalisation. But as we have seen, the multilateral globalisation supposedly championed by Clinton was hardly committed to the expansion of genuine global democracy, and the free-trade policies that he advocated actually undermined such an aspiration. Moreover, as Harvey also points out, there is also substantial continuity between the administration of Bush Jr and other moments of US hegemony – in terms of not only market expansion, but also the use of hard power and unilateralism (Harvey 2003: Ch. 5).

The optimism of the 'globalisation talk' of the 1990s was thus misplaced, and this can be rooted in the weaknesses of globalisation theory. In that decade, globalisation theory tended to be accompanied by a 'cosmopolitan optimism'. The problem was that, just as globalisation theory tended to ignore social relations, so cosmopolitanism tended to ignore the political form that such a philosophy could embrace. In both cases this could be linked to the fetishisation of space, so that globalisation focused on social relations beyond the territoriality of the nation-state, while cosmopolitanism focused on politics beyond the sovereignty of the nation-state. Neither was necessarily wrong, but both failed to specify the forms of social relations or politics beyond the state. Thus, as we saw in Chapters 3 to 6, cosmopolitanism, for example, can be linked to the extension of 'market forces' and global governance, or 'humanitarian' military intervention; equally, however, it could be tied to Marxist conceptions of international labour solidarity or anti-war politics. In the process, the specific content of politics was lost as a result of an over-emphasis on 'globality'. The first argument that the book made, then, is that, contrary to the claims of globalisation theory, there has been considerable continuity in the last 25 years, based on the expansion of *neoliberal globalisation*.

Its second argument was a challenge to claims made by the advocates of neoliberalism and US hegemony. In Chapters 3 and 4, through an examination of contemporary international relations, I characterised the US-led global order as imperialist, and developed this argument in Chapter 5 through an account of the relationship between US hegemony and neoliberalism. However, I also argued that *even on its own terms*, the project of liberal internationalist expansion through the development of sovereign states and market economies was unlikely to work. This was because of the social, political and historical conflicts that have led to 'failed states', and the political and economic hierarchies of the global order, which global 'market expansion' actually intensifies. These arguments were further developed in Chapter 5, which looked at the globalisation of popular culture and of human rights. The argument was made that, contrary to some radical theories of cultural imperialism – and, it should be stressed, the arguments of US neoconservatives – there is no intrinsic link between the consumption of an 'American' commodity and wider support for 'Americanisation'. However, more significant is the debate about universal human rights, whether they exist, and whether the US is the rightful enforcer of such rights. It was suggested that US hegemony has been inconsistent, at best, in promoting human rights, and that, though they are important, liberal rights are also limited. In practice, liberal rights and US hegemony have often combined to mean simply the freedom of the free market. This has meant growing inequality within countries alongside the failure of developing countries to move towards 'developed' status. In other words, the 'globalisation' of the free market has not led to the 'Americanisation' of the world. Insofar as there has been a tendency towards cultural standardisation, it has been through the increased dominance of the commodity. In this respect, the rule of the market has become a realm of global 'un-freedom'. For all these reasons then, 'globalisation' is a deeply flawed project, and it is one that cannot be divorced from the realities of capitalist and state power, and indeed of contemporary *imperialism*.

But to talk of imperialism does not mean that we are simply witnessing a repeat of the economic and political rivalries that occurred in the build-up to the First World War. As I explained in Chapter 3, there is a far greater number of independent nation-states now than in the pre-1914 period. Moreover, these states are more interdependent, partly because of the internationalisation of capital, which means that investment and trade may derive from a wide variety of sources, as opposed to the more exclusive policies of the pre-1914 era. This does not mean that competition between states has ceased to exist, and indeed we have seen how in the post-Cold War period the US has attempted to pursue polices designed not only to police zones outside the liberal order, but also to deter potential competitors to US hegemony. But equally, I also argued that this was unlikely to give rise to a repeat of the inter-imperialist conflicts of the pre-1914 period, or indeed to war. Indeed, it is this interdependence that leads some globalisation theorists to claim that there is no single source of power in the current global order. While this is true, it is still clear that some states have far more power than others. This power is exercised not only through international institutions such as the Security Council and weighted voting at the IMF and World Bank, but also through military and financial power, which are heavily concentrated in the hands of the US. Continued US hegemony actually relies on the continued liberalisation of financial capital, which ensures that capital will flow to the US, so that the widening trade deficit can be financed through capital inflows from overseas.

Despite their misgivings, other countries accept this framework, not least because the US acts as the major market for the goods produced by those countries with trade surpluses. But this 'system' is unstable, and if confidence in the dollar declined and foreign capital stopped flowing to the US, then that country would have to carry out some strict austerity policies in order to balance its payments, which in turn would have considerable knock-on effects for other countries. The current era of globalisation is thus one in which power relations persist, and competition and cooperation between the most powerful nation-states exists in an uneasy alliance. Thus, insofar as this represents an era of imperialism, it is one ultimately based on ultra-imperialist cooperation between the core capitalist states, although this cooperation is led by the most powerful state.

However, it is also a highly unstable international era, not least because this neoliberal order serves to marginalise so many regions and countries from the centres of capital accumulation.[2] For developing countries, the current era is not one that is conducive to rapid development, since free-trade policies in goods and services threaten to undermine their capacity to develop new, competitive industries, while the surge of finance steers investment into speculative rather than productive activity, which is further reinforced by the concentration of finance capital in the US economy. For these countries, then, liberal incorporation is unlikely to take place, as weaker states face a situation that Mann characterises as 'ostracising imperialism', based on the tendency of capital to concentrate in some areas and marginalise others (Mann 2001). This marginalisation is caused not *only* by neoliberal policies, though they remain a significant factor. In some places – those territories often designated as failed or rogue states – political and social instability persists reflecting continued conflict over state formation, politically grounded ethnic rivalry, inter-state conflict, and so on. The US state has led the way in attempting to incorporate some of these territories into the 'liberal core', even using military intervention as a means towards this end. But the rationale for such intervention has been based on 'quick-fix' solutions that ignore these social and historical processes, and which themselves have led to many deaths, usually described as 'collateral damage'. The failure of these states to be incorporated into the liberal 'zone of peace' is then put down to the existence of non-liberal 'evil', which paves the way for ongoing conflict. Contemporary imperialism is thus not based on the pre-1914 era, but can in some respects be described as 'liberal imperialism'. But the liberalism of such an imperialist strategy is neither benign nor effective, as it involves double standards by the core nations so that claims to represent the global good involve 'evil' acts and wholesale slaughter of the non-liberal periphery, or indifference to some non-liberal states so long as they remain allies of the US. Moreover, liberal incorporation fails partly because neoliberal policies themselves militate against it (see Ch. 5).

As we have seen, compared to the pre-1914 period, the present era is characterised by the increased internationalisation of capital – especially productive capital – and the uneven universalisation of the nation-state. These processes have led to the development of new Marxist theories that suggest that the era of classical imperialism has been replaced by a new period of international capitalism (Sklair 2002; Becker and Sklar 1987; Hardt and Negri 2000). These are united in the belief that the development of transnational capitalism has undermined state-based inter-imperialist rivalries, although these may still occur if particular 'hegemonic' fractions of the state managerial class become dominant, as in the case of the Iraq war. The development of a transnational capitalist class has also promoted the nascent development of a transnational state, in which global capital is regulated beyond the archaic boundaries of the nation-state (Robinson 2004). These approaches have perhaps been best developed by neo-Gramscian theories of international relations, which particularly attempt to theorise the idea of hegemony. Gramsci argued that the ruling class rules not only through force, but through the capacity of the ruling class to convince everybody that its ideas are universal, and therefore win the (contested) consent of the lower classes (Gramsci 1971: 182). Cox (1987) and Gill (2003) have attempted to use this idea to historicise the process of hegemonic state formation within international relations. In contrast to realist accounts of hegemony, neo-Gramscians attempts to historicise and periodise both US hegemony and international capitalism.[3] This has led to the criticism that neo-Gramscian theory therefore ignores the totality of capitalist social relations, and separates the historically constructed social forms of capitalist society, thus reifying capitalist social relations (Burnham 1991; Clarke 1992). This criticism is misplaced, because neo-Gramscians accept the totality of capitalist social relations as their starting point, but then attempt to historicise such relations and the changes that occur *within* capitalist social relations (Bieler and Morton 2004; Panitch 2003). Neo-Gramscian perspectives are particularly concerned with theorising the relationship between changing forms of US hegemony and the rise of neoliberal capitalism since the 1970s and 1980s. This task is carried out by attempting to explain the relationship between social forces that are historically constituted *within* capitalism and particular state forms (Cox 1987: 105). Cox uses this approach to explain the movement from US hegemony to the system of transnational capitalism that emerged in the 1970s. The Bretton Woods era, based on liberalism and some regulation of capital, has been replaced by a transnational managerial class (Cox 1981: 147), which has promoted the globalisation of capital. Gill argues that these processes are the product of the replacement of the post-war international bloc of social forces by a new, transnational bloc, albeit one still centred on US hegemony (Gill 1990). This is reflected in the development of new institutional think-tanks such as the Trilateral Commission (Crozier et al. 1975), as well as the transnationalisation of the state in the 1980s.

These theories have usefully attempted to come to terms with the changes that have occurred since 1914, and especially 1945 – not least the increased cooperation between the major capitalist states. They also usefully remind us that current wars cannot be read off from perceived inter-imperialist rivalries, but may be political projects of dominant state actors in the US, as well as manifestations of Cold War legacies and/or of the unevenness of state formation in particular localities. But at the same time, these theories tend to exaggerate the decline of the nation-state, and underestimate the continued centrality of the US state in the ultra-imperialist order of cooperation between the main imperialist powers. Negri's related contention that no state is in control of the world order, but that some states are more powerful than others, begs the question asked of mainstream globalisation theory in Chapter 2, namely: When were states in total control? (Negri 2003) Moreover, the exaggeration of state power in the past is accompanied by an underestimation of state power in the present, and – in relation to the nation-state system at least – much US uncertainty is not so much a product of the mobility of capital (indeed its continued hegemony relies in part on flows to the US economy), but rather the problem of securing hegemony through strategies designed to promote and generalise the nation-state system.[4] While these criticisms do not necessarily apply to all neo-Gramscians, and certainly not to Gill in particular, considerable problems remain. While neo-Gramscians are certainly correct to recognise the change from neo-Keynesian to neoliberal capitalism, and indeed the ways in which this has been promoted by the US state, they tend to do so in a way that overestimates the structural power of the dominant social forces, and underestimates the ways in which neoliberalism is resisted. In particular – like the transnational class theory of Sklair – neo-Gramscians tend to theorise class in isolation from social relations of exploitation *and resistance*. These points in turn can be related to the fact that neo-Gramscians tend towards an overly descriptive account of the international order, which never quite succeeds in linking the general features of capitalism to their specific manifestations in the post-war order, and in its transition to neoliberal capitalism. In these respects at least, the criticisms made by Burnham and others are convincing.

Nevertheless, these newer theories attempt to address the nature of contemporary global capitalism, which has been the main focus of this book. My account has tried to forge a path between classical theories of imperialism and contemporary theories (mainstream and Marxist) of globalisation. There is greater interdependence through the (uneven and unequal) diffusion of capital in the nation-state system, but this has not eroded the power of some nation-states. The role of states has changed, but this is a product of the movement from neo-Keynesian to neoliberal capitalism, a shift that was led by the US, but which has won widespread support among ruling classes and states in the world order. This support is sometimes contested, for instance through trade conflicts and debates over financial liberalisation, but such conflict is very different from old inter-imperialist rivalries. On the other hand, and contrary to theories of cosmopolitan capital (Desai 2002; Harris 2003), neoliberalism has not led to global convergence through the progressive diffusion of capitalism throughout the globe, but has instead actually intensified uneven development based on the concentration of capital. Insofar as there are counter-tendencies to this process, they have operated through the continued interventionist role of the state, and have therefore occurred *despite* rather than because of neoliberalism (see Chapter 5). This can perhaps best be described as an 'imperialism of free trade', rather than of colonial state capitalist trusts (Gallagher and Robinson 1953).[5]

If it is an imperialism of free trade, then it is one that is ultimately backed by the US, and this brings us back to the question of hegemony. The US has acted as the hegemonic power in the capitalist world since 1945. In the post-war period, this hegemony was guaranteed by overwhelming military and economic dominance, which left even the most powerful of the other capitalist countries dependent on the US. This dependence was reinforced by the perceived threat of the communist alternative. The US's hegemonic position since 1945 has experienced two significant changes 'from above' in the period. The first was the challenge from revived capitalist powers – particularly Japan and Germany – from the late 1960s onwards, which was reinforced by the end of the Bretton Woods agreement and the gradual shift towards neoliberal policies from the late 1970s. As we have seen, this shift led to the US securing its hegemonic role through reliance on foreign capital inflows, secured partly by the neoliberal turn, which was broadly accepted (albeit with some resistance[6] at times) by the other major capitalist states. The second change occurred with the end of communism, which secured the US's dominant, unipolar position in the global order – albeit in the context of continued concern about revived economic competitors, including China. The question of securing US hegemony in the post-Cold War world has been a matter of considerable debate, with Clinton focusing more on 'geo-economics' and Bush Jr on military power. However, as we have seen, this distinction is sometimes made too sharply, as it ignores the military power exercised by Clinton and the neoliberal economics promoted by both presidencies.

But this leaves us to ponder one further question – namely: What is the future for US hegemony? As we have seen, some argue that we are in an era of US super-imperialism (Gowan 1999; Hudson 2003), based on the US's dominant military role, the continued strength of US companies in key economic sectors such as information technology, and the continued dominance of the US domestic economy and transnational companies, and of the dollar internationally. On the other hand, others argue that US hegemony has weakened (Arrighi 1994; Mann 2003; Wallerstein 2003; Harvey 2003), as a result of the comparative decline of the US economy, at least since the 1940s and 1950s, the limitations of military power in a world of sovereign states and capitalist interdependence, the rise of East Asia, increased hostility to the US under Bush Jr, the US budget and trade deficits, the bubble economy in the US (stock markets in the 1990s, housing in the 2000s), and the possible rise of the euro as an alternative international currency. Certainly there are convincing arguments made by both sides in this debate, and while there are clear signs of US vulnerability, there remain considerable sources of strength.

These tensions will continue and possibly intensify in the second presidency of George W. Bush. The election victory of 2004 has reinvigorated the Bush administration, including the neoconservatives within it. The changes in personnel suggest a further shift to the right, but how this will relate to future policy direction is unclear. Certainly we can be sure that many in the administration would like to see an extension of military power, into Iran at the very least. Bush himself has attempted to link al Qaeda leaders to the leadership in Iran, an argument as vacuous as the supposed Saddam–al Qaeda connection. The supposed voice of moderation in the first administration, Colin Powell, argued immediately after the election victory that the president had won a mandate to continue to pursue an aggressive foreign policy, and was unlikely to be held back (Pena 2004). Wesley Clark, former Supreme Commander of NATO and unsuccessful Democrat nominee in 2004, has alleged that the Pentagon has a five-year plan to remove the governments of Iraq, Syria, Lebanon, Iran, Somalia and Sudan, as well as now presumably discarded Libya (Clark 2003). On the other hand, while the fiasco in Iraq may not have undermined the ambitions of the neoconservatives, it may have left the US considerably overstretched.[7] This point applies not only to the continued conflict in Iraq, but also to wider issues that relate back to the wider questions of the strengths and weaknesses of US hegemony. These include the expanding budget deficit, which Bush at least claims will be cut during his second term; continued economic tensions in the world economy, which relate back to the question of the dollar and the US deficit; and popular opposition to US policies, not least within the deeply divided US itself (Mann 2003).

These, then, are some of the tensions that exist in the neoliberal, US-led, international order. But pointing to these weaknesses is not the same thing as suggesting anything like an imminent collapse. For one thing, US hegemony is relational, and depends partly on the actions of other states and capitals in the world order. These are bound to provoke competition, and even hostility at times, but equally, as I have argued, the neoliberal years have been characterised by remarkable levels of cooperation too, which are rooted in the interdependent nature of the contemporary capitalist world. The rapid fall in the dollar in late 2004 has undoubtedly fuelled tensions between Europe and the US, not least because the unilateralism of the latter has ruled out multilateral cooperation to manage exchange rates, as occurred for instance in 1995, when the dollar was revalued. The US appears to be relying on a strategy of relatively painless adjustment, as the falling dollar increases competitiveness and exports, even at a cost of its European competitors. But this strategy is likely to lead to capital flight from the US economy, with the result that overseas investors will no longer finance the twin deficits. Adjustment then would be much more painful – and unilateralism would be likely to give way to multilateralism. But this future scenario is one in which Europe does not so much present an alternative to US hegemony as seek the US's active cooperation in a system which is ultimately led by the US. This has important implications, including the fact that alternatives to US hegemony and liberal capitalism are unlikely to be found 'from above' (Grahl 2004). We therefore need to examine the questions of alternatives 'from the bottom up'.

THE NEW SUPERPOWER?
THE POLITICS OF 'ANTI-GLOBALISATION' AND GLOBAL JUSTICE[8]

If globalisation is not independent of questions of power, then neither is it independent of the questions of agency and resistance. Such resistance takes a number of forms in a number of movements, usually captured by broad terms like the 'anti-globalisation' movement, or the movement for 'global justice'. This movement became very visible through the protests at the Seattle meeting of the WTO in late 1999, although its origins can be traced back to protests in the South against structural adjustment policies in the 1980s. Representing a great variety of interests and agendas, anti-globalisation politics was initially critical of the neoliberal agendas of the World Bank, IMF and WTO, certain manifestations of global exploitation, such as the use of sweat-shop labour, and global environmental destruction. Seen by many as a kind of travelling circus of activists, the movement was often criticised for its alleged lack of concrete alternatives to 'actually existing globalisation' and its tendency to celebrate resistance as an end in itself. The movement was also challenged by the events of 11 September 2001, and the US state's response to them. This was important, as many activists, particularly those in the west, tended to internalise the argument that global flows had undermined the nation-state, and that therefore the focus of resistance should be transnational capital and international institutions. The war drive of the Bush administration showed in a particularly stark form the continued relevance of the nation-state, and the hierarchies of the international system of nation-states.

The anti-globalisation movement has thus had to respond to the challenge of proposition as well as opposition, alongside the questions of the continued importance of nation-states and war. This has led to vigorous debates at World and European Social Forums, perhaps most notably over questions of the 'space' for reforms at the level of nation-states, and 'anti-imperialist' solidarity in the face of US imperialism and reactionary opposition movements (Fisher and Ponniah 2003). Perhaps as important is the manner in which these debates have arisen, as the movement demonstrates an awareness that while anarchism tends to celebrate lack of organisation, Leninism has a history of intolerance to dissent that has encouraged authoritarian forms of politics. The key organisational task of the movement has therefore been to find a compromise between effectiveness and democracy, which itself entails recognition that the separation of means and ends has been disastrous in the history of socialism. The concluding section can provide only a taster of the kinds of debates that have taken place within the 'movement of movements'. I do this by returning to the themes of the previous chapters – politics, economics and culture – and focusing on some of the critiques made, and alternatives proposed by 'anti-globalisation' movements. This separation is made for analytical purposes, and in no way means that priority should be accorded to any of these themes.

The global economy

Critique

The anti-globalisation critique of the global economy is quite straightforward. Its essential claim is that it has led to increased inequality, exploitation and instability. These processes have occurred because of the nature of global free-market competition, transnational production and international finance. The increase in free trade has led to an increase in inequality, because competition is intrinsically unequal. First, the commitment to free trade is selective, discriminating against those products in which developing countries may have potential competitive advantages. Thus, tariffs for developing world exports to the advanced countries are on average four times greater than the tariffs for goods that originate from First World countries (Oxfam 2002). The WTO may be committed to changing these discriminatory practices, but this may be little more than rhetoric. Negotiations at the WTO tend to be dominated by the most powerful countries, leaving poorer countries with little more than 'take it or leave it' options. This 'choice' is further narrowed by the time and cost of settling disputes, and above all by the fact that weaker trading nations that retaliate against discriminatory practices of powerful trading nations are bound to have little or no effect on the practices of the latter. The institutional principle of one member one vote, even if it was actually employed by the WTO (as opposed to its current rhetorical commitment to the principle), is largely irrelevant in the context of such political and economic inequality. A second point, which follows from the first, is that even if free-trade policies were more consistently adopted throughout the world, it would not lead to a level playing field. As I argued in Chapter 5, free trade ignores enormous inequalities in structures of production, so that some locations, regions and countries can generally out-compete others, even if the 'losers' may still find the odd niche in the world market. Capital tends to concentrate in certain areas, and not disperse in such a way as to promote global governance. In free-market situations, 'late developers' thus find it hard to break into established world markets for many goods. Moreover, as pro-free-trade policies also mean liberalisation of domestic trade policy, this can have devastating effects for countries attempting to establish reasonably efficient domestic production, as they can be put out of business through import competition from established overseas producers. Free trade therefore protects the interests of the powerful, and it is for this reason that *all* successful developers have (selectively) protected domestic producers from overseas competition. Of course, this has not been through blanket protection to all producers regardless of economic performance, but neither has it been through neoliberal policies. There is some controversy over the extent to which the WTO undermines the ability of 'late developers' to continue to protect domestic producers but, given that selective protection will be outlawed, it appears that the WTO undermines at least one basis for the replication of new 'East Asian miracles'. Instead, it is assumed that economic growth and social advance will be achieved through the 'one size fits all' neoliberal policies of free trade, in which all countries exercise their respective comparative advantages. Unfortunately, while this may promote some growth and other advances, it is unlikely to alleviate global inequalities, or even absolute poverty.

The second argument is that globalisation has led to increased exploitation. The basis for this charge is that capital investment flows are now so mobile that investors can move from one country to another in order to avoid regulations and controls on capital. Such factors may include environmental regulations, or pressure for employers to pay higher wages. To avoid these problems, capital moves on, or at least threatens to do so, to lower-cost, less regulated countries or regions. But this threat of unemployment means that areas lower their standards and wages in order to attract and retain capital investment in the first place. The globalisation of production therefore leads to a race to the bottom, in which countries compete to attract investment through low wages or lack of controls on capital.

It is certainly true that many workers have seen an erosion of their bargaining position over the last 20 to 30 years. Real wages have fallen, the threat and reality of unemployment has increased, and protection at work has often been undermined. However, it is far from clear that the mobility of capital is the main cause of this downward trend. Real wages have often declined most in sectors in which capital mobility is not particularly great, such as local services. Moreover, as we saw in Chapter 5, the relocation of investment to the developing world has been very limited, and in fact in many respects there has been an increase in the concentration of capital investment in established areas of accumulation, together with a few select countries of developing countries (including where there has been substantial development of trade unionism). 'Race to the bottom' rhetoric implies that there should be a dispersal of capital throughout the globe in order to take advantage of cheap labour, but this has not occurred, and the tendency has been towards increased concentration – one of the reasons why there has been an intensification of inequality in recent years. None of these points disprove that there has been some relocation of capital investment in recent years, and Naomi Klein has done a valuable job in exposing the conditions faced by workers in the Mexican *maquiladoras* and in factories producing for the world market throughout the globe (Klein 2000). But it must be remembered that these factories do not generally utilise capital-intensive techniques or produce goods in the fastest-growing manufacturing sectors. (It also needs stressing that, for similar reasons, the use of such factories cannot constitute a model for the developing world in general for, leaving aside the awful working conditions, the goods that are produced eventually come up against limited market demand.) Again, this is not to deny the erosion of labour and social standards for workers in many countries, but this has at least as much to do with national (state) restructuring of labour relations and work organisation as it has to do with the global mobility of capital in some sectors. Such restructuring includes technological change that displaces full-time workers, and the use of suppliers in preference to in-house production. Such cost-saving satisfies short-term shareholder profits, which in turn encourage financial speculation in favour of profitable company stock.

In this respect, the more significant 'relocation' has not been from First to Third Worlds, but from productive to financial capital. Indeed, the contemporary global economy is associated with the intensification of financial flows, which in turn are a product of liberalisation policies that stretch back to the 1970s. This liberalisation is often justified on the grounds that it increases access to savings, and therefore stimulates investment. However, as we have seen, most financial flows are used to generate income through investment in further financial instruments, rather than to increase productive investment. In other words, financial liberalisation encourages unproductive speculation rather than growth of the 'real economy'. This is further reinforced (at times) by high interest rates designed to attract flows, and by the risks associated with a rapid withdrawal of funds at the first sign of weakness in the real economy. Such withdrawals can exaggerate trends in the real economy, and therefore have a devastating impact on the real economy. Moreover, financial flows tend to concentrate in established areas and bypass poorer economies. Financial flows are therefore at best a mixed blessing, and their global impact reflects less considerations of economic efficiency and more the interests of financial capital, and the need of the US state to preserve its hegemony through allowing the free flow of capital into the US.

Alternatives

It is simplistic to argue that anti-globalisation politics are always based on a simple opting-out from globalisation. Instead, what is proposed is a restructuring of the relationship between global, national and local levels. Probably the movement's leading intellectual, Walden Bello has characterised this restructuring as part of a process of 'deglobalisation' (Bello 2002: 114–17). Such a strategy focuses on the development of an alternative and more progressive global structure. This would include: production based first on the local market; local finance (not foreign investment); less emphasis on growth per se; the subjection of the market to social control; and the development of community-based and public-sector initiatives, along with the continued development of the (local) private sector. Bello argues that, to facilitate deglobalisation, there needs to be a reconstruction of global institutions, which rejects the monolithic approach of the IMF, World Bank and WTO, and instead adopts a more pluralistic system. These institutions would be weakened or abolished, and replaced by strengthened UN institutions such as the UN Economic and Social Council of the General Assembly and the UN Conference on Trade and Development, a new United Nations International Insolvency Court to negotiate debt settlements, and a United Nations International Financial Organisation to implement controls on finance.

The desired effects of these policies can be seen if we examine some of the proposals in a little more detail. Thus, in the field of international finance, the proposed new regulations are designed to alleviate the inequality and instability associated with current international financial transactions. National capital controls – including those actually implemented in the 1990s by Malaysia and Chile, for example – would give states some leverage over otherwise volatile financial flows, stabilise exchange rates, and prevent an over-valuation of currency. An international tax on transactions in the foreign exchange market would reduce speculation, and thereby further increase the possibility of states pursuing expansionary economic policies, and the revenues generated from the tax could be used to finance aid to poorer countries (ATTAC 2003). Other financial reforms could include cancellation of international debt, and new public institutions such as a World Financial Authority that could more effectively distribute financial flows, so that they tended to move from richer to poorer countries, rather than vice versa. Deglobalisation policies therefore do not necessarily mean a rejection of globalisation per se, but rather a rejection of neoliberal globalisation.

These proposals are not without their problems (see below), but what is also clear is that they involve substantial reorganisation of the world economy and its forms of regulation. Alongside such ambitious demands, the anti-globalisation movement also makes more immediate demands, such as the call for a reversal of the privatisation of goods and services, of the liberalisation of trade, and of the expansion of patents. This amounts to a defence of 'the commons' against the threat of commodification. 'Commonly owned goods' denotes not only commonly owned land and public goods, but also the modern commons such as health, water, education, and so on. This represents a cultural revolution in terms of the values that determine economic activity. In contrast, the WTO, and in particular its GATS and TRIPS agreements, advances a new round of 'primitive accumulation', in which new sectors of society are privatised – a process in which, to recall Karl Polanyi, the economy becomes disembedded from society. A new global regime would therefore explicitly limit the right of private appropriation of the commons.

A more extreme version of deglobalisation is associated with the strategy of localisation. Colin Hines argues that actually existing globalisation leads to a race to the bottom and cultural homogenisation (see above and Chapter 6). In addition to the race to the bottom, there is the environmental cost of transporting goods from one location to another (known in orthodox economics as an 'externality'). The alternative, as well as the race to the bottom, is a strategy of localisation. Although there is disagreement on how this perspective would be applied in practice, all of its advocates are agreed that the problem is partly one of 'gigantism' (Bello 2002: 112–18; Hines 2000: 62–8). As we have seen, Walden Bello advocates the alternative of 'deglobalisation', in which new or heavily reformed global institutions guarantee the right to develop through state-directed, neo-Keynesian policies. Bello's particular brand of localisation is thus one of allowing a return to import-substitution industrialisation based development strategies which, contrary to neoliberal myth, were crucial to the success of the East Asian newly industrialising countries. For Bello, then, deglobalisation does not represent an alternative to development; rather, it proposes global reform as a means of making sufficient space to allow development to take place.

There is considerable overlap – but also difference – between Bello's conception of deglobalisation and more decentralised strategies that are more explicitly localist. The basic principle of localisation is to discriminate in favour of the local, so that 'all decisions should be made at the lowest level of governing authority competent to deal with them' (IFG 2002: 107). This means that international trade will only occur where it promotes the reconstruction, rather than destruction, of local economies. Therefore, while total delinking from the world economy is not advocated, the principle of self-sufficiency would be applied wherever possible. Some global institutions would be needed in order to preserve local autonomies, and therefore protect the principle that 'small is beautiful'.

Local autonomy is thus seen as a desirable alternative, because it maintains diversity and avoids the undesirable consequences of global free trade – namely, environmental destruction and a race to the bottom. In contrast, local communities can develop a 'subsistence perspective', regarded as being closer to nature than industrial society. Vandana Shiva regards pre-colonial India as an ideal model based on the subsistence perspective (Shiva 1989). Subsistence production is said to guarantee food for the local population, rather than production for export, and its simplicity means that the eco-feminist principle of respect for 'Mother Earth' is embraced. For the extreme localisers, the problems of globalisation are thus transcended by re-establishing local 'community', and therefore they (unlike Bello) reject development. This account tends to ignore inequalities within and between localities (not least in terms of access to food), and can often lead to a justification of hierarchy and exploitation, so long as they are 'embedded' in local cultures.

The proposals discussed in this section are thus not without their problems. As we have seen, localisation can easily lead to a local-first strategy that can pave the way for all kinds of reactionary parochial-isms, despite the best intentions of its proponents. The less explicitly localist strategy of deglobalisation can suffer from similar problems, as it tends to assume that many of problems are caused by *foreign* rather than *local* capital. Marxists on the other hand, tend to argue that the problem is less one of foreign or local capital, but one of *capital itself*. That is, faced with similar circumstances, capitalists tend to behave in similar ways, exporting capital, speculating rather than investing productively (and exploiting cheap labour in the latter case). In other words, all capitalists, regardless of origin, have little motive in pursuing local or national interests per se, as their primary motivation is to make a profit. This has implications for how we think about struggles both globally and within particular localities, and by implication about the role of the state as a site of struggle that can win reforms for exploited classes and oppressed groups. It also has implications for how we think about the relationship between institutional reform and systemic critique. Briefly, institutional reform may be necessary and welcome, but in the absence of wider social and political change it is unlikely to challenge the dominant tendencies of global capitalism. This is not to say that reform is irrelevant, or that meaningful social change can only come about through a classical Marxist revolution (Kiely 2005: Ch. 9). But neither can the centrality of uneven capitalist development in the world order be ignored (T. Smith 2003).

Global governance

Critique

Since the terrorist attacks of 9/11 and the US response to them, the anti-globalisation movement has developed a more explicit critique of the state system and of global governance. The anti-globalisation movement is moving beyond a critique of corporate globalisation to one that includes the state system, militarism and (less economically based) international institutions in its analysis (Social Movements Manifesto 2003). Thus, at the second World Social Forum at Porto Alegre, Brazil, in 2002, there was considerable debate about the need to reform the UN, and especially the Security Council. As discussed in Chapter 3, this institution allows veto powers for its five permanent members, and the UN itself is often bypassed by leading powers – the US in particular. The double standards of some states perhaps reached the nadir in 2003, when the US and Britain introduced the spurious concept of 'unreasonable veto', which essentially argued that war with Iraq would occur if the other permanent members of the Security Council vetoed any decision to go to war. This concept is not recognised in international law, and moreover it is one that ignores the US's use of the veto throughout the Cold War, and six times since the end of the Cold War in 1990. For some Marxists, such behaviour means that the UN should be disbanded, as it is a toothless organisation at best and an instrument of western imperialism at worst (Anderson 2002). But in the absence of wider changes, this proposal would lead to a step back into a more starkly hierarchical system of nation-states. But what is also clear is that movement towards a system of democratic global governance, operating beyond the specific interests of nation-states, is far from a reality. Indeed, George W. Bush's administration is quite blatantly unilateralist in its behaviour, and has done much to undermine any optimism concerning the politics of globalisation.

So the basic critique of actually existing global politics is that they have not escaped the reality of state power, and of how some states continue to exercise power over others. Indeed, the most powerful states use international organisations when it suits them, but discard them when it does not. This criticism applies to institutions of global economic governance such as the WTO, as much as to political organisations such as the UN.

Alternatives

As I have said, some Marxists see no hope for existing international institutions and therefore welcome the decline of the UN and the WTO. But it can be argued in response that, in the absence of any concrete replacement, this could actually make matters worse, as there would then be no countervailing power to the interests of the most powerful states and transnational companies. Of course, such countervailing power is already weak, and even sometimes non-existent, but this is an argument for strengthening institutions – an International Clearing Union, for example, would have far more power and independence from nation-states than the IMF. A strengthened system of global regulation does not necessarily mean that all of the current international institutions should continue to exist, but neither does it mean that they should all be abolished. As we have already seen, many anti-globalisers propose a whole host of new institutions and the strengthening of some existing ones, as well as the abolition of others.

In the realm of global politics, a reformed UN is one obvious proposal. Concrete programmes are thin on the ground, but they would include at the very least the end of the veto power of the five permanent members of the Security Council. This arrangement could be replaced by a reformed Security Council with far more members, or even one that worked according to the principle of one member one vote. In practice, this would remain far from perfect – as we saw in the build-up to the war in Iraq in 2003, the US attempted to buy the votes of non-permanent members of the Security Council through promises or the threatened withdrawal of aid programmes. This is not, of course, an argument against the extension of democracy to the Security Council; but it does emphasise the limitations of the potential of democracy in such an unequal global order. But such expansion of democratic practices within the sphere of global governance limitations make the expansion all the more imperative.

However, there is a further proposal that seeks to transcend the interests of nation-states, and that is the call for a global parliament. Such a parliament would not be international, as representatives would be independent of specific nation-states. In this respect, a global parliament would constitute a genuine attempt to globalise – rather than simply internationalise – politics. George Monbiot suggests that such a parliament could comprise representatives of constituencies of around 10 million people, who would not necessarily all live in the same nation-state (Monbiot 2003b). He also (somewhat optimistically) hopes that such a parliament could gradually bypass existing institutions such as the Security Council, and thereby increase its powers.

Objections to this view are based on both principle and strategy. Some argue that a global parliament would undermine diversity, and that democracy is only possible at a local level. But as we have seen, this perspective can ignore power relations within and between local communities; and it still ultimately accepts some role for global governance in order to ensure local diversity. Thus, a global parliament is not necessarily incompatible with diversity – indeed, it may actively encourage it (though presumably such diversity would not include acceptance of local hierarchy and exploitation). The strategic objection is perhaps more convincing, as it is far from clear that such a parliament is either a feasible short-term goal or an immediate priority. More local and national demands may be of greater immediate importance, such as democratisation within nation-states. This does not, of course, mean a rejection of globalist principles – still less that the local or national should always be prioritised as a matter of priniciple over the global; but it does involve some prioritising of short- and medium-term political aspirations.

Related to this debate is the issue of whether institutions of global economic governance should be reformed ('fixed') or abolished ('nixed'). These are important debates, and the anti-globalisation movement has no single position on these issues. For critics, this is a sign of the movement's incoherence. But, there are two responses to this criticism. First, why should there be a single position? Any movement that wishes to promote social and political change is bound to be divided in some ways, and singular answers often carry their own political danger. Second, pointing to some (alleged) inconsistencies in terms of alternatives is not the same as justifying the existence of the current order. Too often, defenders of the status quo assume that the one leads to the other. But as we have seen in earlier chapters, actually existing globalisation works in ways that are very different from how its advocates hope, and it is hierarchical, exploitative and unstable. It is therefore imperative that the – difficult and sometimes inconsistent – work of finding alternatives continues.

Of course, these debates tend to focus narrowly on international institutions. This book has argued that nation-states remain central to understanding the reality of intensified capitalist globalisation, and that the hierarchical nation-state system is still highly relevant. Nation-states therefore continue to remain central sites of conflict, and while transnational solidarity is important it should not be at the expense of politics that continue to focus on the nation-state (Kiely 2005: Ch. 8). This point is now increasingly recognised by many in the global justice movement, although there remain important dissenters (Hardt and Negri 2000). The reality of the wars launched by the Bush administration after 2001 partly explains this renewed focus on the state, and it has been reinforced by growing disillusionment with the limitations of summit-stalking by activists. This of course does not mean that politics focused on the nation-state should simply replace 'global politics', but it does undermine the ways in which the dichotomy was sometimes presented in the late 1990s, so that global resistance was seen as progressive and national resistance as parochial.[9]

Global culture

Critique

The anti-globalisation movement's critique of culture argues that it has been colonised by consumer capitalism. This has taken a variety of forms, such as the increased visibility of global products like Coca Cola and McDonald's, through to the advocacy of GNP and GDP as supposedly objective measures of progress. As I argued in Chapter 5, this critique can sometimes lead to a politics that romanticises the past, or local cultures in the Third World, in the name of a spurious authenticity. But, shorn of such romanticism, it can promote a radical approach to politics based on a challenge to the inequality, alienation and growth fetishism of contemporary global capitalism.

Alternatives

The basic alternative offered by anti-globalisation movements is a commitment to the principle of 'reclaiming the commons' – in other words, a rejection of the increased privatisation, commodification and rationalisation of the planet. As the prominent French activist, Jose Bove insists, 'The world is not for sale' (see Bove and Dufour 2001). This notion of the commons, and even more the claim that they can be reclaimed, can certainly sometimes be associated with a romantic notion of local communities, in which peasantries are said to be at one with nature, and inequality and poverty are either romanticised or ignored. This position is often proposed in the context of the localisation strategies discussed critically above.

However, the idea of reclaiming the commons need not be backward-looking, localist and romantic. Perhaps we should talk about democratisation of the commons, rather than reclamation, as it is difficult to conceive of a time when there was a genuinely democratic commons. Seen in this light, the anti-globalisation movement is based less on a romantic attachment to the past (though such tendencies certainly exist), and more on a position that is united through opposition to increasing commodification, privatisation and rationalisation, and to the institutional arrangements that promote these practices. This entails nothing less than a cultural revolution – a new way of life. This does not mean a simple 'New Age' change in consciousness, but a change at one and the same time in people's consciousness *and* in the social circumstances in which they live. Moreover, this cultural revolution does not occur in some distant future, but starts in the here and now, in everyday struggles against privatisation, deregulation, war, and so on. Many anti-globalisation activists therefore argue that there is a cultural revolution in the ways in which they 'do politics', so that, in the famous slogan, there is 'one no, but many yeses'.

This involves commitment to the principles of democracy, diversity and even open-endedness. Certainly there can be no rigid blueprints, as the future cannot be predicted precisely, the outcome of struggle being open-ended. But having said that, a politics that is so open-ended as to avoid *any* decisions is one that ultimately evades the question of politics (Kiely 2005: Ch. 7). Politics does involve the making of decisions, and a politics that avoids any 'closure' ceases to be politics. There is clearly a need for commitment to some principles, policies, and indeed political programmes, even if these should not become ahistorical blueprint. Similarly, anarchists tend to downgrade organisation and fetishise direct action. In this approach, organisation is regarded as something that inevitably gives rise to hierarchy and the domination of minority leadership. This is certainly a danger, but it is true of all political action, not least the 'unorganised', leaderless direct action supported by anarchists and autonomists. In this system of 'unstructured tyranny', leadership is effectively in the hands of those that are most politically active, and there is no accountability precisely because there is no formal organisation (Ross 2002). Moreover, politics tends to be reduced to the deed, and direct action is celebrated as an end in itself. The result is that resistance becomes just another spectacle – something ignored in the ongoing dominance of neoliberal capitalism. For the anti-globalisation 'movement of movements' to grow and have a wider impact, there is a need to learn from the authoritarian lessons of the 'socialist' past, but no lesson will be learned through a total rejection of leadership, organisation and political programmes.

CONCLUSION: PROGRESSIVE ALTERNATIVES TO
US HEGEMONY AND NEOLIBERAL CAPITALISM

I want to link the question of the relationship between neoliberal global capitalism, US hegemony and political alternatives by returning to the work of Karl Polanyi. He argued that the rise of the 'market economy' was distinct from the market as one particular means of allocating resources. The market economy did not arise naturally or spontaneously, but was in fact the deliberate creation of the state. A separate market economy was thus the product of historical social struggles, such as the enclosure of land. Once a 'separate' economic sphere was created, it tended to dominate all aspects of social life – instead of economy being embedded in social relations, social relations are embedded in the economic system' (Polanyi 1944: 57). Profit-maximisation thus becomes the main goal of economic activity, and capital tends to commodify ever more aspects of social life, with destructive consequences. As Polanyi argued, 'To allow the market mechanism to be sole director of the fate of human beings and their natural environment ... would result in the demolition of society.' (Polanyi 1944: 73) Unsurprisingly, this tendency for capital to penetrate into new areas was resisted in the nineteenth century, and attempts were made to 're-embed' the economy within wider social relations. There thus occurred what Polanyi called a 'double movement':

> While on the one hand markets spread all over the globe and the amount of goods involved grew to unbelievable proportions, on the other hand a network of measures and policies was integrated into powerful institutions designed to check the action of the market relative to labour, land and money. (Polanyi 1944: 76)

So, in phase one of the double movement the market became separated from social control, which led to intensified inequality and conflict, while in phase two society restored some control over the market economy. Such means of control included universal suffrage, the rise of 'mass politics', trade unions, and so on. The 1930s saw a challenge to the democratic potential of the double movement, in the shape of Stalinism and fascism, but the post-Second World War period constituted a democratic second phase of this double movement.

Although we should be careful not to romanticise the post-war settlement, or to overestimate the re-embedding of the economy in that period,[10] it is still useful to think of the current period in terms of a renewed double movement. With the breakdown of neo-Keynesian welfare and developmental states, and the resurgence of a global 'market economy', neoliberal capitalism can be regarded as the first phase of a new double movement. Until the rise of the anti-globalisation movements can thus be seen as its second phase, constituting an attempt to reassert social control over the capitalist economy. Thus, 'global' protests against the IMF, World Bank and WTO, and 'local' protests against privatisation and deregulation, are clearly part of a protest against the tendency of capital to become disembedded from wider social relations. Although many protestors are probably unaware of Polanyi's work, placards at May Day anti-globalisation protests in Sydney and Melbourne in 2001 most clearly expressed the Polanyian influence on anti-globalisation politics. They read: 'We live in a Society, not an Economy' (*Daily News* 2001). The politics of anti-globalisation recognises that this must be the starting point in constructing alternatives to 'actually existing globalisation'.

But when talking of a new double movement, there is a strong need for political caution. We should remember that, like the first double movement, responses to the dominance of what Polanyi called 'market society' are not necessarily progressive. This has implications for how we think about responses to the dominance of contemporary neoliberal capitalism. Chapter 5 challenged the idea that the world can be reduced to a clash of civilisations, but equally we need to avoid simplistic divisions based on a binary division between a homogeneous imperialist bloc and a homogenous anti-imperialist bloc. Moreover, anti-globalisation and anti-imperialist politics are not automatically progressive. As we saw in Chapter 3, some anti-imperialist politics have promoted alliances purely on the basis that 'my enemy's enemy is my friend' – a mirror-image of the world outlook of George W. Bush. Indeed, some political movements in the periphery have a great deal in common in this respect with the populist right in the US and Europe, and of course some ostensibly anti-US movements have in the past made strategic alliances with their own current enemy. The idea of a clash of civilisations must be rejected, and this point is as relevant to ideologues who espouse this view outside US as for those within it. But the search for a European, social democratic alternative to US hegemony is also problematic. This perspective, advocated by Jürgen Habermas, ignores the ways in which European states are integrated into the world capitalist order, and how this has led to a sustained reliance on the US domestic market for exports, and on US transnational companies for investment within Europe. France and Germany may have opposed the war in Iraq, but such disagreements over military strategy have largely been tactical, and have not challenged US hegemony in any sustained way. Moreover, Europe's record in relation to the developing world – in terms of protectionism, aid levels and conditions, limited debt initiatives, support for the penetration of domestic markets, and so on – leaves little room for optimism. These brief comments illustrate the fact that anti-American politics are not necessarily progressive politics. If the global justice movement represents the best agency for challenging actually existing globalisation, then that reflects the fact, that while US hegemony may rightly be opposed, then so too should many reactionary anti-Americanisms: opposition to US hegemony should not be made because it is American, but because of the role played by the dominant capitalist state in the neoliberal, global order.

Notes

1 INTRODUCTION

1. A distinction should be made between globalisation theory and theories of globalisation. This will become clear in the argument that follows, but for now my focus is on the former, which suggests that globalisation, rather than being the outcome of social processes, actually determines other factors. Not all globalisation theorists are necessarily optimistic – Castells could be considered a pessimist, for instance. See further Chapter 2.

2 GLOBALISATION THEORY OR CAPITALIST GLOBALISATION?

1. These observations also have implications for debates over the relevance of classical Marxist theories of imperialism to the current era of globalisation – a point taken up in Chapter 3.
2. Interestingly, in more recent work, Held and his colleagues have slightly amended their three-fold divide in the globalisation debate. Instead, we have a divide between those who see globalisation as a myth and those who see it as a reality (Held and McGrew 2002; 2003). However, there are still massive divisions within the two camps, and still the question of agency is downplayed. This point is all the more true of Giddens' (1999) survey of globalisation, which divides the debate between radicals (who believe – like Giddens himself – that strong globalisation is an established fact) and sceptics (who dispute this claim).
3. This paragraph draws heavily on Kiely 2005: Ch. 2.
4. This is the subject of later chapters, particularly Chapter 5, but also Chapters 3, 4 and 6.
5. This does not imply that 'global civil society' is meaningless, nor that transnational solidarity or cosmopolitan politics are not laudable aspirations. It is merely to suggest that progressive politics cannot be measured in terms of space. These issues are addressed further in Chapters 5 and 7.
6. In fairness to Held and his colleagues (see especially Held 1998), they are critical of accounts that regard globalisation as simply impacting on nation-states, in the way that Tony Blair (selectively) argues his case. However, the transformationalist account still has little to say about the question of agency.
7. See Kiely 2005: Ch. 2.

3 GLOBALISATION AND POLITICS I: STATE SOVEREIGNTY, IMPERIALISM AND COSMOPOLITANISM

1. At first sight, this statement appears to confirm Giddens' view that there is no escape from globalisation. But as I argued in chapter 2,

this statement is made at such a high level of generalisation that it is effectively meaningless.

2. See also the outline of the position of optimistic Marxist hyper-globalisers in Chapter 2.

3. For a full analysis see Kiely (2005: Ch. 9).

4. As we will see in Chapter 6, US policy after the Cold War has been influenced by the objective of pre-empting potential competitors. The fact that such concerns have influenced US policy-makers does not, however, confirm the relevance of Lenin and Bukharin for the current era. As my argument makes clear, analyses based on inter-imperialist rivalry ignore the interdependence and cooperation between major powers, and ignores the local reasons for these conflicts.

5. For one very useful analysis of state formation along these lines, see Bromley 1994: Chs. 4 and 5. For all its (economistic and functionalist) faults, see also the 'modes of production' literature of the 1970s, discussed in Kiely (1995: Ch. 4). Unfortunately, development studies rarely concerns itself with such issues these days.

6. This point is not made to absolve the US state from its responsibility for past (and present) actions, but equally these actions alone cannot explain tragic events like those of September 11 2001. Arguments of this kind simply reproduce the 'us' and 'them' thinking of George W. Bush's axis of evil speech. On this point, see Gregory (2004: 45–6) and Mamdani (2004: 14). See also the discussion of rights in Chapter 6.

7. These criticisms are not meant to imply that Shaw is an advocate of 'liberal imperialism', or 'humanitarian military intervention'. Indeed, his work has argued strongly against the latter, and has usefully argued that 'anti-imperialism is not enough'. My disagreement is that this valid point does not make imperialism irrelevant.

8. Crude Marxist assertions that global governance is simply capitalist governance neglect the institutional forms that make up such governance, and the ways that capitalism can change over time. In this respect they closely parallel the Stalinist dogma of the 1930s, which denied any difference between social democracy and fascism.

9. It therefore follows that some international institutions, no matter how imperfect, may act as restraints on the most powerful states. Arguments like those made by Tariq Ali (2004) appear to be close to the realist position that the dominant state *always* secures its interests. Faced with this never-ending triumph of imperialist power, the question of how we move to a more democratic and indeed socialist world is left unanswered. This reflects Ali's crude mixture of third-worldism (whereby all resistance is assessed as anti-imperialist and therefore of equal value – a mirror image of the Bush-Blair homogenisation of terrorism), anti-institutionalism (see note 8) and realist defences of state sovereignty. The rejection of institutionalism leads to ultra-leftist dismissals of all institutions, and the failure to see any difference between, say, Clinton and Bush – a position increasingly advocated by the *New Left Review*. Certainly there are significant continuities, but there are differences too, even if much of the globalisation thesis is hopelessly nostalgic for the Clinton era. Indeed, Perry Anderson (2001) effectively advocated support for Bush in

the 2000 election, showing an ultra-leftism that drifts towards despair or admiration for the right. The political trajectory of Christopher Hitchens can be regarded as a kind of twisted cousin of this perspective – and Ali does a useful job in demolishing that particular rightward drift.

4   GLOBALISATION AND POLITICS II:
INTERNATIONAL RELATIONS AND THE POST-9/11 WORLD

1. Neoconservatives were divided on the war over Kosovo. Robert Kagan and William Kristol, for instance, supported it, and Charles Krauthammer opposed it. But even those who supported it argued that Clinton was not exercising US hegemony in a decisive way.

2. This was not always the view taken by neoconservatives, especially prior to Bush's nomination as Republican candidate for the 2000 election. Many neocons initially gave their support to John McCain. See Kristol and Brooks (2000).

3. The probably doomed efforts to impeach Blair for misleading Parliament have led to the production of a devastating indictment. See Rangwala and Plesch (2004).

4. This point applies not only to US hegemony, but to the British Empire too. In 1900, Fabian Society member George Bernard Shaw wrote: 'a great power must, consciously or unconsciously, govern in the general interests of civilization', and that any state 'large or small, which hinders the spread of international civilisation must disappear'. (quoted in Ali 2004: 179)

5. Kagan does this by contrasting Kantian Europe with the Hobbesian US. This ignores the co-operation between Europe and the US prior to 2003, and rests on a woeful understanding of Hobbesian political philosophy, which most certainly does not give a free licence to the exercise of power. The idea of a US constitution without the influence of Kant is similarly ludicrous, as is the idea of international law based solely on the exercise of 'good power'. As Hardt and Negri argue, '[t]he idea of republican virtue has from its beginning been aimed against the notion that the ruler, or indeed anyone, stands above the law. Such exception is the basis of tyranny and makes impossible the realization of freedom, equality and democracy.' (Hardt and Negri 2004: 9) These themes are explored further in relation to rights in Chapter 5.

6. Advocates of the war have argued that even its most prominent opponents believed that Saddam had WMD on the eve of war, and so everyone was mistaken. However, at the time many cast doubt on the so-called intelligence presented to the UN and to the US and British publics, which was precisely why liberal opponents of the war argued that the UN inspectors should be given more time.

7. Among the counts available are www.iraqbodycount.net, the Brookings Institution (O'Hanlon and de Albuquerque 2004), and Iraqi Peoples Kifah. Some of the data below can be found at IPS (2004). According to Iraq Body Count, whose estimates tend to be lower than others, civilian deaths as a direct result of the invasion and occupation (measured in terms of

the failure of the occupying forces to carry out their security obligations as laid down by the Geneva Convention) stood at between 14,181 and 16,312 at 29 October 2004 (insurgent deaths accounted for a further 6, 000 deaths at least). In addition, morgues in Baghdad have reported massive increases in deaths through violent crime – from an average of 14 a month in 2002, compared to 357 a month (a total of 4,279) in the first year of occupation. In October 2004, a new report, published by the medical journal *The Lancet,* estimated that the figure could be as high as 194,000 (Roberts et al. 2004). This report caused enormous controversy and criticism on its publication, particularly the headline figure of almost 100,000 deaths. In fact, the 100,000 figure (actually 98,000) was based on an estimate of deaths that stretched from one as low as 8,000 to one as high as 194,000. This high margin for error was used by critics to rubbish the report's findings (see, for instance, Kaplan 2004). But in fact the report went to great lengths to incorporate probabilities and eliminate uncertainties (for details, see Soldz 2004), particularly those likely to bias the figures upwards. Indeed, the headline 98,000 figure excluded the findings from some outlier areas (such as Fallujah), where death rates were much higher than the average, and did not include other areas with high rates of conflict such as Ramadi and Najaf. It is for such reasons that the report's authors suggested that the headline figure may be conservative. There is no way of verifying this statement, but critics of the report, including (to return a term of abuse) the 'usual suspects' such as the British Prime Minister's office and liberal pro-war newspaper *The Observer,* simply did not engage with its findings, resting content with assertions that a figure closer to the lowest estimation was the true figure.

8. Of the 30 states willing to be identified as being part of the coalition (a further 15 preferred to remain anonymous), the US State Department's own survey of human rights identified 18 as having 'poor or extremely poor' human rights records (IPS 2003, *Coalition of the Willing or Coalition of the Coerced,* cited in Gregory 2004: 184, 321).

9. Many neoconservatives therefore opposed the Blair–Bush road map to peace in the Israel–Palestine conflict. See for instance Krauthammer (2003a) and Muravchik (2003).

10. A failure to recognise this distinction between nation-states and the international system of nation-states lies at the heart of liberal cases for humanitarian military intervention. See for instance the journalism of Johann Hari. Notwithstanding his one-dimensional view of US state power, it is precisely a recognition of this distinction that lies at the heart of Chomsky's case that the US state is the main terrorist in the world today (Chomsky, 2001).

11. For a neoconservative statement along these simplistic lines, see Perle and Frum (2003).

12. The US military budget for 2004 was $399 billion. This is almost as large as that of the rest of the world combined, and 29 times as large as the combined spending of those Bush identified as rogue states that comprised the axis of evil (Cuba, Iran, Iraq before 2003, Libya before

2003, North Korea, Sudan and Syria). See Centre for Defense Information (2004) and www.globalissues.org/Geopolitics/ArmsTrade.

13. There is a whole list of such states, not all of which neocons agree on. These include Syria, Iran and North Korea, on which there is general agreement. More divisive are states such as Saudi Arabia, Pakistan and Egypt, all of which are allies of the Bush administration.

14. See also Ferguson (2003) and Ferguson and Kagan (2003).

15. Thus, to paraphrase a famous definition of neoconservatism, we can distinguish between those neocons outside the administration and those inside it, the latter of which have been hit by the reality of the limits of US power. Even Krauthammer complained that 'If the world wants us to play God, especially in godforsaken places, it had better help' (Krauthammer 2003b).

16. Callinicos provides some useful substantive discussion of the current order. However, this discussion leaves one at a loss as to why he continues to defend the relevance of Bukharin and Lenin in the current era (Callinicos 2003).

17. This point relates to a wider problem with Marxist theories of imperialism – namely their tendency to regard wars as necessities of imperialism rather than policy choices in the context of an imperialist world order. In other words, specific strategies cannot be 'read off' from the general reality of imperialism, not least because imperialism does not only involve war (Nederveen Pieterse 2004: 27).

18. The Blair government's efforts to link its foreign policy to the Report of the International Commission on Intervention and State Sovereignty (ICISS 2001), which attempts to provide a clear basis for humanitarian intervention and respect for state sovereignty, is therefore unconvincing. This report may suffer from some of the optimistic fallacies of liberal cosmopolitanism, but equally its clarity on the principles necessary for intervention to be classified as humanitarian are in stark contrast to Blair's case for war in Iraq. This point applies in particular to the 'right authority' principle (the UN), but also to the principles of last resort, proportional means, and perhaps, with hindsight, reasonable chances of success. Given the contorted and changing justifications for the war, 'right intention' also seems problematic.

5   THE GLOBAL ECONOMY:
US HEGEMONY FROM BRETTON WOODS TO NEOLIBERALISM

1. The HIPC initiative was introduced in 1996 to give debt relief to some of the poorest countries in the world. The countries that qualify are low-income countries that are not considered credit-worthy by international capital markets, and that have unsustainable debt. The countries qualifying are those with an annual debt service ratio of 15 per cent (initially set at 25 per cent in 1996, but changed in 1999). However, in practice the amount of debt relief actually committed has been limited, as has the movement of countries from unsustainable to sustainable debt.

2. This strategy of pre-emption has also influenced more specific aid policy, such as the refusal to channel money through NGOs who advocate birth control. This is likely to have devastating effects on the spread of HIV/AIDS, thus undermining the increase in aid money to AIDS-stricken territories in Africa.
3. Of course such setbacks are not irreversible, and the East Asia region may continue its rise to prominence. But globalisation theory, with its emphasis on flows that transcend location, cannot hope to explain this phenomenon. The rise of East Asian capitalism clearly points to the continued importance of location, as do state strategies that have facilitated this process..
4. Ironically, such an anti-sociological argument is made in Giddens (2002).

6   GLOBALISATION, CULTURE AND RIGHTS: LIBERAL INTERNATIONALISM, IMPERIALISM AND UNIVERSALISM

1. This is probably only a rumour, which may have been started by Matt Groening himself.
2. For a highly informative account of current neoconservatism, emphasising common positions and differences within the neoconservative camp, see Dorrien (2004).
3. China remains a major concern of US neoconservatives and of the Bush administration, but the issue was far less visible in the 2000 election campaign than in 2004. Indeed, Democrat candidate John Kerry was much more vocal on the issue of China.
4. Indeed, prominent neoconservative intellectual Charles Krauthammer distinguishes between the 'democratic globalism' of Bush and Blair, and the 'democratic realism' advocated by those who regard strategic considerations as a condition for intervention. This division reflects the different emphases placed on (perceived) global democratisation alongside a more realist strategy of dealing with US enemies (who happen to be non-democratic), while still possibly including non-democratic states as allies. For Krauthammer, the main enemy is said to be 'Islamic/Arab radicalism'. This strategy is at least honest about the double standards that are promoted by either strategy, and the fact that neither can ultimately advocate a genuine universalism (Krauthammer 2004).
5. Although, as we saw in Chapter 4, military power has its limits, and it is hard to see how it could be used against China, for example.
6. From 1992 to 2000, military spending as a percentage of GDP fell from 4.72 per cent to 2.99 per cent (Pollin 2003: 29).
7. This point is most clearly made by the leading neoconservative realist, Charles Krauthammer (1990; 2002/3).
8. Isolationist ideas do, however, continue to influence the ways in which the US interacts with other states, not least in the unilateralism of the Bush administration. The argument that US interventionism can be rigidly contrasted to isolationism – advanced by Christopher Hitches as justification for his support for Bush – is guilty of the spatial fetishism

that was criticised in Chapter 2. In particular, in proposing an 'isolation bad/intervention good' dichotomy, it tells us nothing about the different forms – the politics – of interventions.

9. Indeed, post-Saddam Iraq has provoked considerable conflict among neoconservatives. See for instance Krauthammer (2004) and Fukuyama (2004a).

10. These orders have not, however, been implemented, because of both the chaos in Iraq and the end of the CPA.

11. In a poll conducted in May 2004, commissioned by the US-led Coalition Provisional Authority, 92 per cent of Iraqis considered the coalition forces to be 'occupiers'. The poll, taken just before Iyad Allawi was appointed as Prime Minister in the 'return to sovereignty', found that he had the support of just 23 per cent of Iraqis, compared to opposition from 61 per cent (IPS 2004: 5–6).

12. Or indeed by some on the anti-imperialist left, who have accused Iraqi trade unions of collaboration with the occupation. Indeed, some crude anti-imperialists are completely indifferent to internal developments in Iraq, both before and after the US invasion. This reflects the wider problems of a strand of anti-imperialism, discussed in previous chapters.

13. This is especially evident in the neoconservative cynicism of Charles Krauthammer, which is essentially characterised by indifference to the idealist neocon project of liberal democratic expansion abroad. Fearing active citizenship within the US, Krauthammer also finds indifference to the political process within the US to be desirable.

14. This conflation is the ultimate weakness of the BBC series of 2004, called *The Power of Nightmares*. Having noted this weakness, I should stress how this brilliant, thought-provoking programme rightly points to areas of convergence between neoconservatism and some political Islamist strands, and the functionality of each for other.

15. The survey was carried out by Gallup International and Environics International, and reported by the World Economic Forum. It included a survey of the trust ratings of 17 different institutions, of which parliaments had the lowest rating, closely followed by global companies. In terms of the regional breakdown for responses to the idea of being governed by the will of the people, the Middle East saw an 82 per cent negative response, Latin America 78 per cent, Asia and the Pacific 74 per cent, Eastern and Central Europe 70 per cent, Africa 69 per cent, the EU 61 per cent, and North America 52 per cent (compared to 43 per cent positive).

16. This argument is made in order to question the one-sided emphasis on growth, but not to reject growth outright. There is a great deal of envisionmentalist hubris that must be rejected, including the deep green perspective that argues against *any* growth and industrialism. The problems of romantic 'localist' utopias are briefly discussed later in the text.

17. As Thomas Friedman, one of the most prominent US advocates of globalisation argues, 'Globalization-is-U.S.' (cited in Bacevich 2002: 40)

18. But we should be careful not to homogenise this political clash. Neoconservatives are clearly generally committed to liberal democratic and market expansion, but they are ultimately cynical about the former

and tend to suggest that the latter leads to complacency and indifference (see also note 12). This is yet another way in which neoconservatism's advocacy of liberal expansion rapidly becomes support for conservative elitism, whether in the form of imperialism, the pacification of the citizenry, the limiting of democracy, or a hierarchical nation-state system. Ultimately, neocons have contempt not only for the Iraqi, but also the US, 'masses', not to mention other countries. Ultimately, this can be traced back to the problems of (versions of) liberalism, and its implicit support for the market over politics.

7   CONCLUSIONS: US IMPERIALISM, ACTUALLY EXISTING GLOBALISATION, AND THE QUESTION OF ALTERNATIVES

1. Of course not all globalisation theorists accept the argument for neoliberal free trade, although Giddens comes closest to this position. Held, Kaldor and others reject neoliberalism and suggest reforms of global governance to promote a level playing field. Nevertheless, they remain optimistic that institutions of 'global governance' can alleviate these inequalities, and that they can do so more effectively than the nation-state. (See Chapter 2).

2. This is not an argument that necessarily involves advocacy of some crude versions of dependency. I accept that the world can be divided into cores and peripheries, but this division is more than a binary one, and it changes over time. Most important, the division intro core and periphery reflects the latter's marginalisation from global capital flows, and not their incorporation. Contrary to neoliberal theory (which, like crude dependency theory assumes that capital will flow from core to periphery), this is not because of market imperfections, but rather reflects the ways that markets work in the real world. See Chapter 4.

3. A project that overlaps with the concerns of regulation theory. See Aglietta (1976) and Jessop (2002).

4. Hardt and Negri's characteristically brilliant but fundamentally flawed account of war should be seen in this light. They rightly emphasise that the 'war on terror' is not simply a war against territorial states, and from the point of view of the purveyors it must involve 'the continuous, uninterrupted exercise of power and violence' (Hardt and Negri 2004: 14), and thus argue that this constitutes a war that transcends the older idea of war between sovereign nation-states. While much of this is true, Hardt and Negri also underestimate the extent to which the advocates of such a war believe that it can be won through the policing of sovereign nation-states, and the extension of the 'liberal zone of peace'. This weakness can be traced back to their exaggeration of the decline of the nation-state system, first outlined in *Empire*. See the interesting review of Hardt and Negri (2004) by the (ex?) neoconservative Francis Fukuyama (2004b). See also Fukuyama (2004c) and Lal (2004).

5. This is not the place for a full consideration of the work of Gallagher and Robinson, and their critical account of Marxist theories of imperialism. (This will be undertaken as part of the author's long-term project on

comparative state formation, capitalist development, imperialism and globalisation over the next few years.) Whatever the status of their work, what is useful is their emphasis on the fact that free trade is fully compatible with the domination of some states by others, and that such domination may be accepted by some dominant agents in the subordinate states – a central argument of this work.

6. This is reflected in the ending of many capital controls in the 1980s and 1990s, which became all but inevitable once the dominant state had itself liberalised in the 1970s and 1980s. Some states, however, continue to regulate their capital accounts, including China, India and Malaysia.

7. The outcome of proposed elections in Iraq, both in early 2005, and (after the construction of a new constitution) late 2005 or early 2006, will have an important impact on US policy. The best-case scenario is likely to be the development of a kind of low-intensity democracy, as discussed in the previous chapter. The worst case is likely to be a full-scale civil war. The most likely scenario is somewhere between these two extremes – a 'low, low-intensity democracy' accompanied by ongoing conflict. This will obviously have very significant implications for the US occupation and future US foreign policy.

8. This phrase is taken from a *New York Times* article of 17 February 2003, in response to the massive, global, anti-war protests of 15 February. The article actually regarded 'world public opinion' as the second superpower.

9. In this way the movement tended to accept the arguments of neoliberalism and globalisation theory regarding the increased irrelevance of the nation-state.

10. The post-war period was after all one in which mass production and consumption were developed to unprecedented levels, at least in the western world. Nevertheless, there was important non-market protection against the full effects of the market economy, such as full employment and the welfare state, which have been undermined in recent years.

References

Achcar, G. (2002) *The Clash of Barbarisms* (New York: Monthly Review Press).

Aglietta, M. (1976) *A Theory of Capitalist Regulation* (London: Verso).

Ali, T. (2002) *The Clash of Fundamentalisms* (London: Verso).

——. (2004) *Bush in Babylon* (London: Verso).

Allen, T. (1992) 'Prospects and Dilemmas for industrialising nations', in T. Allen and A. Thomas (eds), 1992 *Poverty and Development into the Twenty-First Century* (Oxford: Oxford University Press), pp. 379–90.

Anderson, J. (2003) 'American Hegemony after 11 September: Allies, Rivals, Contradictions', *Geopolitics* 8(3), pp. 35–60.

Anderson, P. (1974) *Lineages of the Absolutist State* (London: Verso).

——. (2001) 'Testing Formula Two', *New Left Review* 8, pp. 5–22.

——. (2002) 'Force and Consent', *New Left Review* 17, pp. 5–30.

——. (2003) 'Casuistries of peace and war', *London Review of Books* 25(5).

Archibugi, D. (2002) 'Demos and Cosmopolis', *New Left Review* 13, pp. 24–38.

Archibugi, D. (ed.) (2003) *Debating Cosmopolitics* (London: Verso).

Archibugi, D. and D. Held (eds) (1995) *Cosmopolitan Democracy* (Cambridge: Polity).

Arrighi, G. (1994) *The Long Twentieth Century* (London: Verso).

ATTAC (2003) 'Financial Capital', in Fisher and Ponniah (2003), pp. 41–50.

Bacevich, A. (2002) *American Empire* (Cambridge, Mass.: Harvard University Press).

Baker, D., G. Epstein and R. Pollin (1997), 'Introduction', in D. Baker et al. (eds) 1997, pp. 1–34.

Baker, D., G. Epstein and R. Pollin (eds) (1997) *Globalization and Progressive Economic Policy* (Cambridge: Cambridge University Press).

Bangkok Declaration (1993) *Bangkok NGO Declaration on Human Rights* (Vienna: World Conference on Human Rights).

Baran, P. and P. Sweezy (1966) *Monopoly Capital* (New York: Monthly Review Press).

Barber, B. (1996) *Jihad vs McWorld* (New York: Random House).

Barnet, R. and J. Cavanagh 2001 'Homogenisation of Global Culture', in Goldsmith and Mander 2001, pp. 169–74.

Barnett, T. (2003) 'The Pentagon's New Map', *Esquire*, March 1.

Bartholomew, A. and J. Breakspear (2003) 'Human Rights as Swords of Empire', in *Socialist Register* 2004 (London: Merlin) pp. 125–45.

Baudrillard, J. (1993) *Symbolic Exchange and Death* (London: Sage).

——. (2002) *The Spirit of Terrorism* (London: Verso).

Baxter, J. (2003) 'United Nations' in F. Reza (ed.) (2003) *Anti-Imperialism: A Guide for the Movement* (London: Bookmarks), pp. 259–69.

Becker, D. and R. Sklar (1987), 'Why Postimperialism?', in D. Becker, J. Frieden, S. Schatz and R. Sklar (1987) *Postimperialism* (Boulder: Lynne Rienner), pp. 1–18.

Beetham, D. (1985) *Max Weber and the Theory of Modern Politics* (Cambridge: Polity).

——. (1999) *Democracy and Human Rights* (Cambridge: Polity).

Bello, W. (2002) *Deglobalization* (London: Zed).

Berlin, I. (1969) *Four Essays on Liberty* (Oxford: Oxford University Press).

Bieler, A. and A. D. Morton (2004) 'A critical theory route to hegemony, world order and historical change: neo-Gramscian perspectives in international relations', *Capital and Class* 82, pp. 85–113.

Blair, T. (2003) 'The left should not weep if Saddam is toppled', *Observer*, 10 Februrary.

Bobbit, P. (2002) *The Shield of Achilles* (New York: Knopf).

Boot, M. (2003a) 'The Case for American Empire', *Weekly Standard*, 15 October.

——. (2003b) 'What Next? The Bush Foreign Policy Agenda beyond Iraq', *Weekly Standard*, 5 May.

Bove, J. and R. Dufour (2001) *The World is not for Sale* (London: Verso).

Brenner, R. (1976) 'Agrarian Class Structure and Economic Development in Pre-Industrial Europe', *Past and Present* 70, pp. 30–74.

——. (1986) 'The social basis of economic development', in J. Roemer (ed.) (1986), *Analytical Marxism* (Cambridge: Cambridge University Press), pp. 23–53.

——. (2003) 'Towards the Precipice', *London Review of Books* 25(3) (www.lrb.co.uk).

Brett, E. (1985) *The World Economy since the War* (London: Macmillan).

Bromley, S. (1991) 'Crisis in the Gulf', *Capital and Class* 44, pp. 7–14.

——. (1994) *Rethinking Middle East Politics* (Cambridge: Polity).

——. (2003) 'Reflections on *Empire*, Imperialism and United States Hegemony', *Historical Materialism* 11(3), pp. 17–68.

Bukharin, N. (1972) *Imperialism and World Economy* (London: Merlin, first published 1914).

Burnham, P. (1991) 'Neo-Gramscian Hegemony and the International Order', *Capital and Class* 45, pp. 73–93.

Burnheim, J. (1995) *Is Democracy Possible?* (Cambridge: Polity).

Bush, G. (1992) 'State of the Union Address', *Congressional Quarterly Almanac: 102nd Congress, 1st session, 1991* (Washington: US Govt), vol. xlvii, pp. 6E–8E.

Callinicos, A. (2003) *The New Mandarins of American Power* (Cambridge: Polity).

Callinicos, A., C. Harman. M. Gonzalez and J. Rees (1994) *Marxism and the New Imperialism* (London: Bookmarks).

Castells, M. (1993) *The Informational City* (Oxford: Blackwell).

Castells, M. (1996) *The Rise of the Network Society* (Oxford: Blackwell).

Centre for Defense Information (2004) 'World Military Spending 2004' (www.cdi.org).

Chace, J. (1992) *The Consequences of the Peace* (Oxford: Oxford University Press).

Chandler, D. (2000) 'International Justice', *New Left Review* 6, pp. 55–66.

Chandler, D. (ed.) (2002) *Rethinking Human Rights: Critical Approaches to International Politics* (London: Palgrave).

Chang, H.-J. (2002) *Kicking Away the Ladder* (London: Anthem).

Chomsky, N. (2002) *9/11* (New York: Seven Stories Press).

Clark, W. (2003) *Winning Modern Wars: Iraq, Terrorism and the American Empire* (New York: Public Affairs).

Clarke, S. (1992) 'The Global Accumulation of Capital and the Periodisation of the Capitalist State Form', in W. Bonefeld (ed.) (1992) *Open Marxism*, vol. 1 (London: Pluto Press), pp. 133–50.

Clinton, B. (1993) 'Inaugural Address', *The Times*, 21 January.

——. (1994) *A National Security Strategy of Engagement and Enlargement* (Washington: US Government).

Coates, D. and J. Krieger (2004) *Blair's War* (Cambridge: Polity).

Comninel, G. (1987) *Rethinking the French Revolution* (London: Verso).

Cooper, R. (2002) 'Why we still need empires', *Observer*, 7 April.

Corbridge, S. (1993) *Debt and Development* (Oxford: Blackwell).

Corrigan, P. and D. Sayer (1985) *The Great Arch* (Oxford: Blackwell).

Cox, R. (1981) 'Social Forces, States and World Orders: Beyond International Relations Theory', *Millennium* 10(2), pp. 126–55.

——. (1987) *Production, Power and World Order* (New York: Columbia University Press).

Crouch, C. (2004) *Post-Democracy* (Cambridge: Polity).

Crozier, M., S. Huntington and J. Watanuki (1975) *The Crisis of Democracy: Report on the Governability of Democracies to the Trilateral Commission* (New York: New York University Press).

Daily News, 2 May 2001 (Sri Lanka).

Dean, K. (2003) *Capitalism and Citizenship* (London: Routledge).

Desai, M. (2002) *Marx's Revenge* (London: Verso).

Deudney, D. and J. Ikenberry (1999) 'The nature and sources of a liberal international order', *Review of International Studies* 25(2), pp. 179–96.

Dicken, P. (2003) *Global Shift* (London: Sage).

Dicken, P., J. Peck and A. Tickell (1997) 'Unpacking the Global', in R. Lee and J. Willis (eds) (1997) *Geographies of Economies* (London: Edward Arnold), pp. 147–57.

Dorrien, G. (2004) *Imperial Designs: Neoconservatism and the New Pax Americana* (New York: Routledge).

Dowd, D. (2000) *Capitalism and its Economics* (London: Pluto Press).

Doyle, M. (1983) 'Kant, liberal legacies and foreign affairs: Part One', *Philosophy and Public Affairs* 12(3), pp. 205–35.

Drury, S. (1997) *Leo Strauss and the American Right* (New York: St. Martins Press).

Emmanuel, A. (1974) 'Myths of Development versus Myths of Underdevelopment', *New Left Review* 85, pp. 61–82.

Escobar, A. (1995) *Encountering Development* (Princeton: Princeton University Press).

Evans, T. (2001) 'If democracy, then human rights?', *Third World Quarterly* 22(4), pp. 623–42.

Ferguson, N. (2003) *Empire: The Rise and Demise of the British World Order and the Lessons for Global Power* (New York: Basic Books).

Ferguson, N. and R. Kagan (2003) 'The United States Is and Should Be, an Empire: A New Atlantic Initiative Debate', American Enterprise Institute for Public Policy Research (www.aei.org/events).

Fine, B., C. Lapavitsas and J. Pincus (eds) 2001, *Development Policy into the Twenty-First Century* (London: Routledge).

Fisher, W. and T. Ponniah (eds) (2003) *Another World is Possible* (London: Zed).

Fiske, J. (1989) *Reading the Popular* (London: Unwin Hyman).

Foner, E. (1998) *The Story of American Freedom* (New York: Norton).

Frank, A. G. (1969) *Capitalism and Underdevelopment in Latin America* (New York: Monthly Review Press).

Frankel, J. (2000) *Globalization of the Economy*, NBER Working Paper Series, no. 7858 (New York: National Bureau of Economic Research).

Frobel, F., J. Heinrichs and O. Kreye (1980) *The New International Division of Labour* (Cambridge: Cambridge University Press).

Fukuyama, F. (1992) *The End of History and the Last Man* (London: Penguin).

——. (2004a) 'The Neoconservative Moment', *The National Interest* 76, pp. 57–68.

——. (2004b) 'Review of Hardt and Negri's *Multitude*', New York Times, 25 July.

——. (2004c) *State Building* (Ithaca: Cornell University Press).

Gallagher, J. and R. Robinson (1953) 'The Imperialism of Free Trade', *Economic History Review* vi(i), pp. 1–15.

Giddens, A. (1990) *The Consequences of Modernity* (Cambridge: Polity).

——. (1991) *The Transformation of Intimacy* (Cambridge: Polity).

——. (1997) 'Interview with John Lloyd', *New Statesman*, 10 January.

——. (1999) *Runaway World* (Cambridge: Polity).

——. (2002) *Which Way for New Labour* (Cambridge: Polity).

Gill, S. (1990) *American Hegemony and the Trilateral Commission* (Cambridge: Cambridge University Press).

——. (2002) *Power and Resistance in the New World Order* (Basingstoke: Palgrave Macmillan).

Gills, B., J. Rocamora and R. Wilson (1993) *Low-Intensity Democracy* (London: Pluto Press).

Glyn, A., A. Hughes, A. Lipietz and A. Singh (1990) 'The Rise and Fall of the Golden Age', in S. Marglin and J. Schor (eds) (1990) *The Golden Age of Capitalism* (Oxford: Clarendon), pp. 39–125.

Golding, P. (2000) 'Forthcoming features: information and communications technologies and the sociology of the future', *Sociology* 34(1), pp. 165–84.

Goldsmith, E. and J. Mander (eds) (2001) *The Case Against the Global Economy* (London: Earthscan).

Gowan, P. (1999) *The Global Gamble* (London: Verso).

——. (2001) 'The State, Globalisation and the New Imperialism', *Historical Materialism* 9 (with L. Panitch and M. Shaw) pp. 3–38.

Grahl, J. (2004) 'The European Union and American Power', *Socialist Register 2005* (London: Merlin), pp. 284–300.

Gramsci, A. (1971) *Selections from the Prison Notebooks* (London: Lawrence and Wishart).

Gregory, D. (2004) *The Colonial Present* (Oxford: Blackwell).

Habermas, J. (2001) *The Post-national Constellation* (Cambridge: Polity).

Halliday, F. (1989) *Cold War, Third World* (London: Hutchinson Radius).

Halper, S. and J. Clarke (2004) *America Alone: The Neoconservatives and Global Order* (Cambridge: Cambridge University Press).

Hardt, M. (2002) 'Today's Bandung', *New Left Review* 14, pp. 112–18.

——. (2000) *Empire* (Harvard: Harvard University Press).

——. (2004) *Multitude* (New York: Penguin).

Harman, C. (2003) 'National Liberation', in F. Reza (ed.) (2003) *Anti-Imperialism: A Guide for the Movement* (London: Bookmarks), pp. 65–77.

Harris, J. (2003) 'Transnational Competition and the End of US Economic Hegemony', *Science and Society* 67(1), pp. 68–80.

Harris, N. (2003) *The Return of Cosmopolitan Capital* (London: I B Taurus).

Harvey, D. (1989) *The Condition of Postmodernity* (Oxford: Blackwell).

——. (2003) *The New Imperialism* (Oxford: Oxford University Press).

Hayek, F. (1960) *The Constitution of Liberty* (London: Routledge and Kegan Paul).

Heffer, R. (1976) *A Documentary History of the United States* (New York: Mentor).

Held, D. (1996) *Democracy and the Global Order* (Cambridge: Polity).

——. (1998) 'Globalization: The timid tendency', *Marxism Today* Nov/Dec, pp. 24–7.

——. (2003) 'Violence, Law and Justice in a Global Age', in D. Archibugi (ed.) (2003) *Debating Cosmopolitics* (London: Verso), pp. 184–202.

——. (2004) *Global Covenant* (Cambridge: Polity).

Held, D. and M. Koening-Archibugi (2004) 'Whither American Power?', in D. Held and M. Koening-Archibugi (eds) (2004) *American Power in the 21st Century* (Cambridge: Polity), pp. 1–20.

Held, D. and T. McGrew (2002) *Globalization/Anti-Globalization* (Cambridge: Polity).

Held, D. and T. McGrew (eds) (2003) *The Global Transformations Reader* (Cambridge: Polity), second edn.

Held, D., T. McGrew, J. Perraton and D. Goldblatt (1999) *Global Transformations* (Cambridge: Polity).

Helleiner, E. (1994) *States and the Re-emergence of Global Finance* (Ithaca, NY: Cornell University Press).

Henwood, D. (2003) *After the New Economy* (London: New Press).

Hilton, R. (1973) *Bond Men Made Free* (London: Routledge).

——. (1976) 'A Comment', in R. Hilton (ed.) (1976) *The Transition from Feudalism to Capitalism* (London: Verso), pp. 109–17.

Hines, C. (2000) *Localization: A Global Manifesto* (London: Zed).

Hines, C. and T. Lang (2001) 'The New Protectionism of "Localization"', in Goldsmith and Mander 2001, pp. 289–95.

Hirst, P. and G. Thompson (1999) *Globalization in Question* (Cambridge: Polity), second edn.

HM Government (2002) *Iraq's Weapons of Mass Destruction: The Assessment of the British Government* (www.number-10.gov.uk).

Hobsbawm, E. (1962) *Age of Revolution* (London: Weidenfeld and Nicholson).

Howe, S. (2003) 'American Empire: the history and future of an idea' (www. openDemocracy.net).

Hudson, M. (2003) *Super Imperialism* (London: Pluto Press).

Hulsman, J. (2004) 'The coming foreign policy civil wars: Part Two – The Republicans' (www.openDemocracy.net).

Huntington, S. (1989) 'The Modest Meaning of Democracy', in R. Pastor (ed.) (1989) *Democracy in the Americas* (New York: Holmes and Meier), pp. 5–28.

——. (1996) *The Clash of Civilisations and the Remaking of World Order* (New York: Simon and Schuster).

ICISS (2001) *The Responsibility to Protect* (Ottawa: International Development Research Centre).

IFG (2002) *Alternatives to Economic Globalization* (San Francisco: Berrett Kohler).

Ignatieff, M. (2003) 'The Burden', *New York Times Magazine*, 5 January.

Independent (2004) 'Britain's "broken pledges on aid cost the poorest £9.5 billion"', 28 July.

IPS (2004) *Paying the Price: The Mounting Costs of the Iraq War* (Washington: Institute of Policy Studies: Foreign Policy in Focus, www.ips-dc.org/iraq/ costsofwar).

Jessop, B. (2002) *The Future of the Capitalist State* (Cambridge: Polity).

Johnson, C. (2002) *Blowback* (London: Time Warner).

Juhasz, A. (2004) *The Handover that Wasn't: How the Occupation of Iraq Continues* (www.fpif.org).

Kagan, R. (1998) 'The benevolent empire', *Foreign Policy* 111, pp. 24–35.

——. (2002) 'Power and Weakness', *Policy Review* 113 (www.policyreview. org).

——. (2003) *Paradise and Power* (London: Atlantic).

Kagan, R. and W. Kristol (ed.) (2000) *Present Dangers: Crisis and Opportunity in American Foreign and Defense Policy* (San Francisco: Encounter).

——. (2000) 'American Power – for What?', *Commentary*, January, pp. 30–2, 35–6.

Kaldor, M. (2002) 'American power: from "compellance" to cosmopolitanism?', *International Affairs* 79(1), pp. 1–22.

——. (2003) *Global Civil Society* (Cambridge: Polity).

Kaldor, M., H. Anheier and M. Glasius (2003) 'Global Civil Society in an Age of Regressive Globalisation', in M. Kaldor, H. Anheier and M. Glasius (eds) (2003) *Global Civil Society Yearbook 2003* (Oxford: Oxford University Press), pp. 3–33.

Kant, I. (1983) *Perpetual Peace, and Other essays on Politics, History and Morals* (Indianapolis: Hackett, first published 1795).

Kaplan, F. (2004) '100, 000 Dead – or 8, 000: How many Iraqi civilians have died as a result of the war?' (http://slate.msn.com/id/2108887).

Kaplan, L. (1998) 'Leftism on the Right: Conservatives Learn to Blame America First', *Weekly Standard*, 9 February.

——. (2003) 'Early Exit: Why the Bushies Want Out of Iraq', *New Republic*, May 26.

Kaplan, L. and W. Kristol (2003) *The War over Iraq: Saddam's Tyranny and America's Mission* (San Francisco: Encounter Books).

Kaplan, R. (1994) *The Coming Anarchy* (New York: Vintage).

Kautsky, K. (2002) 'Ultra-Imperialism', *Workers Liberty* 2(3), pp. 73–9 (first published 1914).

Kiely, R. (1995) *Sociology and Development: The Impasse and Beyond* (London: UCL Press).

——. (1998a) 'Globalisation, (post-)modernity and the "third world"', in R. Kiely and P. Marfleet (eds) (1998) *Globalisation and the Third World* (London: Routledge), pp. 1–22.

——. (1998b) *Industrialization and Development: A Comparative Analysis* (London: UCL Press).

——. (1999) 'Globalization: Established Fact or Uneven Process?', in S. Ismael (ed.) (1999) *Globalization: Policies, Challenges and Responses* (Calgary: Detselig), pp. 45–64.

——. (2004) 'Global civil society and spaces of resistance', in J. Eade and D. O'Byrne (eds) (2004) *Global Ethics and Civil Society* (Aldershot: Ashgate), forthcoming.

——. (2004/5) 'The Changing Face of Anti-Globalisation Politics: Two (and a half) tales of globalisation and anti-globalisation', *Globalizations* 1(2), 2004/5, forthcoming.

——. (2005) *The Clash of Globalisations: Neo-liberalism, the Third Way and Anti-Globalisation* (Leiden: Brill).

Kirkpatrick, J. (1982) *Dictatorships and Double Standards* (New York: Simon and Schuster).

Kitching, G. (2001) *Seeking Social Justice through Globalization* (Pennsylvania: Penn State University Press).

Klare, M. (2004) *Blood and Oil* (London: Hamish Hamilton).

Klein, N. (2000) *No Logo* (London: Flamingo).

——. (2001) 'Reclaiming the Commons', *New Left Review* 9, pp. 81–9.

Krauthammer, C. (1990) 'The unipolar moment', *Foreign Affairs* 70(1), pp. 23–33.

——. (2002/3) 'The unipolar moment revisited', *National Interest* 70, pp. 5–17.

——. (2003a) 'Shades of Oslo', *Washington Post*, 6 June.

——. (2003b) 'Help Wanted: Why America Needs to Lean Hard on its Allies to Lend a Hand in Iraq', *Time*, no. 162, 1 September.

——. (2004) 'In Defense of Democratic Realism', *National Interest* no. 77, pp. 15–25.

Kristol, W. (2000) 'American Power – For What?', *Commentary*, January, pp. 35–6.

Kristol, W. and D. Brooks (2000) 'The Politics of Creative Destruction', *Weekly Standard*, 13 March.

Kristol, W. and R. Kagan (2003) 'Exit Strategy or Victory Strategy', *Weekly Standard*, 17 November.

Lacher, H. (2003) 'Putting the state in its place?', *Review of International Studies* 29(4), pp. 521–41.

Lal, D. (2004) *In Praise of Empires* (Basingstoke: Palgrave).

Lenin, V. (1975) *Imperialism: The Highest Stage of Capitalism* (Moscow: Progress, first published 1916).

Lewis, B. (1990) 'The Roots of Muslim Rage', *Atlantic*, September 1990 (www. theantlantic.com/issues/90Sep).

Lieven, A. (2004) *America Right or Wrong?* (London: Harper Collins).

Litwak, R. (2000) *Rogue States and US Foreign Policy* (Washington: Woodrow Wilson Center Press).

Lloyd, J. (2001) *The Protest Ethic* (London: Demos).

Mamdani, M. (2004) *Good Muslim, Bad Muslim* (New York: Pantheon).

Mann, M. (2001) 'Globalization and September 11th', *New Left Review* 11, pp. 51–72.

——. (2003) *Incoherent Empire* (London: Verso).

Marquand, D. (2004) *Decline of the Public* (Cambridge: Polity).

Marx, K. (1976) *Capital*, vol.1 (London: Penguin, first published 1867).

Marx, K. and F. Engels (1977) *Manifesto of the Communist Party* (Peking: Foreign Languages Press, first published 1848).

Mazarr, M. (2003) 'George W. Bush, Idealist', *International Affairs* 79(3), pp. 503–22.

McGrew, A. (2000) 'A Second American Century? The United States and the New World Order?', in A. McGrew (ed.) (2000) *Empire* (London: Hodder and Stoughton), pp. 211–50.

McGuigan, J. (1992) *Cultural Populism* (London: Routledge).

McKinnon, R. (1973) *Money and Capital in Economic Development* (Washington: Brookings Institute).

Milanovic, B. (2002) 'True World Income Distribution, 1988 and 1993: First Calculations Based on Household Surveys Alone', *Economic Journal* 112, pp. 51–92.

Mill, J. S. (1974) *On Liberty* (London: Penguin, first published 1869).

Mittelman, J. (1997) 'How does globalization really work?', in J. Mittelman (ed.) (1997) *Globalization: Critical Perspectives* (Boulder: Lynne Rienner), pp. 220–39.

Monbiot, G. (2002) 'What do we really want?', *Guardian*, 27 August.

——. (2003a) 'The moral myth', *Guardian*, 25 November.

——. (2003b) *The Age of Consent* (London: Flamingo).

Monthly Review 'Editorial: What Recovery?' (2003), 54(11), pp. 1–14.

Muravchik, J. (2003) 'The Road Map to Nowhere', *Weekly Standard*, 31 March.

National Security Strategy (2002) *The National Security Strategy of the United States of America* (www.whitehouse.gov).

Nederveen Pieterse, J. (2004) *Globalization or Empire?* (New York: Routledge).

Negri, T. (2003), 'Empire and the Multitude', *Radical Philosophy* 120, pp. 20–37.

Negus, K. (1996) *Popular Music in Theory* (Cambridge: Polity).

NEPDG (2001) *Reliable, Affordable and Environmentally Sound Energy for America's Future* (National Energy Policy Development Group, www.whitehouse. gov/energy).

Nye, J. (1990) *Bound to Lead* (New York: Basic).

——. (2002) *The Paradox of American Power* (Oxford: Oxford University Press).

O' Brien, R. (1992) *Global Financial Integration: The End of Geography* (London: Pinter).

O'Hanlon, M. and A. de Albuquerque (2004) 'Iraq Index: Tracking Variables of Reconstruction and Security in Post-Saddam Iraq' (www.brooking.edu/fp/saban/iraq/index.pdf).

Ohmae, K. (1995) *Borderless World* (London: Fontana).

Oxfam (2002) *Stop the Dumping: How EU Agricultural Subsidies are Damaging Livelihoods in the Developing World* (Oxford: Oxfam).

Panitch, L. (2003) 'Globalization and the State', in L. Panitch, C. Leys, A. Zuege and M. Konings (eds) (2003) *The Globalization Decade* (London: Merlin), pp. 9–43.

Panitch, L. and S. Gindin (2003) 'Global Capitalism and American Empire', *Socialist Register 2004* (London: Merlin), pp. 1–42.

Pena, C. (2004) 'After Baghdad, Tehran' (www.openDemocracy.net).

Perle, R. and D. Frum (2003) *An End to Evil: How to Win the War on Terror* (New York: Random House).

Phillips, A. (1987) *The Enigma of Colonialism* (London: James Currey).

Podhoretz, N. (1999) 'Strange Bedfellows: A Guide to New Foreign Policy Debates', *Commentary*, December, pp. 19–31.

Pogge, T. (2002) *World Poverty and Human Rights* (Cambridge: Polity).

Pogge, T. and S. Reddy (2002), 'Unknown: The Extent, Distribution and Trend of Global Income Poverty' (www.socialanalysis.org).

Polanyi, K. (1944) *The Great Transformation* (New York: Beacon).

Pollin, R. (2003) *Contours of Descent* (London: Verso).

Porter, D. and D. Craig (2004) 'The third way and the third world: poverty reduction and social inclusion in the rise of "inclusive" liberalism', *Review of International Political Economy* 11(2), pp. 387–423.

Project for the New American Century (1997) *Statement of Principles* (www.newamericancentury.org).

——. (1998) *Letter to President Clinton on Iraq* (www.newamericancentury.org).

——. (2000) *Rebuilding America's Defenses* (www.newamericancentury.org).

Rahnema, M. (1997) 'Towards Post-Development: Searching for Signposts, A New Language and New Paradigms', in M. Rahnema and V. Bawtree (eds) (1997) *The Post-Development Reader* (London: Zed), pp. 377–403.

Rangwala, G. and D. Plesch (2004) *A Case to Answer: A first report on the potential impeachment of the prime minister for high crimes and misdemeanours in relation to the invasion of Iraq* (www.impeachBlair.org).

Redefining Progress (2003) *Genuine Progress Indicator* (www.rprogress.org).

Reich, R. (1983) *The Next American Frontier* (Harmondsworth: Penguin).

Reus-Smit, C. (2004) *American Power and World Order* (Cambridge: Polity).

Rice, C. (2000) 'Campaign 2000 – Promoting the National Interest' (www.foreignpolicy2000.org).

Ritzer, G. (1993) *The McDonaldization of Society* (London: Sage).

——. (2004) *The Globalization of Nothing* (London: Sage).

Roberts, L., L. Riyadh, R. Garfield and J. Khundhairi (2004) 'Mortality before and after the 2003 invasion of Iraq: cluster sample survey' (http://image.thelancet.com/extras/04art10342web.pdf).

Robertson, R. (1992) *Globalization: Social Theory and Global Culture* (London: Sage).

Robinson, W. (1996) *Promoting Polyarchy* (Cambridge: Cambridge University Press).

Robinson, W. (2004) *A Theory of Global Capitalism* (Baltimore: Johns Hopkins University Press).

Rosenberg, J. (1994) *The Empire of Civil Society* (London: Verso).

——. (2000) *The Follies of Globalisation Theory* (London: Verso).

Ross, S. (2002) 'Is This What Democracy Looks Like? The Anti-Globalization Movement in North America', *Socialist Register* 2003 (London: Merlin), pp. 281–304.

Rostow, W. (1960) *The Stages of Economic Growth* (Cambridge: Cambridge University Press).

Rueschmeyer, D., E. Stephens and J. Stephens (1992) *Capitalist Development and Democracy* (Cambridge: Polity).

Russett, B. (1990) *Controlling the Sword* (Cambridge, MA: Harvard University Press).

Sahlins, M. (1999) *Waiting for Foucault and Other Aphorisms* (Chicago: University of Chicago Press).

Sardar, Z. and M. Wyn Davies (2004) *American Dream, Global Nightmare* (Cambridge: Icon).

Sayer, D. (1991) *Capitalism and Modernity* (London: Routledge).

Schiller, H. (1979) 'Transnational Media and National Development', in K. Nordenstreng and H. Schiller (eds) (1979) *National Sovereignty and International Communication* (New Jersey: Ablex), pp. 17–25.

Scholte, J. A. (1999) 'Globalisation: Prospects for a Paradigm Shift', in M. Shaw (ed.) (1999) *Politics and Globalisation* (London: Routledge), pp. 55–76.

——. (2000) *Globalization: A Critical Introduction* (London: Palgrave).

Schor, J. (2001) *Understanding the New Consumerism* (www.2bc.edu/~schorj).

Schumacher, E. (1973) *Small is Beautiful* (London: Blond and Briggs).

Scott, A. (1997) 'Introduction – globalization: social process or political rhetoric?', in A. Scott ed. (1997) *The Limits of Globalization* (London: Routledge), pp. 1–22.

Seabrook, J. (2004) *Consuming Cultures* (London: New Internationalist).

Shaw, E. (1973) *Financial Deepening in Economic Development* (New York: Oxford University Press).

Shaw, M. (2000) *Theory of the Global State* (Cambridge: Cambridge University Press).

——. (2002) '10 Challenges to Anti-War Politics', *Radical Philosophy* 111, pp. 11–19.

——. (2003) 'The Global Transformation of the Social Sciences', in M. Kaldor, H. Anheier and M. Glasius (eds) (2003) *Global Civil Society* (Oxford: Oxford University Press), pp. 35–44.

Shiva, V. (1989) *Staying Alive* (London: Zed)

Singer, P. (2004) *The President of Good and Evil* (London: Granta).

Singh, K. (2000) *Taming Global Financial Flows* (London: Zed).

Sklair, L. (2002) *Globalization* (Oxford: Oxford University Press).

Smith, N. (2003) 'After the American *Lebensraum*', *Interventions* 5(2), pp. 249–70.

Smith, T. (2003) 'Globalisation and Capitalist Property Relations: A Critical Assessment of David Held's Cosmopolitan Theory', *Historical Materialism* 11(2), pp. 3–36.

Social Movements' Manifesto (2003) 'Resistance to Neoliberalism, War and Militarism: For Peace and Social Justice', in Fisher and Ponniah (2003), pp. 346–53.

Soederberg, S. (2004) 'American Empire and "excluded states": the Millennium Challenge Account and the shift to pre-emptive development', *Third World Quarterly* 25(2), pp. 279–302.

Soldz, S. (2004) '100,000 Iraqis Dead: Should we believe it' (www.zmag. org).

Strinati, D. (1992) *An Introduction to Theories of Popular Culture* (London: Routledge).

Sutcliffe, B. (1999) 'The Place of Development in Theories of Imperialism and Globalization', in R. Munck and D. O'Hearn (eds) (1999) *Critical Development Theory* (London: Zed), pp. 135–54.

Teschke, B. (2003) *The Myth of 1648* (London: Verso).

——. (2004) 'The origins and evolution of the European states system', in W. Brown, S. Bromley and S. Athreye (eds) (2004) *Ordering the International* (London: Pluto Press), pp. 21–65.

Thompson, G. 2000 'Economic globalization?', in D. Held (ed.) (2000) *A Globalizing World? Culture, Economics, Politics* (London: Routledge), pp. 85–126.

Thompson, G. (2003) *Between Hierarchies and Markets: The Logic and Limits of Network Forms of Organization* (Oxford: Oxford University Press).

Thrift, N. (1996) 'A hyperactive world', in R. Johnston, P. Taylor, and M. Watts (eds) (1996) *Geographies of Global Change* (Oxford: Blackwell), pp. 18–35.

Tomlinson, J. (1991) *Cultural Imperialism* (London: Pinter).

——. (2000) *Globalization and Culture* (Cambridge: Polity).

Tunstall, J. (1977) *The Media are American* (London: Constable).

UNCTAD (1998) *World Investment Report* (Geneva: United Nations).

——. (1999) *World Investment Report* (Geneva: United Nations).

——. (2002) *World Investment Report* (Geneva: United Nations).

——. (2003) *World Investment Report* (Geneva: United Nations).

——. (2004) *Development and Globalization: Facts and Figures* (Geneva: United Nations).

UNDP (1995) *Human Development Report* (Geneva: United Nations).

——. (1997) *Human Development Report* (Geneva: United Nations).

Urry, J. (2002) *Global Complexity* (Cambridge: Polity).

Wade, R. (2003), 'The Disturbing Rise in Poverty and Inequality: Is It All a "Big Lie"?', in D. Held and M. Koenig-Archibugi (eds) (2003) *Taming Globalization* (Cambridge: Polity), pp. 18–46.

Wallerstein, I. (2003) *The Decline of American Power* (New York: New Press).

Watson, M. and C. Hay (2003) 'The discourse of globalisation and the logic of no alternative: rendering the contingent necessary in the political economy of New Labour', *Policy and Politics* 31(3), pp. 289–305.

Weber, M. (1970) *From Max Weber: Selected Writings*, H. Gerth and C. Wright Mills (eds) (London: Routledge).

——. (1978) Economy and Society (London: Routledge, first published 1921).

Weinberg, A. (1963) *Manifest Destiny* (Chicago: Quadrangle).

Weisbrot, M., D. Baker, E. Kraev and J. Chen (2002) 'The Scorecard on Globalization, 1980–2000' (www.cepr.net).

Weisbrot, M. and T. Tucker (2004) 'The Cancún Ministerial and the US: Public Perception, Reality and Implications' (www.cepr.net).

Williams, R. (1958) *Culture and Society* (London: Chatto and Windus).

Williams, W. A. (1980) *Empire as a Way of Life* (Oxford: Oxford University Press).

Wolfowitz, P. (2000) 'Remembering the Future', *National Interest* 59, pp. 35–45.

Wood, E. M. (1991) *The Pristine Culture of Capitalism* (London: Verso).

——. (1995) *Democracy against Capitalism* (Cambridge: Cambridge University Press).

——. (2002) *The Origins of Capitalism* (London: Verso).

——. (2003) *Empire of Capital* (London: Verso).

World Bank (1981) *Accelerated Development in sub-Saharan Africa* (Washington: World Bank).

——. (1989) *Sub-Saharan Africa: From Crisis to Sustainable Growth* (Washington: World Bank).

——. (1990) *World Development Report* (Oxford: Oxford University Press).

——. (1993) *The East Asian Miracle* (Oxford: Oxford University Press).

——. (1994) *Adjustment in Africa* (Oxford: Oxford University Press).

——. (1997) *World Development Report* (Oxford: Oxford University Press).

——. (1999) *Global Economic Prospects and the Developing Countries* (Washington: World Bank).

——. (2001) *Global Economic Prospects and Developing Countries* (Washington: World Bank).

——. (2002a) *Global Economic Prospects and Developing Countries – Making Trade Work for the Poor* (Washington: World Bank).

——. (2002b) *Globalization, Growth and Poverty* (Oxford: Oxford University Press).

World Economic Forum (2003) 'Press Release: Trust will be the Challenge of 2003' (Davos: WEF).

www.globalissues.org/Geopolitics/ArmsTrade

www.iraqbodycount.net

www.mca.org (Millennium Challenge Account website).

Index